Julian of Norwich

Julian of Norwich
Mystic and Theologian

Grace M. Jantzen

Paulist Press
New York/Mahwah

jul set 2/25/88
Paulist Press
Julian of Norwich
PPRESS 90086 FM

First published in Great Britain 1987
SPCK
Holy Trinity Church
Maryleborne Road
London NW1 4DU, England

Thanks are due to Penguin Books for permission to quote from *The Prayers and Meditations of St. Anselm* translated by Sr. Benedicta Ward (penguin 1973), and to Cambridge University Press for permission to Quote from *St. John of the Cross: His Life and Poetry* by Gerald Brenan (CUP 1973).

Library of Congress Cataloging-in-Publication Data

Jantzen, Grace.
    Julian of Norwich / by Grace Jantzen.
        p.   cm.
    Bibliography: p.
    Includes index.
    ISBN 0-8091-2992-2 (pbk.):
        1. Julian, of Norwich, b. 1343.   2. Mystics—England—Biography.
3. Hermits—England—Biography.   I. Title.
BV5095.J84J36 1988
248.2'2'0924—dc19
[B]   88-2417
                                                                      CIP

Published by Paulist Press
997 Macarthur Boulevard
Mahwah, NJ 07430

Printed and bound in the
United States of America

To Enid B. Mellor

'Ingenua et verecunda confessio est quo ipse careas id in aliis praedicare.'

JEROME

Contents

Abbreviations   viii

Preface   ix

Part One: Background and Biography
 1 Julian in her Context   3
 2 Education and Enclosure   15
 3 The Life of an Anchoress   28

Part Two: Julian's Spirituality
 4 Julian's Prayers   53
 5 Julian's Visions   74

Part Three: Julian's Theology of Integration
 6 'Love was his Meaning': Julian's Theological Method   89
 7 The Trinity: Attributes of Love   108
 8 Creation and Asceticism: Expressions of Love   127

Part Four: Wounds into Honours
 9 Sin and Suffering   167
10 Spiritual Growth and Healing   203

Appendix: Note on Texts   220

Bibliography   221

Index   228

Abbreviations

AR   Morton, James, ed., *The Ancrene Riwle* (London, Chatto & Windus, and Boston, John W. Luce & Co., 1907).

C & W   E. Colledge o s a, and James Walsh s j, eds., *A Book of Showings to the Anchoress Julian of Norwich* 2 volumes (Toronto, Pontifical Institute of Medieval Studies, 1978).

LT   The Long Text contained in E. Colledge o s a, and James Walsh s j, *Julian of Norwich: Showings*, Classics of Western Spirituality (London, SPCK, and Paulist Press, New York, 1978).

RR   Aelred of Rievaulx, 'A Rule of Life for a Recluse', in *Treatises and the Pastoral Prayer*, Cistercian Fathers Series No. 2 (Kalamazoo, Michigan, Cistercian Publications, 1971).

ST   The Short Text contained in E. Colledge o s a, and James Walsh s j, *Julian of Norwich: Showings*, Classics of Western Spirituality (London, SPCK, and Paulist Press, New York, 1978).

PL   *Patrologia Latina, Cursus Completus* ed. J.-P. Migne (Paris 1844f).

Preface

That a philosopher of religion should write a book on the theology and spirituality of a medieval mystic is rather unusual. Mystics do not offer arguments of the sort to which philosophers are accustomed; and what they do offer is so different from contemporary philosophy that it is inevitable that I will have made many mistakes in trying to understand it. I have no expertise in Middle English or fourteenth-century history or even medieval theology, though I have tried to learn what I can about them; and while I alone am responsible for the errors in this book, I hope that those who do have these specialities will help to correct them.

I have written this book for two interconnected reasons. The first is that, as a Christian philosopher, it is important to me to learn to receive the love of God, to pray, and to love God and my neighbour. Julian of Norwich is a model for this: she provides both example and instruction. As I became more aware of her teaching, it seemed important to me to try to make more widely known her insights into human personhood and its healing in rootedness in God, her depth of prayer, and her delight in God. I have tried to be true to her own meanings, but if I have read her writings from a late twentieth-century perspective it is because, both in the hours I spent in her anchorhold and when I returned to everyday activity, her words ring true in our own context, and it is this truth above all which I should like to share.

This book is therefore an effort to integrate the findings of scholarship with the interests of contemporary spirituality. By an exploration of Julian's theology and her own religious experiences, based primarily on her own writings but also gleaning perspectives from her social and intellectual context and background, we can understand more about one strand of the fourteenth century. More importantly, however, we can understand more about spiritual growth for ourselves. Though we must of course be careful not to transpose ideas without regard for the social and intellectual contexts that modify them (and I hope that anachronisms that remain will be pointed out), this book is written with the presupposition that Julian's spirituality, and indeed all genuine spirituality, is not of merely antiquarian interest, but has a bearing on our own life before God. Here as elsewhere, scholarship and spiritual development must be colleagues, not competitors.

ix

Preface

The second reason for writing the book is my conviction that if one is going to do philosophy of religion, one ought to know something about religion, not least about the life of prayer, and about giving and receiving love of God and neighbour. There is a considerable amount of philosophy of religion written, especially about mysticism, which shows no first-hand acquaintance with mystical literature, and is content to repeat slogans about absorption of selfhood in God, or the four (highly questionable) characteristics listed by William James. I want to examine philosophical questions about mysticism: questions about language, epistemology, and certainty, about selfishness, evil and freedom, about context and interpretation and whether there could be a mystical core of religion. But it seems to me imperative to precede such philosophical investigation with as thorough a study as I could make of one actual mystic, and, through her, of the spiritual tradition in which she is situated. This book is the result. It is not a philosophical book, but is, *inter alia*, a preparation for one. One immediate discovery is that many mystics in the Christian tradition would not be able to recognize themselves in philosophical writings about mysticism; another was that these spiritual giants do indeed have much to contribute to philosophical concerns with knowledge and truth. The dialogue between mystics and philosophers will be pursued in *Mysticism, Philosophy, and Christianity*.[1]

The two reasons for writing are not separable. A Christian tries to pray, and to learn from giants of prayer in her tradition. A philosopher tries to think, and to understand what is true. A Christian philosopher tries to pray thoughtfully and to think prayerfully. In this effort of integration, Julian is a splendid guide.

Far more people than I can list here have helped me in writing and conversation. Robert Llewelyn and Michael McLean offered not only their deep acquaintance with Julian, but also their friendship and guidance. Mother Violet, CAH, and the sisters of All Hallows showed me something analogous to Julian's joyful welcome. Aunt Miriam Jantzen read and corrected part of the typescript. Nancy Tapper made especially helpful comments. Friends, colleagues, and students, especially those in the lectures and seminars on mysticism at King's College, have given me stimulation and encouragement. Judith Longman has gone far beyond her duties as editor in kindness and help. Anne Cotton and Enid Mellor have given constructive friendship and support beyond measure. The cat Pepper has smudged quite a lot of ink. Merle Adams holds it all together. Thank you.

Note to Preface

1. Forthcoming. Blackwell's, Oxford, 1988.

PART ONE

Background and Biography

1 Julian in her Context

Julian of Norwich, an anchoress of the fourteenth century, has captured the imagination of our time in a remarkable way.[1] Scholars are fascinated by her life and writings, of course; but ordinary men and women also find her writings helpful in developing their own spirituality. Julian is full of good sense and theological insight, and is found to speak to our own concerns and offer guidance for our own spiritual growth.

Apart from a brief reference to Julian in a book by a younger contemporary, Margery Kempe,[2] and some mention of her in wills,[3] all we know about Julian comes from her own book, *The Showings of the Love of God*. This book exists in two versions, known as the Short Text and the Long Text.[4] Both begin by telling of how Julian prayed, how her prayers were answered in a severe illness which she suffered, and of a series of sixteen visions she had when she was *in extremis*. The Short Text largely restricts itself to a narration of the contents of each vision, including the teaching Julian received in them, and her responses to them. The Long Text repeats much of this material, but adds a good deal more commentary and theological reflection, and is obviously the result of much pondering.[5] By its own account it was written more than twenty years after the illness and the visions.[6]

It is impossible to be certain, but it seems likely that after the visions Julian recovered quite quickly from her illness, and wrote down the contents of her visions soon thereafter in what we know as the Short Text. Perhaps this was so that she would remember them correctly, though it seems from internal evidence that she was also aware from the start that the revelations were not for her benefit alone, and she intended them to be read by others. She then spent twenty years pondering their meaning and praying for further enlightenment, and afterwards wrote the expanded version which incorporates the insights she received in the intervening period.[7] At some stage she became an anchoress.

Julian is therefore one of the figures of history whom we feel that we can come to know very well, and yet who simultaneously remains an enigma. Her book recounts in detail the most intimate experience of her life: 'a revelation of love which Jesus Christ, our endless bliss,

3

made in sixteen showings'.[8] She is forthright in talking about her own thoughts and feelings insofar as they develop that theme of the love of God. She speaks of her prayers, her severe illness and her whole-making, her perplexity and delight, her experiences of wretchedness and joy. Yet she never dwells on the experiences or sensations, unusual as they are, for their own sake: she says nothing about them except what is germane to understanding the central theme of the message of God's love. Where talking about herself furthers this purpose she is utterly uninhibited. Where it does not, she is silent.

This means that in one sense it is possible to come to know her very well: she shares with her readers the deepest and most significant experience of her life, and her sustained reflection upon it. Yet in another sense we hardly know her at all. She tells us nothing of what was going on around her at the time, though it was a tumultuous age. She says nothing about where she lived or in what conditions she grew up. She does not mention how or when she came to be an anchoress, or what she did before that time; nor anything about how, if at all, she was educated. She does not so much as tell us her name: it was almost certainly not Julian!

In the twentieth century, however, we cannot afford to ignore all these facts of her background to whatever extent we can discover them, despite Julian's own silence on the matter. As with all writers, the background and context affect the interpretation of what Julian wrote. Unless we have some awareness of the context in which she wrote, it is easy to abstract juicy devotional passages from her book, or make pronouncements about the nature of her mysticism, without a proper understanding of what she herself meant. Besides, we are curious.

As already stated, Julian was probably not her given name, though it was used of her in her own time (with possible variations Lady or Dame or Mother Julian or Juliana). The custom was for an anchoress to adopt as her name the name of the church to which she was attached, which in this case was the Church of St Julian, built in the reign of Canute on a site reaching back to the tenth century. From ancient times it had been known as St Julian's, though it is not clear which of the several saints of that name was originally intended as its patron. One possibility that commends itself is that the saint in question was Julian the Hospitaller, the patron saint of ferrymen, because of the ferry which ran across the River Wensum near which the church stands.[9]

One of the things Julian does note is the exact date of the experiences which precipitated the writing of her book: 8 May, 1373;[10] and she says that she was then 'thirty and a half years old'. Accordingly, she must have been born about December 1342. With this as a fixed point of reference, it is possible to glance back at the history of the period, to discover some of the characteristics of the time, and the significant events which would have impinged on Julian and her readers.

The ruling monarch, Edward III, had come to power as a very young man in 1330 by a series of scandalous intrigues in which his mother Isabella and her lover Mortimer toppled his inept and unpopular father. They were in turn deposed, Mortimer executed, and Isabella set free but deprived of power. In Norfolk, where presumably Julian grew up, the memory of these events was kept green by the fact that Isabella was allowed Castle Rising near King's Lynn as one of her chief residences. Now Isabella had a taste for luxurious living, and became a resented burden on the burgesses of the area, from whom she received 'gifts' of meat, swans, turbot, wine, wax, lampreys, and other delicacies. It is almost inevitable that Julian knew of Isabella. It seems plausible, in view of factors to be discussed later, that Julian's family was a relatively wealthy one;[11] if this was the case, they may have felt directly the financial bite of having a queen in the county, and must also have been aware of the scandals surrounding the royal household. Yet increasingly Isabella developed a religious side as well. She went on a pilgrimage to Walsingham, and gradually became known more for her good works than for her past record. In her last decade, she entered a convent of the Poor Clares.[12] The queen's increasing piety did not altogether escape the notice of the residents of Norfolk, and gave another dimension to her portrait in their eyes, an example of the sort of person Julian was to admire greatly.[13]

Edward III, who was king until Julian was 35, was a much more competent monarch than his father had been. He had a taste for adventure and military exploits, and courage and ability in battle the lack of which had earned his father the scorn of the nobility. Though these characteristics made him popular, however, they increased the turbulence of the period. Trouble with Scotland on one side and France on the other was never far away in the late medieval era, and when these two countries formed the Franco-Scottish alliance in 1334, war seemed inevitable. Pope John XXII and his successor Benedict XII attempted to avert a conflict by proposing that France take the leadership in a crusade in which England was to participate. Philip IV, King of France, agreed; but just when he was ready to commence, the Pope vacillated. Philip diverted his waiting ships to the Channel, English fears were aroused, and the military energies which had been building up on both sides erupted into the beginning of the Hundred Years' War.[14] No one in medieval England escaped its consequences.

There was in the first place the draining of manpower, as knights and squires, peasants and bondsmen went off to battle. At first, enthusiasm ran high. The English forces under Edward III won a decisive victory at Crécy in 1346 and took Calais in 1347, while a Scottish invasion to Durham was repelled and the Scottish king, David II, was captured. Although the popes and preachers denounced the hostilities, the English Church with its warlike bishops in general blessed the expeditions of Edward and his sons the Black Prince and John of Gaunt. The bearing of arms was, after all, an honourable profession; and the chivalric ideals of truth, honour, freedom and courtesy were semi-religious in inspiration: we shall meet Julian frequently referring to Christ as her 'courteous Lord'. Whatever the actual practices of the pillaging armies, part of whose military ambition was the riches they would attain through looting, the ideals, at least in theory, had the hearts of the religious population.[15]

In spite of initial enthusiam, however, English fortunes declined and English taxes and manpower seemed to be poured into a bottomless pit which offered few returns. By the time of Edward's death in 1375, most of the initial gains had been taken from him, and the morale of the country was low. Why should endless men and money be wasted on this unpromising enterprise?[16]

For Norwich in Julian's time, however, the war and the methods of taxation had some economic benefits as well as hardships. Because of the hostilities with France, the ports of the south coast were in constant danger of piracy, and were in any case not so well situated for commerce with England's chief allies and trading partners, Flanders and the Rhineland. Norwich, on the other hand, was sufficiently inland to be protected from pirates, and yet was served by the River Wensum, a river of sufficient size to allow Norwich to become an increasingly important port. The mouth of the Wensum in the north east of Norfolk made it geographically convenient for her continental neighbours, and Norwich became the gateway to England, connected by roads and waterways to London, York, Lincoln, and other important centres. The taxation and customs measures of Edward III and his successor Richard II caused a growth of first wool and then cloth trade, much of which was shipped via Norwich to Flanders. Foreign cloth workers, especially Flemish, who wished to settle in England, were given special royal franchises: some of these settled in Norwich itself, while a great many more passed through her streets on their way to other parts of England.[17]

Julian shows keen awareness of colours and textures of cloth, describing them with a precision which has caused speculation that her family may have been involved with the wool or cloth trade.[18] Whether or not this is so, once Julian was in the anchorhold, there cannot have been many daylight hours free of the sounds of carts and their drivers taking their loads to the barges or returning with goods to the city and beyond; the Church of St Julian is only a few hundred yards from the main road which linked the centre of Norwich with Conisford, a bend in the Wensum which made a natural docking place for vessels of trade.

Naturally more than just cloth and wool passed between East Anglia and the continent. Along with other more exotic material items of trade, there was a flourishing trade of ideas, not least of them religious. All the main religious orders recognized the strategic importance of Norwich and developed their houses in the city. It is interesting to note also that Norwich had a house of Béguines – the only English city to do so.[19] The Béguines were an informal sisterhood which flourished in the Low Countries in the late Middle Ages. Their male counterparts, the Beghards, supported themselves by occupations such as weaving and dying cloth, and it may have been because of this that some of them came to England. The Béguines devoted themselves to caring for the sick and poor, combining prayer and personal austerity with social action in a way that made them attractive to the lower classes but a threat to the ecclesiastical establishment, whose wealth and too frequent unconcern they repudiated by word and example.[20] Consequently, they were suspected of heresy (a suspicion not mitigated by their affinities with the Spiritual Franciscans in their emphasis on the poverty of Christ) and in the fourteenth century they were fiercely persecuted on the continent. Yet in the Norwich of Julian's youth their devotion to care for the sick and dying would have been urgently needed and appreciated, because of the violence of the plague commonly known as the Black Death which swept through the land. In the absence of any concrete evidence, one can only speculate about what, if any, Julian's relations to the Béguines might have been: certainly she shared their compassion for human wretchedness (but so, of course, did many others), and it is not impossible that she might have been more closely affiliated to them.

The Black Death itself had begun in Dorset, in August, 1348, presumably imported from the continent. By November it had spread to London, and reached Norwich the following January,[21] when Julian was a girl of six or seven. People died, horribly and suddenly and in great numbers. It was so contagious that one contemporary witness describes how anyone who touched the sick or the dead immediately caught the disease and died himself, so that priests who ministered to the dying were flung into the same grave with their penitents.[22] It was impossible for the clergy to keep up with all those who required last rites, and to die unshriven was seen as a catastrophe of eternal proportions. Nor could the people who died be buried with dignity. At nightfall carts would lumber through the city with the cry, 'Bring forth your dead', and men, women and children who had been in robust health only that morning were carted away to mass graves.

The psychological impact on the survivors was incalculable, made worse in subsequent years by the further outbreaks which occurred at unpredictable intervals. When Julian was nineteen, a form particularly savage to young children developed, and in 1369 there was yet another severe outbreak. In all, the population of the country as a whole was drastically reduced. Towns like Norwich were affected worse than the countryside, because of the unsanitary methods of medieval drainage and waste-disposal; probably more than a third of the population succumbed.[23] Clergy were especially severely decimated because their ministry to the dying made it impossible for them to avoid contact with the disease. At least fifty per cent of Norwich clergy perished[24] – thus increasing the strain on those who survived. Julian does not speak of the plague directly (or for that matter of any other social or political events) but her book shows, as we shall see, a deep sensitivity to suffering and dying, not least in her persistent questioning of why suffering should be permitted at all in a universe loved by God. It is obvious that she had pondered deeply on suffering and death: the events of her childhood and youth indicate some of the factors which must have prompted her to do so.

The calamities of the Black Death were exacerbated by murrains of cattle in 1348, 1363, and 1369; and by a series of bad harvests: 1369 was the worst for fifty years. The country was in a condition of famine; and in the already socially difficult situation, further upheavals were inevitable. Tensions mounted as landlords tried to keep serfs and bondsmen tied to their old terms of service to avoid the high wages, while bondsmen struggled to escape the yoke.[25]

At last violence flared; open revolt was led in Kent by Wat Tyler, who approached London from the south, while Essex men moved in along the north bank of the Thames. Turmoil erupted throughout England, with peasants in rebellion against their lords, secular and ecclesiastical. In East Anglia, especially, there was much anger against the large landowners of the church, the monasteries.[26] Peasants ran amok, pillaging churches and monasteries, and in some cases killing their leaders.[27]

Trouble began in Norfolk itself in June. On the seventeenth of that month, a rebel band led by Geoffrey Litster forced the magistrates of the city of Norwich to open its gates to them. Litster set himself up in Norwich Castle, banqueting and revelling while his mobs plundered the city and neighbouring monasteries, destroying the Rolls on which the records were kept, and staging mock trials immediately followed by executions of the victims. In the midst of all this, news arrived that the uprising in London had been quelled through the bravery of the boy king. Litster, still in the castle, thought it prudent to send a delegation to ask the king's pardon. But the Bishop of Norwich, Henry Despenser, who had been away when trouble flared, was by this time on his way back, restoring order in East Anglia on his way. He intercepted and executed the peasant delegates to the king, and then proceeded to Norwich, arriving on 24th June. Litster fled, but was soon captured, summarily tried and sentenced to death by the Bishop, by whom he was first shriven and then led to the gallows.[28]

Nothing had been sacred in the city of Norwich. Property was looted, monasteries ransacked, and even churches pillaged. We do not know where Julian was during this period; there is a possibility that she was already in the anchorhold.[29] If she was, she would have been near the street which formed the most direct route from the Castle to the east gate of the city – hardly a position of security.

Although the population of Norwich was relieved and grateful when order was restored to the street, the Bishop aroused resentment as well. He was ruthless and merciless in the way he quelled the riots; yet the revolt would never have occurred at all if the peasantry had not been pushed over the brink of despair, first by calamities of plague and famine, and then by harsh taxation tactlessly imposed. Their griev-ances were not alleviated by their awareness of how their Bishop shared in the ostentation and extravagance of the royal household. Perhaps in part because Norwich was a rapidly growing port city, relations between the populace and the civic and ecclesiastical admin-istration were in any case often strained, and the Bishop, by his arro-gance and harsh administration of which this was only one example, did not ease the tensions.[30]

It was this Bishop who would have been responsible for judging Julian suitable for the life of an anchoress. Although in such matters episcopal authority was considered essential, popular respect for re-ligion was on the decline through a series of events which cumula-tively discredited ecclesiastical authority. As already noted, papal ineptitude had been one of the precipitating causes of the Hundred Years' War. Then in 1377 came the Great Schism, the unholy spectacle of the Church with one claimant to the papal throne in Rome and another in Avignon, pope and antipope indulging in slanging matches and mutual excommunications.

As the exchange became more heated, swords as well as words were called into action. Urban VI, the Roman claimant to the papacy, encouraged a general crusade against supporters of his rival, Clement, to be led by none other than the Bishop of Norwich, Henry Despenser. Urban VI promised full remission of sins to those who gave military or financial support to his cause: later these indulgences were extended even to the dead relatives of those who would contribute. At first, enthusiasm was wild. Men volunteered, perhaps for some partly as an escape from their conditions of servitude at home; and gold and silver piled up for the bishop, as people bought the forgiveness of God for themselves and their beloved dead, including, no doubt, plague victims who had died unshriven.

When Despenser and his army reached the continent, however, things went less well. After some initial successes, reverses set in, and it became apparent that the crusaders had no clear strategy for their campaign. Some were killed in battle; some were captured; many deserted. Those who survived, including the Bishop himself, straggled home in disgrace, having failed utterly in their projects. No one had been converted, no one had moved an inch nearer to furthering the Urbanist cause. Instead, the Bishop, the Pope, and the Church as a whole were made to stink in the nostrils of the people by this gross abuse of the system of indulgences, and by the indecent behaviour of an army of looters pretending to be soldiers of the cross.[31]

It is in this context that we must view the continuous tension with the church which we find in Julian's writing. As we shall see, Julian continually protests her loyalties to 'Holy Church', but what she stands for in her life and writings was often hopelessly at odds with the ideals of her warlike Bishop. Although she tried her best to be a faithful daughter of the Church, that faithfulness consisted partly in recalling it to its ideals, rather than acquiescing in its current practice; though Julian is at pains not to be negative about the church as she sees it, using gentler methods, as we shall see.

The disaster of the crusade was not entirely unforeseen. John Wyclif, an influential Oxford scholar and preacher who had earlier been at the royal court as an ally of John of Gaunt, openly and vigorously attacked such a blatant misuse of indulgences in the promotion of war. Wyclif himself, however, was under attack. He had opposed the corruption and worldliness of the ecclesiastical hierarchy, and had become involved in quarrels about the doctrines and lifestyle of bishops. Many thought that he was connected with the Peasants' Revolt, and with some justice, for although he would not have supported the peasants in their violence or their looting of the churches and monasteries, their behaviour was a translation into rough action of Wyclif's anti-clericalism. A synod at Blackfriars in 1382 condemned his teachings, and Wyclif himself retired to Lutterworth from whence his influence spread through the tracts he and his followers wrote.

Wyclif's followers were called Lollards, a term derived from a combination of a Middle Dutch word meaning 'a mumbler of prayers' and a Middle English word meaning 'loafer', and made even more abusive by a pun with the Latin 'lolia' which means 'tares'.[32] The Lollards, like Wyclif, condemned clericalism and religious abuses; but this ought not to be seen merely as the response of disgruntled human beings looking for something to attack, but as the only recourse of men who genuinely believed that the outward abuses practised by the church barred men and women from experiencing the inner truth of the gospel.[33]

Like Wyclif, they had a deep devotion to the human Jesus – a devotion which Julian also came to share. She also shared with them in the move to popularize the English vernacular. Consistent with their belief that the church should expose people to religion, not bar them from it, they translated the whole Bible into English, the first complete translation being published in 1390. There had been moves to the vernacular before this time, both in secular literature (especially in the midlands and the north)[34] and in translations of the Psalter and sections of the New Testament, but this was the first completely English Bible. Because it was done by followers of Wyclif, it – and with it presumably any religious writing in the vernacular – carried with it the odour of heresy.[35] This can hardly have escaped Julian's notice; yet she too wrote in English, not in Latin, expressly intending her writings for *all* her fellow-Christians, not just for the educated, Latin-reading few.[36] Although she protested frequently her intended loyalty to the church, she must had had a view of the good of the church which would not altogether have coincided with that of some of its bishops, not least her own.

Julian herself, of course, would have been aware of these differences. Furthermore, she would not have been ignorant of the severe persecution of the Lollards. From 1385 onwards, sheriffs had the power to arrest and imprison Lollards, and in 1397 a group of bishops with Henry Despenser much to the fore requested the authorization of the death penalty, which was granted after Henry IV's accession.[37] The place of execution in Norwich, known as the Lollard Pit, where heretics were burned to death, was only just out of sight of Julian's cell.[38] Her book had been written by the time authorization for the burning of Lollards was granted, but she would surely have been aware of the direction of the wind long before this. So when she says,

> But in everything I believe as Holy Church teaches, for I beheld the whole of this blessed revelation of our Lord as unified in God's sight, and I never understood anything from it which bewilders me or keeps me from the true doctrine of Holy Church[39]

we must surely see this in the context of her book as a whole and indeed of her overall situation, and not as a solemn pronouncement of fidelity to every aspect of the teachings and practices of the ecclesiastical hierarchy which in her time constituted itself as the church.

Her emphasis on the importance of love and unity among Christians may well have been deliberately intended as a direct counter to the disunities of the empirical church, both in terms of the local situation of the persecution of the Lollards and in the wider terms of the Great Schism. Whether or not this was her intention is impossible to say; but her readers would inevitably have understood her this way:

> It is in this unity of love that the life consists of all men who will be saved. For God is everything that is good, and God has made everything that is made, and God loves everything that he has made, and if any man or woman withdraws his love from any of his fellow Christians, he does not love at all, because he has not love towards all.[40]

This, of course, is no foreign teaching; it is an echo of the biblical comment that 'if anyone says "I love God" and hates his brother, he is a liar; for he who does not love his brother whom he has seen, cannot love God whom he has not seen'.[41] Nevertheless it is not inappropriate to wonder what someone going off [under one Pope] to fight his fellow Catholics in the army of another Pope might have made of her words. And surely if they came to the attention of Julian's Bishop, it is safe to assume that Henry Despenser would not be amused. Julian might well have been putting herself into grave danger. But she proceeds to say (is it not consummate irony?) that it is precisely this loveless one who

> is in danger, because he is not at peace; and anyone who has general love for his fellow Christians has love towards everything which is ... and he who loves thus is safe. And thus will I love, and thus do I love, and thus I am safe ...[42]

No Catholic bishop could disagree with this in principle; but it was far from Despenser's actual practice, and Julian surely knew it. But she insisted that the canons of safety and danger were quite other than what he supposed, having to do with integrity and inner peace rather than with any display of force which the *episcopus martius* (a nickname for Henry Despenser in his own time) might have enjoyed.

We will see more clearly in subsequent chapters how Julian's theology and spirituality were firmly rooted in the history of Christian thought and prayer, and constituted simultaneously an expression of loyalty to its ideals and a protest at its unworthy behaviour. Before we turn to this, however, it is useful to consider how Julian's personal biography insofar as we can ascertain it emerged from this general context and expressed itself in her experience and her writing.

Notes to Chapter One

1. cf. Michael McLean, 'Introduction' to Robert Llewelyn, ed., *Julian, Woman of our Day* (London, DLT, 1985). There are at the time of writing at least 150 'Julian groups' all around Britain: groups who meet together for prayer and spiritual companionship, and who draw their inspiration more or less

closely from Julian's writings: particulars are available from 'Julian Meetings', 5 Geale's Crescent, Alton, Hants GU34 2ND. These groups are also active in North America, where a religious Order of Julian of Norwich is developing in the American Episcopalian Church (P.O. Box 912, Norwich, CT, USA 06360).

2. *The Book of Margery Kempe*, ed. W. Butler-Bowden (Life and Letters Series No. 103, Jonathan Cape, London, 1936), Ch. 18. pp. 72–4.
3. Norman P. Tanner *Popular Religion in Norwich with Special Reference to the Evidence of Wills, 1370–1532* (Oxford D. Phil. dissertation, 1973). See below, p. 20.
4. Neither the Long Text nor the Short Text exist in autograph. For extant manuscripts, as well as editions and translations, see Appendix I.
5. cf. Simon Tugwell, 'Julian of Norwich', in his *Ways of Imperfection* (London, DLT, 1984).
6. LT 51.
7. C & W pp. 18–25; cf. Anna Maria Reynolds, CP, *A Showing of God's Love, The Shorter Version of Sixteen Revelations of Divine Love by Julian of Norwich* (London, Longmans, Green, 1958), Introduction p. xii; Paul Molinari, *Julian of Norwich, The Teaching of a 14th Century English Mystic* (Longmans, Green and Co., London & New York, 1958), pp. 4–5.
8. LT 1.
9. Michael McLean, *Guidebook to St Julian's Church and Lady Julian's Cell* (Norwich, 1979, rev. 1981).
10. LT 2. But even this is disputed. Colledge and Walsh follow the Paris manuscript of the Long Text which reads, 'the xiij. Daie of may' and suggest that a misreading resulted in 'the viij . . . .' However, the Sloane MSS can be taken to read 'viij', and the direction of error is debatable. 8th May in 1373 was the third Sunday after Easter in the Old Calendar, and the day after the feast of St John of Beverley: this makes it an attractive date, but of course proves nothing. For a fuller discussion see Brant Pelphrey, *Love was His Meaning: The Theology and Mysticism of Julian of Norwich*, Salzburg Studies in English Literature (Institut für Anglistik und Amerikanistik, Universität Salzburg, Austria, 1982), p. 1n.
11. See below, p. 6.
12. See *Dictionary of National Biography*, vol. IX (OUP, 1917f), p. 504.
13. cf. LT 38.
14. cf. May McKisack, *The Fourteenth Century 1307–1399*, Ch. 4. The Oxford History of England vol. 5 (Clarendon, Oxford, 1959).
15. cf. Sr Isabel Mary, 'The Knights of God: Citeaux and the Quest of the Holy Grail', in Sr Benedicta Ward, ed., *The Influence of St Bernard* (SLG Press, Oxford, 1976).
16. cf. G. M. Trevelyan, *England in the Age of Wycliffe*, Ch. 1 (Longman, London, 1972; first publ. 1899).
17. cf. J. L. Bolton, *The Medieval English Economy 1150–1500*, Ch. 6 (J. M. Dent, London, and Rowman & Littlefield, Totawa, New Jersey, 1980); cf. McKisack, Ch. 12.
18. LT 51.
19. F. I. Dunn, 'Hermits, Anchorites and Recluses: A Study with Reference to Medieval Norwich', in F. D. Sayer, ed., *Julian and Her Norwich*, Commemorative Essays and Handbook to the Exhibition 'Revelations of Divine Love' (Norwich 1973), p. 27.

Background and Biography

20. R. W. Southern, *Western Society and the Church in the Middle Ages*, The Pelican History of the Church, vol. II. (Harmondsworth, Middlesex, 1970), pp.318–58.
21. Possibly independently, by way of the ports Yarmouth and King's Lynn. cf. Robert S. Gottfried, *Epidemic Disease in Fifteenth Century England* (Rutgers University Press, New Brunswick, New Jersey, 1978), pp.142–4.
22. The account is from Clyn, a chronicler of the period, cited in Charles Creighton, *A History of Epidemics in Britain*, vol. I (Barnes and Noble, New York, 2nd edn 1965), p.121.
23. McKisack, p.322; cf. Gottfried, op. cit.
24. John Hatcher, *Plague, Population and the English Economy 1348–1530* (Macmillan, London and New York, 1977), pp.21–6; cf. David Knowles, *The Religious Orders in England*, vol. II, *The End of the Middle Ages* (Cambridge University Press, Cambridge, 1955) pp.8–13.
25. cf. Bolton, op. cit., pp.207–45.
26. McKisack, Ch.13.
27. Richard de Cambridge, for instance, who was prior of Bury St Edmund, was captured and beheaded at Mildenhall.
28. McKisack, p.418.
29. See below, pp.21–5.
30. McKisack, p.382. A special royal charter in 1380 empowered the council of Norwich to make ordinances for the city because of the 'contrariousness' of the populace.
31. McKisack, p.432.
32. McKisack, Ch. 16; cf. Oxford English Dictionary, s.v. 'Lollard'.
33. cf. Trevelyan, op. cit., esp. Chaps. 4 and 5.
34. cf. Derek Brewer, 'The Social Context of Medieval English Literature', in Borsi Ford, ed., *Medieval Literature: Chaucer and the Alliterative Tradition*, vol. I (Part One of the New Pelican Guide to English Literature, Penguin, 1982).
35. McKisack, Ch.16.
36. LT 8, 9, 79, etc.
37. McKisack, Ch.16.
38. cf. R. A. Flindall, 'The Lady Julian and her City', in Sayer, p.17.
39. ST 6.
40. ibid.
41. 1 John 4.20 RSV.
42. ST 6.

2 Education and Enclosure

> But God forbid that you should say or assume that I am a teacher, for that is
> not and never was my intention; for I am a woman, ignorant, weak and frail.
> But I know very well that what I am saying I have received by the revelation
> of him who is the sovereign teacher.[1]

Julian's protestations of ignorance in the first presentation of her experiences have given rise to much puzzlement. She reinforces them in
her statement in the second, much longer account of her experiences
and subsequent reflections on them, written some fifteen to twenty
years later,[2] when she says,

> This revelation was made to a simple, unlettered creature . . .[3]

A usual understanding of 'unlettered' would be illiterate, unable to
read or write. Two of the ancient manuscript traditions strengthen this,
having, instead of 'unlettered', 'to a symple creature that cowde no
letter'.[4] On the face of it, it would seem that Julian is telling us that she
was utterly uneducated, without even the most elementary of literary
skills. If this was so, then we would have to surmise that she dictated
her book to a scribe – a common enough practice in the Middle Ages.[5]
This is not impossible, and some scholars are prepared to take her at
her word.[6]

The internal evidence of her book, however, casts doubt upon this
literal acceptance of her words. She is clearly a woman of profound
intellect; and her book, especially in the Long Text, shows such
meticulous organization and literary skill that she has been ranked
with Chaucer as a pioneering genius of English prose.[7] It might be
barely possible that she was capable of all this using only dictation, but
the many references and allusions backward and forward in her text
and the skilful handling of the material make this seem implausible.

Accordingly, it has been suggested that her disclaimers need not be
taken at face value. Perhaps she was picturing herself in this way out of
a deep humility, recognizing her unworthiness to receive divine revelations. Perhaps also she did not want to antagonize her readers,
especially male readers in the ecclesiastical hierarchy, who might have
been offended if she had made pretensions to being a teacher.[8] Alternatively, Simon Tugwell makes the interesting suggestion that the

implications of denying her own authority might not after all be totally modest, for if she does not claim authority of her own, then her teaching comes from the far greater authority of God himself, and cannot be lightly dismissed.[9]

However this may be, it is possible to throw some light on her comments by two observations. First, 'unlettered' or 'illiterate' in the Middle Ages did not necessarily mean the inability to read and write, but rather not having had a classical education and therefore not having formal training in Latin. There was a whole class of such 'illiterati' who were not unlettered in the modern sense, but who wrote in the vernacular[10] – as of course Julian herself did. It is likely, therefore, that her comments about not being a teacher and being an ignorant, unlettered woman, should be taken in the context of her time to indicate the lack of formal education such as would have been available to men in monastic or cathedral schools and universities. We need not take these terms literally in their modern sense, but neither need we say that she was telling a 'palpable untruth'.[11]

Secondly, it is noteworthy that in the long version of her book, Julian no longer describes herself in this way. Even her comment that the revelation was given to a woman who 'cowde no letter' is in the past tense: she does not say that she is still unlettered, even in the formal sense, by the time she writes this. A comparison of the two texts shows, in fact, an impressive intellectual deepening. She has spent much effort in the intervening years pondering the content of the revelation, especially with reference to the problem of sin and suffering, and she is prepared to pursue her questioning and probing much farther than she went in the short text.[12] The long text also shows deepened solidarity with the tradition of spirituality in the treatment of its themes, and immersion in Scripture which is brought to bear on her reflection on her experiences.[13]

It is possible that Julian, though formally without the sort of education available to men in her time, either knew Latin already or, more plausibly, learned it in the fifteen years between the two versions of her book. Colledge and Walsh in fact argue that she knew the Vulgate Bible before she wrote even the short text, that she had an exceptionally good education in Latin, Scripture, and liberal arts, and that she read widely, and was deeply influenced by Augustine, Gregory, and especially William of St Thierry, as well as by English spiritual and secular writers:[14] a far cry from her own disclaimers!

Colledge and Walsh might be right, but the evidence they give is inconclusive. Their argument for her use of the Vulgate, for instance, rests on the fact that she makes plentiful use of Scripture, sometimes reproducing the precise Latin syntax in her translations. It is indeed true that such translations occur; but we must remember that the

Vulgate was standardly used in the churches in her time, and an intelligent, devout woman such as Julian clearly was would have been able over the years to pick up a good deal of the text and its meaning without having formal Latin training.

Her solidarity with the patristic and spiritual writings of the early and medieval Christian tradition, similarly, might but need not indicate that she had read these authors herself. In some respects, particularly in her treatment of the problems raised by sin, she is profoundly Augustinian[15] – but Augustinian theology was the common legacy of the Middle Ages,[16] and Julian could have absorbed a great deal of teaching by discussions with learned clerics.[17] The same is true of the other alleged influences, like Thomas Aquinas, to whose thought Julian sometimes bears striking similarity[18] or the Cistercians. She does not name or cite any authors explicitly, and though it is clear that she has absorbed much from the tradition, it is not demonstrable (though it might well be true) that she was able to read Latin for herself.[19]

Nevertheless, it is clear that Julian had at least received instruction, that she could probably read and write in the vernacular, and perhaps could read some Latin, at least by the time of the Long Text. It is therefore worth asking where she might have received the training which enabled her to express herself in masterful English – let alone study Latin tomes of theology and spirituality. She herself, as usual, tells us nothing; but from the history of Norwich in the mid-fourteenth century several possibilities emerge. Norwich was a flourishing centre for religious life: all the major orders had houses in the city and many of them had long recognized the importance of scholarship, particularly in this key city. Foremost among these was the Benedictine cathedral priory, which may have had an emphasis on intellectual endeavour reaching back to the previous century.[20] Certainly by the fourteenth century it was a distinguished centre of learning and possessed a magnificent library: one of the best in medieval England.[21] When Julian was a girl, one of its members, Adam Easton, was a popular preacher in Norwich. He studied at Oxford and became a doctor of theology especially famous for his Greek and Hebrew. Easton eventually became a Roman curial cardinal with the title of St Cecilia:[22] one can only speculate about whether or not it was a coincidence that St Cecilia impressed Julian so deeply that it was by reflection on her that she came to pray for the 'three wounds':[23] certainly her legends were popular during this time. In any case Adam Easton and his older contemporary in the Norwich cathedral priory, Thomas Brunton, had been singularly uncorrupt men in a corrupt age. Easton rebuked Pope Urban VI and suffered imprisonment for it; and Brunton criticized the moral and social decay of England, beginning with the royal court.[24]

17

Background and Biography

It is easily possible that Julian heard either or both of these preachers in her youth; but she could not, of course, have been educated as they were in the cathedral priory and then at Oxford. However the Benedictines also had a house for nuns at Carrow, just outside Norwich city walls. This convent, significantly, held the benefice of St Julian's Church and would therefore have had a voice in who inhabited its anchorhold. Thus it is virtually certain that Julian had dealings with them at some point, though there is no evidence that she was ever a nun.[25] Many English nunneries in medieval times had boarding schools for girls (and often for boys too, up to at least the age of ten: there are letters from bishops protesting that the nuns are not to have the little lads sleeping in their beds!). Carrow Abbey was 'one of the most famous nunneries of England'[26] and had a boarding school which took in exclusively girls and boys from high social class or wealthy bourgeois families. We cannot be sure that Julian went to school here, but it seems not at all improbable. If she did, it argues for either an upper class or prosperous merchant or middle class family background. Both these classes, incidentally, provided Carrow Abbey with its nuns – it, like most medieval nunneries, was an essentially aristocratic institution and provided the main alternative to marriage for well born women.[27]

Supposing Julian did attend the boarding school at Carrow Abbey, what would she have learned? What would the nuns have been able to teach her? Nuns were expected to be able to read and write when they were admitted to a Benedictine convent, but it seems clear that the general standard of education among nuns was declining through the fourteenth and fifteenth centuries. In many English nunneries the majority knew no Latin, and had to recite their offices by rote; probably some could not write.[28]

The whole trend of medieval thought was against learned women, and even in Benedictine nunneries, for which a period of study was enjoined by the rule, it was evidently considered altogether outside the scope of women to concern themselves with writing. While the monks composed chronicles, the nuns embroidered copes; and those who sought the gift of a manuscript from the monasteries, sought only the gift of needlework from the nunneries.[29]

It would be tempting (though without any foundation in evidence) to indulge in the whimsical speculation that this was just what dissuaded Julian from becoming a nun: she had far too keen an intellect to be content to spend her life doing high class embroidery!

Judging from the low educational standards in convents, one might suppose that if Julian did go to school at Carrow, she would have learned little more than reading (French) and perhaps writing. Yet it

18

may be that that is too black a picture. Historians admit that some nuns retained Latin, and indeed an altogether higher educational standard; and these, of course, would have been the ones likely to be involved in the education of students. With the scholarship at the cathedral priory being high at this time, it is not unlikely that some stimulation for higher standards was passed on to Carrow Abbey. It is also possible that if this was the source of Julian's education and she had thereby come to the notice of the cathedral priory, she might have been eligible for a special arrangement which made books from their library of theology and spirituality available to her.

There are other possibilities which could account for Julian's ability to read and write, even perhaps in Latin. There was a proliferation of schools in the late Middle Ages; more and more young men were given the basic training needed for entrance into the growing universities. Some of the schools were attached to a church or cathedral, but many others by this time were regular grammar schools, perhaps supported by a guild, though even in these all teachers would be clerks in holy orders until the fifteenth century. These schools would teach reading, writing, religion, spoken and written Latin, and possibly rhetoric and logic.[30] If Julian had had a brother who went to such a school (she could not have gone herself, of course, since they would be open only to boys) she could have learned from him: it would not be the first time that a girl of intellectual ability availed herself of her brother's opportunity. But this is at most a possibility; and it has the disadvantage that it leaves out any connection with Carrow Abbey which could provide the link with the anchorhold at St Julian's Church.

Other religious orders besides the Benedictines had houses and centres of scholarship with libraries in Norwich. Once Julian was seriously embarked on her life of prayer and meditation, arrangements might have been made for her to use their books. The most likely in this respect is the house of the Augustinian friars which was just across the street from St Julian's Church and which possessed an excellent library. In 1456 a rule was promulgated that in Austin friaries in future only *duplicate* copies of their books could be lent out. The fact that such a rule was necessary indicates that before this time single copies had been lent; and the fact that it was possible indicates that libraries possessed duplicate copies of at least some of their books.[31]

The Franciscans, the Carmelites and the Dominicans also had major houses in Norwich and were easily accessible to influences from abroad, especially from the Rhineland and the Low Countries, from whence the thought of Eckhart, Tauler, and other Rhineland mystics penetrated English thinking. Also, of course, came the influence from

Paris with its university where Thomas Aquinas had become notable and notorious. From the rest of the continent came many strands, predominant among which was the Cistercian spirituality of Bernard of Clairvaux and his friend and biographer William of St Thierry, whose *Golden Epistle* to the Carthusian monastery of Mont Dieu was a much loved spiritual treatise, widely read and treasured in four-teenth-century England.[32] Thus there was no shortage of religious stimulation and literature in Norwich during Julian's time, if she had the education to use it, and themes from all these writers appear also in her book.

We know almost nothing about Julian's own youth, but she does let one detail drop. She tells us that at one point in the visions, the Lord says,

I thank you for your service and your labour in your youth.[33]

A person with any instinct for drawing attention to their own good-ness would have found this a perfect pretext for elaborating on what that service had been. Julian, however, characteristically draws atten-tion instead to the courtesy and generosity of God in his repayment of her service – so we are left wondering what it might have been. Cer-tainly the social upheavals and the outbreaks of the Black Death would have given her plenty of opportunity for social involvement, possibly with the Béguines; alternatively, it might have been a much more personal, perhaps familial service; or she might simply have been referring to the devoutness of her life of prayer which, as we shall see in the next section, had already developed profoundly by the time she was thirty.

We know that she became ill and received her visions in May 1373, when she was 'thirty and a half years old'[34] and we know that although she probably wrote them down in what we now have as the Short Text very soon after the revelations, she pondered their meaning for at least twenty years before completing the expansion of the original version into the Long Text, which can therefore be pro-visionally dated at about 1393.[35] We can gain some further clues about her life by examining the wills of the period. In March of 1393 a man named Roger Reed, who was rector of St Michael's Church at Coslany in Norwich, left two shillings to 'Julian anakorite'.[36] It is however impossible to be absolutely certain that this was the same woman, as 'Julian' was a common name at this time. Indeed, several inhabitants of the cell at St Julian's Church seem to have taken this name in subsequent years. This might have been partly because of their esteem for her, but it might also have been, as is likely in her own case, simple adoption of the name of the church; and thus could well have been a tradition already before her time. Confusion has resulted from this practice which produced several 'Julians', and has led to the idea that Julian lived to be more than one hundred years old.[37] For instance, Francis Blomfield, writing his *History of Norwich* in 1745 stated that

> In the east part of this Church-yard stood an Anchorage, in which an Ankress or Recluse dwelt 'til the Dissolution, when the house was demolished, tho' the Foundations may still be seen: In 1393, Lady Julian the Ankress here, was a strict Recluse, and had 2 servants to attend her in her old age, A° 1443. This woman in those Days was esteemed one of the greatest Holynesse.[38]

But although the 1393 reference was very probably Julian, the elderly lady of 1443 was most likely another woman of the same name.

The scribe from whose hand comes the introductory paragraph of the Short Text, however, does speak of Julian as still alive in 1413,[39] and a bequest in November 1415, by one John Plumpton, a citizen of Norwich, left forty pence to the 'ankeres in ecclesia sancti Juliani de Conesford in Norwice', as well as twelve pence each to her serving maid and to her former maid named Alice. Julian is again mentioned in a will of 1416.[40] If as is thought probable these do all refer to Mother Julian and not a later namesake, she lived to be at least seventy-four years old: a very advanced age in medieval times. When she died and where she was buried nobody knows. No doubt she would have preferred it that way.

It is intriguing to speculate on when she became an anchoress. As usual, it is impossible to fix a date, but from the information we have several alternatives emerge. First, she could have been an anchoress before she was thirty, that is, before the visions occurred. Secondly, she might have entered the anchorhold sometime between 1373 and 1393, perhaps soon after her recovery from her illness, to pray and meditate on the revelations, and eventually write the Long Text. Or, third, she might not have been an anchoress until after she had completed the writing of the Long Text.

The third possibility has seemed attractive because of Julian's comment at the end of the Long Text, after she has expounded the meaning of the visions as well as she was able, when she says,

> This book is begun by God's gift and grace, but it is not yet performed, as I see it. For charity, let us all join God's working in prayer, thinking, trusting, rejoicing, for so will our good Lord be entreated ...[41]

Some scholars suggest that this indicates that she was only now ready to take the step of entering an anchorhold: having completed the writing of the book, she will now accept its implication and devote the rest of her life to contemplative prayer.[42] However, in the context, that which is 'not yet performed' is the wider dissemination of the knowledge of God's love. Not enough of Julian's fellow-Christians have recognized that he is 'the foundation of your beseeching', and thus she invites them 'to love him and to cleave to him'.[43] It is this which is the consequence of the understanding which she has received; and it is for all her fellow-Christians, as she emphasizes throughout.[44] Even in the passage quoted above, she says, 'let us *all* join God's working in prayer ...': unless she is (absurdly) inviting everyone to enter an anchorhold, this text would be very slender evidence upon which to base an argument that it was the announcement of her own retirement.

A further puzzle arises if one supposes that Julian did not become an anchoress until after completion of the Long Text. If this were the case, she was at least fifty-two before she entered the anchorhold: what might she have been doing before this time? Whatever it was, she must have had a good deal of time for the reading or at least instruction and reflection that went into the composition of the Long Text; and arguably she must have had access to books. One obvious possibility is that she was a nun at Carrow Abbey,[45] and thereby had access to books from the excellent Norwich Cathedral priory library. Since, as already mentioned, Carrow Abbey held the benefice of St Julian's Conisford, they would in any case have been involved in granting permission for her entrance; and what could have been more natural than that the anchoress should have been of their own number?

This is an initially attractive suggestion, except for one thing: her book itself. It bears no marks of having been written in a convent, or of Julian ever having been a nun. She writes for all her fellow-Christians, not just for professional religious, and makes no reference whatever to sisters in an order: this contrasts sharply with, for example, St Teresa of Avila's *Interior Castle*, or other books written by nuns. Nor is there any reference to monastic vows of poverty, chastity, and obedience; no discussion of or even allusion to a rule; no hint of observance of a monastic timetable or of set hours of prayer; no discussion of deference to a prioress. It simply does not breathe the air of a convent, let alone a Benedictine convent; and her emphasis on all her fellow-Christians suggests (but does not prove) close identification with them as a lay person.[46] This is no more than an argument from silence, and cannot be decisive; but it does prompt us to consider other alternatives to the question of what she might have been doing for the first fifty-two years of her life.

Not many such alternatives commend themselves. It is just possible that she was a Béguine; but the argument from silence would apply here too, though perhaps to a lesser extent, since the Béguines were much less tightly organized along traditional monastic principles than, say, Benedictine convents.[47] She might perhaps have been a devout lady of independent means, possibly a widow, and spent her time in good works, meditation and writing. But the norms of the fourteenth century were different from our own; and although this cannot be altogether ruled out, it would have been very much out of the ordinary. Would she have had access to instruction, or to libraries for the books she probably read, if she were a laywoman? These libraries, after all, were not modern public lending libraries but the treasured collections of priceless handwritten manuscripts of the religious orders: would they have allowed a laywoman to borrow books? It is not completely impossible; she would have had a confessor or spiritual director who would have recognized her as an unusual woman and seen her need for theological resources, and he might have helped to make the necessary arrangements, particularly if she had been initially educated at Carrow Abbey or some other convent school. But it does not seem very likely. Added to this difficulty is the fact that if she had lived as a laywoman of sufficient means for a retired life of study and prayer and good works, it seems odd that we do not know her name or any of her past record from independent sources. And if she really was living a retired life of prayer and meditation all this time, would it not have been likely that she would have entered the anchorhold much earlier? That, after all, is precisely the vocation of an anchoress.

This brings us to the question of whether Julian might have become an anchoress before writing the Long Text, perhaps soon after recovering from the illness which was the occasion for the visions. She writes at one point of the chastisement which we receive from Christ, and in this context says that she had no revelation of specific penances which one would take on oneself, but only the revelation that God can use any of our circumstances for this purpose. She says that it is better to accept his chastening than to develop self-inflicted penances, which would too easily degenerate into self-indulgence; and in this context she continues,

> And therefore I want you wisely to understand the penance which you are continually in, and to accept that meekly for your penance. And then you will truly see that all your life is a profitable penance. This place is prison, this life is penance, and he wants us to rejoice in the remedy.[48]

The comment that 'this place is prison' has been taken as a hint that she was already in the anchorhold at the time of writing.[49] It seems unlikely in the context, however, that this was what she was referring to. We must remember again that she is writing for all her fellow-Christians; 'this place', therefore, probably means the place in which we find ourselves, this life, as contrasted to the heaven to which Julian looks forward; it is not a reference to her particular circumstance, anchorhold or otherwise.[50] She immediately speaks of our Lord's remedy, which is his protection as he leads us 'into the fulness

23

of joy' in which he himself is our heaven. She does accept this for herself personally, certainly; but she intends it to have wider application as well, saying,

> Let us flee to the Lord, and we shall be comforted. Let us touch him, and we shall be made clean. Let us cleave to him, and we shall be sure and safe from every kind of peril.[51]

Although they cannot be based on this text, however, arguments advanced against her entry into the anchorhold only after the Long Text was written do point to the likelihood that she was already enclosed by the time that she composed it. The question then arises whether she entered it some time after recovery from her illness, or whether she might have been enclosed before the illness and the revelations took place. She tells us that when it was thought that she was dying, her curate was sent for to assist in her last moments, and that he brought a little boy with him.[52] This curate was probably a secular priest, for later on when another priest comes she specifies that he was a 'man of religion',[53] that is, a member of a religious order. Her mother was also present,[54] and so, it seems, were a number of others.[55] This has been used as an argument against the possibility that she was a recluse at the time of her revelations: she could not have had all these people in an anchorhold.[56]

However, this argument does not stand up. It was not at all unusual even for nuns and monks to have the service of secular priests rather than only the services of monks and friars, especially at this time of shortage of priests after the toll taken by the Black Death. We find Chaucer's prioress in the *Canterbury Tales*, written at about the same time, having 'Sir John', a decidedly secular priest, among her retinue. If Julian had been an anchoress at the time of her illness, it would have been entirely likely that the curate of the church to which she was attached should have come to attend her dying. It is of course true that men were forbidden to enter the cell of an anchoress, but it would be silly to suppose that this rule would apply to her priest when the anchoress was *in extremis*. The same could be said of the presence of her mother. We have, in fact, evidence from an earlier (and probably stricter) period: an anchorite, St Wulfric of Haselbury in Somerset, died 20th February 1154, having been enclosed for twenty-nine years. His observance was rigorous throughout his life; yet when he died he was attended by at least one friend, and no impropriety was attached to this company.[57] Thus the presence of the priest, her mother, and some others (who could have been her serving women) does not by itself tell against her being an anchoress at this time.

The main reasons for supposing that she might have been are two. First is the depth and profundity of her prayer life and devotion to

Christ, who was her entire focus already at the time of her illness.[58] It is clear that this depth of prayer had been developed over some considerable time; and although it is of course possible that this could occur in a secular situation (or in a convent) it might well be thought that this points already to the life of deep devotion of a recluse. The second reason is the negative consideration already discussed: if she was *not* an anchoress, what was she? This question would not pose as great a difficulty for one who supposed that she entered enclosure soon after her illness as it would for one who supposed that she waited until she was in her fifties; but even here, a single lay woman of thirty or more in fourteenth-century society would not be usual.[59]

Fancy can supply several alternatives. Perhaps, as already suggested, she was a Béguine. Or possibly she was a devout woman performing works of social compassion. Or she was a woman who looked after her aged mother until the tables were unexpectedly turned. Or possibly she was a widow, whose husband and children had perished in the Black Death: certainly her tender discussion of motherhood points to some first-hand acquaintance with it – though it might as easily be a reflection backward to her own mother rather than to children of her own.[60]

In the end we simply have to say that we do not know when she entered the anchorhold or what she did before that. Consideration of the various possibilities is one way of becoming more aware of the constraints of the time in which she lived, and in that sense is of great value; but one cannot develop more than a tissue of speculation about the external events which preceded the revelations and the subsequent writing of her book. And that, no doubt, is what she desired; for her intention is not to tell us about the affairs of her outer life, but of her prayer, and how it was answered in the revelations of the love of God in Christ for the benefit of all her fellow-Christians.

Notes to Chapter Two

1. ST 6.
2. LT 86 and 51.
3. LT 2.
4. S1 and S2; C & W vol. II, p. 285.
5. Gertrude the Great, Angela of Foligno, Birgitta of Sweden, and Catherine of Siena, for example, all had secretaries to whom they dictated some or all of their works; and that in spite of the fact that at least Gertrude and Birgitta could write themselves. cf. Valerie M. Lagorio, 'The Medieval Continental Women Mystics', in Paul Szarmach, ed., *An Introduction to the Medieval Mystics of Europe* (State University of New York Press, Albany, New York, 1984).
6. For example, Brant Pelphrey, pp. 18–28.
7. Evelyn Underhill, *Cambridge Medieval History vol. VII*, ed. Tanner et al.

Background and Biography

(Cambridge University Press, 1949), p.807; cf. Sister Eileen Mary SLG, 'The Place of Lady Julian of Norwich in English Literature', in *Julian of Norwich: Four Studies to Commemorate the Sixth Century of the Revelations of Divine Love* (Fairacres Publications 28, SLG Press, Oxford, 1973), pp.3–9.

8. C & W I, p.45.
9. Simon Tugwell, *Ways of Imperfection* (Darton, Longman & Todd, London, 1984), p.188.
10. E. Rozanne Elder, *The Spirituality of Western Christendom*, vol. II Cistercian Studies Series 55 (Kalamazoo, Michigan, 1984), p.xi.
11. As does Clifton Wolters in his Introduction to *Julian of Norwich: Revelations of Divine Love* (Penguin, 1966), p.17.
12. cf. Tugwell, pp.189–90.
13. See below, pp.146–9. cf. Sr Anna Maria Reynolds CP, 'Some Literary Influences in the "Revelations" of Julian of Norwich', in *Leeds Studies in English and Kindred Languages* 7 and 8 (1952).
14. C & W I, pp.44–5.
15. See below, Ch. 9.
16. Knowles, vol. II, p.159. It is interesting to note that Augustine was the favourite theologian even of John Wyclif. cf. W. Mallard, 'John Wyclif and the Tradition of Biblical Authority', in *Church History* 30 (1961), pp.54–60.
17. cf. Wolfgang Riehle, *The Middle English Mystics* (Routledge and Kegan Paul, London, 1981), p.29.
18. cf. Conrad Pepler OP *The English Religious Heritage* (Blackfriars, London, 1958), p.306.
19. Colledge and Walsh also make a great deal of Julian's mastery of the rhetorical style of the Middle English alliterative tradition; but again this seems to be going well beyond the evidence. If one will speak or write at all, one will sometimes use alliteration and repetition and other 'literary devices'; and if one writes with as much ability and style as Julian does, one will use such devices often and with effect. There is no doubt that she is a consummate stylist; the question is whether she was deliberately using rhetorical figures and devices. They were the common property of her time; and we need not suppose that every time she uses phrases like 'meek and mild' or 'feeble and frail' she is consciously using a 'literary device' any more than we are when we use such phrases.
20. Knowles, vol. I, p.312.
21. Knowles, vol. II, p.58.
22. ibid., p.57.
23. ST 1.
24. Knowles, vol. II, pp.59–60. cf. G. R. Owst, *Preaching in Medieval England: An Introduction to the Sermon Manuscripts of the Period c.1350–1450* (Russell & Russell, New York, 1965), pp.15–19.
25. See below, p.31.
26. Eileen Powers, *Medieval English Nunneries c.1275 to 1535* (Hafner Publishing, London, and Biblo & Tannen, N.Y., 1922; reprinted by permission of Cambridge University Press, 1964), p.168n.
27. ibid., p.12.
28. ibid., pp.245–6.

29. ibid., p. 238.
30. William Boyd, *The History of Western Education*, 11th edn rev. Edmund J. King (Adam & Charles Black, London, 1975), pp. 154–8.
31. C & W I, pp. 39–40.
32. cf. Walter Shewring, tr., and Dom Justin McCann, ed., *The Golden Epistle of Abbot William of St Thierry to the Carthusians of Mont Dieu* (London, Sheed & Ward, 1930), Introduction, p. ix.
33. LT 14. Middle English has 'servys and travelle', which Clifton Wolters translates as 'suffering', but the chapter as a whole makes 'service and labour' much more plausible.
34. LT 2 and 3.
35. LT 51.
36. cf. Norman P. Tanner, *Popular Religion in Norwich with Special Reference to the Evidence of Wills, 1370–1532.*
37. The confusion is unintentionally exacerbated by the colophon written by the scribe at the beginning of the Short Text, where he draws attention to Julian's long life.
38. Francis Blomfield, continued by Charles Parkin, *An Essay Towards a Topographical History of the County of Norfolk* (5 vols., Fersfield & Lynn, 1739–75); vol. 2, *The History of the City and County of Norwich* (Norwich, 1745), p. 546 – italics removed.
39. ST 1.
40. cf. Tanner.
41. LT 86.
42. Thus C & W I, p. 42.
43. LT 86.
44. And not merely for her fellow contemplatives in the narrow sense, as is suggested by C & W II, p. 731 n3.
45. C & W I, p. 44, believe that she was a nun but leave the question open as to whether she was at Carrow or at some other convent.
46. cf. Pelphrey, pp. 17–18.
47. R. W. Southern, *Western Society and the Church in the Middle Ages*, The Pelican History of the Church 2 (Penguin Books, 1970), pp. 319–31.
48. LT 77.
49. Clifton Wolters, p. 15.
50. It must be admitted, however, that in the literature an anchorhold was sometimes referred to as a prison: AR, 57/14; but cf. Goscelin's *Liber Confortorius*, 'is not the whole world a prison?'
51. LT 77.
52. ST 2.
53. LT 66.
54. ST 10.
55. LT 13.
56. e.g. Pelphrey, p. 18.
57. *Wulfric of Haselbury*, by John, Abbot of Ford, ed. and introd. Dom Maurice Bell (Somerset Record Society vol. 47, 1932).
58. See below, Chapter 4.
59. It could of course be retorted that by any standards Julian was not 'usual' anyway!
60. cf. Wolters, p. 34.

3 The Life of an Anchoress

At whatever stage of her life Julian entered the anchorhold, she had by that time come to believe that the best way for her to develop her life of prayer was in these enclosed circumstances. To us, this attitude may seem somewhat unusual. The vocation of an anchoress was one with which people of late medieval times were rather more familiar than we are today. It is therefore important for us to explore this lifestyle and its purpose in order to understand the theology and spirituality within which Julian developed.

The English word 'anchorite' is derived from the Greek verb meaning 'to retire': an anchorite (male) or anchoress (female) retired from the world to live strictly within the enclosure of their anchorhold. The impulse toward such solitary living had its roots in the tradition of the desert fathers of the fourth century, who retreated from the cities in which the Church was increasingly accommodating itself to the norms of society, and sought, through self-surrender and extreme austerity, to develop a profound relationship with God, conquering the demons which tempted them away from him.[1] This desire for solitude and immediacy of contact with God, having given up social intercourse and the pleasures and responsibilities it entails, was frequently emphasized in medieval spirituality.[2] In fact, however, there was also considerable suspicion of the solitary life, and pressure towards communal living in monasteries and convents, where the development of holiness could be facilitated by obedience to the Rule and the abbot or superior.[3]

In the eleventh century there was something of a revival of the eremitical ideal, but with an important difference: many of the hermits and anchorites did not remove themselves to solitary places away from all contact with humanity, but sought to develop their solitude in towns and villages: being in the world but not of it. As we shall see, this change had important implications for the contemporary understanding of the vocation of an anchoress or anchorite, who were thus in much closer contact with society than earlier recluses had been, and yet preserved strict enclosure in their anchorhold.

In this they were distinguished from hermits, who, though also living a solitary life, did not confine themselves to a single place or cut themselves off from social intercourse to the same extent: in the Middle Ages hermits often repaired bridges and roads, acted as ferrymen, or assisted travellers in other ways.[4] The anchorite, by contrast, had no such function. Their role was to be set apart for prayer and communion with God, to seek his presence and develop holiness of life. If their anchorhold was attached to a church, as was often the case, an anchorite might occasionally preach or assist at the Mass; one of the ancient guides for anchorites encourages this.[5] But this was unusual by the fourteenth century, and would in any case apply only to men, not to women. It was, however, taken for granted that their prayers would include intercession for the town in which they lived, and that they would be available to offer counsel to those who came to the anchorhold seeking it. They might in one sense be 'dead to the world', but they were not to be useless towards it, and their usefulness entailed clearsighted awareness of its doings.[6]

Often their reputation for sanctity spread far and wide, so that even very important people would make a considerable effort to go to see them. The biographer of Wulfric of Haselbury tells us that

> he was above all a doctor of body and soul: crowds came to see him by day and he made it his business not to refuse them his help. Many came to consult him in their perplexities, some for advice about their vocation, others about their ailments. To those at a distance he sent holy water or blessed bread: on those who came to his window he laid his hands or healed them with the sign of the Cross.[7]

Whatever we make of these healings, it is clear both that Wulfric's withdrawal from the world, rigorous though it was, did not include withdrawal from compassionate ministry to those in need, and also that his contemporaries considered Wulfric a very holy man. This high regard was accorded him even by royalty: he was consulted on separate occasions by King Henry I, King Stephen, and Queen Matilda, whom he sternly rebuked for her arrogance and misrule, of which he was evidently well aware.[8]

Julian characteristically says nothing of herself as a counsellor, but we know that her reputation was similarly spreading because she is mentioned in the book of Margery Kempe of King's Lynn, who sought her out for her advice and spiritual guidance in about 1412 or 1413.[9] In any case, the function of counsellor and spiritual mentor of an anchoress was meant to be subservient to her dedication to a life of prayer, and was an outgrowth from it. The desert fathers to whom they looked back for inspiration had tried to escape human society altogether in their efforts towards a single-minded dedication to God: Aelred of Rievaulx, writing a Rule for his anchoress sister in about 1160, makes specific reference to them as her model:

You must first understand the reasons that motivated the monks of old when they instituted and adopted this form of life ... to avoid ruin, to escape injury, to enjoy greater freedom in expressing their ardent longing for Christ's embrace.[10]

By the fourteenth century, when the escape from human society was of a different form from that desired by the desert fathers, the anchoress was perforce much more involved with human concerns; but like them, the sacrifice not only of possessions and reputation but also of human society was meant to facilitate above all their total devotion to God and availability to him. Julian of Norwich makes this her first priority, having from an early age the unqualified prayer that she might develop 'the wound of longing with my will for God'.[11]

The lifestyle of an anchoress was intended to serve the development of this ideal. There was no single rule of life for all recluses. Some anchorites and anchoresses would have come from a religious order and would therefore have a rule already, which they would continue to keep, perhaps with modifications necessary for the anchoritic situation. Laymen and laywomen could also enter an anchorhold, however, and the circumstances were too individual for there to be a single rule applicable in all cases. However, Aelred's Rule already referred to was influential, as also was an earlier document, the Regula Solitariorum written in about 891 by a monk named Grimlaic.[12]

Most significant, however, was the Ancrene Riwle, or rule of life for anchoresses, written early in the thirteenth century for three sisters who had become anchoresses, though the anonymous author clearly intended his book for a wider audience.[13] The anchoresses themselves had requested a Rule; but the author replies with what Linda Georgianna has called an 'antirule'.[14] Monastic Rules of the preceding period, including that of Grimlaic and Aelred, had concentrated on the external circumstances of life. There are instructions about when and what an anchoress was to eat, when she might sleep, what she ought to wear, and what prayers she was to say. The Ancrene Riwle does offer suggestions about these matters in the first and last chapters, which the author treats as the external wrappings of his book; but in his central chapters he insists that the primary concern is the inner life, which cannot be simply regulated with a set of external precepts.

It was this inner life which made the solitary vocation the highest and most demanding to which one could be called.[15] The gospel story of Mary who sat at Jesus' feet while Martha served him is regularly applied to the contemplative and the active life respectively, together with Jesus' words that Mary had chosen the 'better part'; and the anchoress was identified with the contemplative. Thus for instance the *Ancrene Riwle*, though cautioning the anchoresses not to scorn or meddle in 'Martha's business' since it is also a laudable calling, nevertheless says,

> Ye anchorites have taken to yourselves Mary's part, which our Lord himself commended ... Housewifery is Martha's part, and Mary's part is quietness and rest from all the world's din, that nothing may hinder her from hearing the voice of God.[16]

And Aelred calls on his sister to do as Mary did and

> Break the alabaster of your heart and whatever devotion you have, whatever love, whatever desire, whatever affection, pour it all out upon your Bridegroom's head, while you adore the man in God and God in the man.[17]

The life of the anchoress was meant to be an arduous one, but the arduousness was not for its own sake but for the interior life which it developed. Because of this they were unlike the desert fathers who tested the extremes of asceticism. The rules we have for anchoresses, especially the *Ancrene Riwle*, expressly prohibit ascetical heroics, and suggest a moderate lifestyle when measured against the standards of living of the time.

The anchorhold itself would generally consist of a fair-sized room or suite of rooms, and might well be less cramped than the homes of the lower classes. Often, as in the case of St Julian's, it was built against the side of a church, with a window or squint pierced through the wall so that the anchoress could follow the daily service. The *Ancrene Riwle* gives special instruction about this:

> To Priest's hours listen as well as you can, but you should neither say the versicles with him nor sing so that he may hear it.[18]

The anchorhold would probably have an oratory with an altar; if the anchorite were a priest, he might assist in celebration of the Mass, but this would obviously not apply to women. In their case, the altar was to be covered with a white linen cloth, symbolic of chastity and simplicity; upon it was to be a crucifix and, if they wished, a picture of Christ's Mother and his disciple on either side of it.[19] Apart from those, they were not to have pictures or decoration in the anchorhold.

Besides the window to the church there would be a window to the world, where people could come for counsel and guidance. It seems that at least in some cases this window did not open directly to the outdoors, but rather to a small parlour, so that visitors might sit in it and speak to the anchoress through the window, away from prying eyes and pouring rain.[20] We shall consider this window and its various uses and temptations in more detail presently.

From the main anchorhold, a door (or perhaps in some cases a third window) would open into another room or rooms in which stayed a servant or two, and which in turn opened to the outside world. The servant was responsible for all the domestic necessities of the anchoress – cooking, cleaning, shopping, and the like – the 'house-wifery' in which the anchoress was not to allow herself to be involved. It would clearly be very important to the anchoress that her servant would be steady and responsible, and sympathetic to the aims of the anchoritic life; troubles with her domestic staff would be a perpetual source of distraction to an anchoress, and should be pre-empted by taking great care about the servant in the first place. If troubles did arise, they could result either from not getting along, or from getting along rather too well, so that the anchoress would be tempted to spend time chatting which she ought to spend in prayer. Aelred gives the following advice on the choice of the domestic:

> Choose for yourself some elderly woman, not someone who is quarrelsome or unsettled or given to idle gossip; a good woman with a well-established reputation for virtue. She is to keep the door of your cell, and, as she thinks right, to admit or refuse visitors; and to receive and look after whatever provisions are needed. She should have under her a strong girl capable of heavy work, to fetch wood and water, cook vegetables and, when ill-health demands it, to prepare more nourishing food. She must be kept under strict discipline, lest, by her frivolous behaviour she desecrate your holy dwelling-place and so bring God's name and your own vocation into contempt.[21]

The *Ancrene Riwle* lays down rules for the domestic when she goes out shopping or on any other business: 'by the way, as she goeth let her go singing her prayers', and be so dressed and deport herself in such a way that everyone recognizes her as the anchoress's servant and does not attempt to engage her in idle conversation. She is expected to say prayers of her own, not to desire a salary beyond her food and clothing (about which, however, the anchoress is to be liberal), and all in all, to live a life of very considerable devotion to the anchoress and to God. And 'let them by all means forbear to vex their mistress', but if, being human, they do, they are to accept the penance which the anchoress imposes upon them. Having imposed the penance, the anchoress in turn is not to nag at them or 'ever again thereafter upbraid her with the same fault'.[22]

The anchoress thus has a solemn responsibility before God for her domestics, and is to teach them with great diligence and care,

> in a gentle manner, however, and affectionately; for such ought the instructing of women to be – affectionate and gentle, and seldom stern. It is right that they should both fear and love you; but that there should always be more of love than of fear. Then it shall go well.[23]

Prayer will go better in an atmosphere of affection and tranquillity than in an overly solemn and heavy-handed anchorhold. The joy and delicate touch Julian shows in her writings was no doubt also a part of her dealings with her domestics. As we have seen from the wills of the period, Julian had at least one servant who had a sufficiently high reputation to be given a bequest in her own right.[24] It is interesting to note that in her profound reflections on the relationship between God's transcendent greatness and his loving intimacy, Julian applies to our attitude to God this very mixture of love and fear which the domestic is to have toward the anchoress:

> And as good as God is, so great is he; and as much as it is proper to his divinity to be loved, so much is it proper to his great exaltedness to be feared. For this reverent fear is the fairer courtesy which is in heaven before God's face; and by as much as he will be known and loved, surpassing how he now is, by so much will he be feared, surpassing how he now is.[25]

The solitude of the anchoress, therefore, was not absolute, for besides giving counsel to those who consulted her she had a domestic or two in her care. Nevertheless, her special hallmark was her strict enclosure. She never left her cell, and was regularly referred to as dead to the world, shut up as with Christ in his tomb.[26] 'Cell' could be interpreted fairly broadly, to include a garden or perhaps the churchyard where she could take the air.[27] Beyond this, however, there was no release from the anchorhold until death, on pain of excommunication.[28]

The idea of the anchoress's death to the world was symbolized in the rite of enclosure, of which several forms survive. In the Sarum usage, to which others are similar, a requiem Mass was sung at the church. Then there was a solemn procession to the anchorhold. When they arrived, the officiant blessed the anchorhold, and led the anchoress inside. The anchoress was then given extreme unction, after which the bishop scattered dust on the anchoress and the anchorhold, which from henceforward was to be considered her grave. The bishop then left the anchoress inside, and bolted the door on the outside, after which the procession returned to the church. It was a dramatic ceremony; its psychological impact on the anchoress and on any observers was intended to reinforce the conception that she was now dead to the world, and was never again to emerge from her enclosure.[29]

Even the common law courts respected the enclosure of the anchoress, and in any case of litigation, a recluse was allowed to send a proxy rather than leave her cell. But is there not something ironic in the idea that a woman dead to the world would need to be represented at court? What could possibly involve an anchoress in litigation? The *Ancrene Riwle* gives some prohibitions which offer clues – and which indicate that though in one sense the anchoress is dead to the world, in another sense, she is very much alive, and the world entered the anchorhold when she did.[30] In the first place, the anchoress is instructed not to become a repository for other people's valuables, nor even of the chalice and vestments of the church.[31] In those troubled times, when the common people would hardly have had access to banks or safety vaults, it might seem most secure to deposit things with an anchoress for safe-keeping: no one would desecrate an anchorhold and plunder it. Or would they? One need only think of Litster's mobs ravaging the churches and monasteries of Norwich in 1381. If Julian was in the anchorhold at that time, she would have been glad of a reputation for not accepting valuables for deposit, for it seems that at the height of their tumult those mobs would have stopped at nothing. In any case, people have a way of forgetting where they deposited things or how much the deposit was, whether in money, jewels, or other valuables. If an anchoress kept things like this for people, it could easily become a source of contention and potentially even of litigation.

Another possible source of trouble was cows. Apparently anchoresses often kept cows; but the author of the *Ancrene Riwle* considers it a very bad idea.

> For then she must think of the cow's fodder, and of the herdsman's hire, flatter the heyward, defend herself when her cattle is shut up in the pinfold, and moreover pay the damage. Christ knoweth, it is an odious thing when people in the town complain of anchoresses' cattle.[32]

All this seems humorously out of character for one who is supposed to be dead; yet even this author relents a little, and says that if they must have a cow, they are to make sure that it is neither a distraction to themselves nor a public nuisance. A pleasant note creeps into this discussion: the anchoress, though she is to possess no cattle or other animals (Aelred had spoken of flocks)[33] is to have a cat. No doubt the cat was intended for the obvious purpose of catching mice and rats, but it is hard to suppose that the 'gentle and affectionate' anchoress and her servant would not have made a pet of it. The image arises of Julian pondering the meaning of the revelations with pussy curled up at her feet.

A different sort of distraction, against which the anchoresses are warned is that of becoming schoolmistress to little girls in the area.

> An anchoress must not become a schoolmistress, nor turn her anchoress-house into a school for children. Her maiden may, however, teach any little girl concerning whom it might be doubtful whether she should learn among boys, but an anchoress ought to give her thoughts to God only.[34]

Aelred puts it more vividly:

> She (the anchoress) sits at her window, the girls settle themselves in the

porch; and so she keeps them all under observation. Swayed by their childish dispositions, she is angry one minute and smiling the next, now threatening, now flattering, kissing one child and smacking another ...[35]

The fact that these warnings had to be repeated probably indicates that teaching, like keeping cows, was a perpetual temptation, with something to be said on its behalf in that time when very little education was available for girls. Perhaps this is why the *Ancrene Riwle* does allow the anchoress' servant to teach – and she, of course, would be guided by the anchoress. One might even speculate that Julian herself received some of her literary skills in this way.

Some further aspects of the life-style of an anchoress emerge from a comparison of the various rules. Chastity is of course taken as an absolute essential: Aelred places so much emphasis on this that his rule has been called 'an ascetic letter on the preservation of virginity'.[36] Chastity, however, is to include chastity of heart as well as of body. He says ironically,

A recluse of today is quite satisfied if she preserves bodily chastity, if she is not drawn forth pregnant from her cell, if no infant betrays its birth by its wailing,[37]

and asserts (one can only hope that he is exaggerating!) that it is 'all too common' for a cell to be turned into a brothel.[38] Evidence from the medieval period suggests that things were probably not quite as bad as that. Although there is one known catastrophe, where the inhabitant of an anchorhold at Whalley parish church ran away,[39] there is very little other indication of scandal, and the reputation of recluses was on the whole very high indeed. But clearly there was plenty of opportunity for any anchoress who should wish to indulge in immoral behaviour. People would come to see her very privately, and her domestic could be dispatched from the anchorhold on any number of legitimate-looking pretexts if the anchoress wished to devise them. Perhaps this was part of the reason for the frequent and emphatic warnings.

To help her avoid sexual temptation, an anchoress' conversation with members of the opposite sex was to be severely restricted. Aelred allows that she should speak to a priest for confession and spiritual direction, but for no other purposes, and even for these, only infrequently. The priest should be 'an elderly man of mature character and good reputation'[40] and there should always be a witness, though probably out of earshot.[41] Even an abbot or a prior should be spoken to only in the presence of a third person, and the anchoress should be sure to keep her face veiled. She should not accept letters or gifts from a man, and should not send them herself, even to a priest or a monk.[42] The *Ancrene Riwle* apparently takes for granted that men as well as women will come to speak with the anchoress and seek spiritual counsel, as they did to Wulfric of Haselbury,[43] but they are to be spoken to only through the parlour window, which is to have a double curtain of black cloth with a white cross on it.[44] Nor should this curtain be drawn back on any pretext whatever:

> If any man requests to see you, ask him what good might come of it; for I see many evils in it, and no good; and if he insists immoderately, believe him the less; and if any one becometh so mad and unreasonable that he puts forth his hand toward the window cloth, shut the window quickly and leave him ...[45]

It is important to see that the warnings are not given in such a way as to suggest that it is only the other party who represents the risk: it is taken for granted that anchoresses are ordinary women with healthy sexual desires, and therefore never immune from temptations to unchastity. Whatever their death to the world may involve, their instincts are still very much alive.[46] The writer emphasizes that temptations are never far away, and that that, indeed, is a good thing, because it helps the anchoress to a robust self-knowledge and humility.[47] We shall find Julian expanding this point in her teaching that sin and suffering find a place in the development of whole and healthy human development.[48]

As was common in the Middle Ages, the writers of these rules believed that moderation in food and drink was a vital counterpart to sexual purity, partly because self-indulgence in one area would easily spread to others. Judging from both Aelred and the *Ancrene Riwle* in their instructions about food, anchoresses would have had two meals a day from Easter until Holy Cross Day in September; the rest of the year they would have only one. But there were exceptions: every Friday throughout the year was a fast day on which bread and water only were permitted; and every Sunday was a feast day, on which they had two meals. Aelred takes the Rule of St Benedict as a basis. This allows for a pound of bread and a pint of wine per day (these are the times before tea and coffee were available), porridge or vegetables cooked in oil, butter, or milk for the noon meal, followed by fresh fruit in season; for the evening meal some fish or a cheese dish.[49] The *Ancrene Riwle* specifies that

> Ye shall eat no flesh nor lard except in great sickness; or whosoever is infirm may eat potage without scruple ...[50]

All this sounds rather austere, and in some ways it was: most people would have had more than bread and water on Fridays, and would have eaten meat at least occasionally – though we must remember that the exclusion of 'flesh' did not mean that fish and fowl were not permitted the anchoress. Even so, however, the anchoress' diet may well have been better than that which the poorer classes enjoyed, in quality if not in quantity; and since an anchoress led a very quiet life, she hardly needed the amount of food required by a stonemason or a ploughman. Furthermore, both rules specify that they are offering guidelines only, which can be changed according to circumstance.[51]

The point in this as in everything else was that they were to curb any sort of self-indulgence in their single-minded devotion to God. From this it would follow, however, that they were to be sensible about it: the dietary rules are only intended as means to an end, and if they become barriers rather than means, they are to be jettisoned. Especially in any time of illness, the anchoresses were not to place stringent physical austerities upon themselves. When any of them went through the common medical practice of blood-letting (which they were to do whenever necessary) the *Ancrene Riwle* exhorts them to

> do nothing that is irksome to you for three days ... thus wisely take care of yourselves when you let blood, and keep yourselves in such rest that long thereafter ye may labour the more vigorously in God's service, and also when ye feel any sickness, for it is a great folly, for the sake of one day, to lose ten or twelve.[52]

The body is to be disciplined in order to make the life of prayer possible, not destroyed to make it impossible.

The same moderation is encouraged in terms of such things as clothes and bedding. The anchoress is to have as much as she needs to keep warm in winter, including shoes and a warm cape, but she is not bound to wear all this in the summer, and is welcome to go barefoot and keep cool if she wishes. It is unimportant what colour her clothes are, since no one sees her:

> Only see that they be plain, and warm, and well made – skins well tawed; and have as many as you need, for bed and also for back.[53]

Anyone who has spent some hours in a stone church on a damp winter morning will recognize the importance of this permission. The anchorhold would have been heated, of course; probably with a wood-burning fireplace. But the anchoress who rose soon after midnight to say Matins and then pray and meditate quietly until dawn would have been very glad of some warm furs to keep away the cold.

In all these things, anchoresses were to be adequately provisioned. If an anchorite was left to starve, the bishop of the area was held responsible. Aelred suggests that a recluse should if possible live by the labour of her own hands, chiefly needlework,

> but if poor health or a delicate constitution forbids this she should, before being enclosed in her cell, find someone to provide her with what is necessary for each day.[54]

Other writers, however, consider needlework a method of staving off idleness, but not a method by which the anchoresses were expected to earn their living, since this would be yet another distraction from the life of prayer to which they were called. The anchoresses for whom the *Ancrene Riwle* was written seem to have been well provided for, and their needlework was accordingly not to be sold but to consist of making clothing for the poor, and church vestments.[55] Sometimes anchorites were provided with food by the monastery or convent that had responsibility for the anchorhold. Wulfric of Haselbury, for example, was provided with daily food from the nearby Cluniac monastery of Montacute, usually oaten bread and porridge; this was supplemented by gifts from private persons of bread, cakes, fish, and wine (which he kept for holy days only!) – again, not a bad diet by the standards of the time.[56] It is possible, though again we cannot be sure, that Julian received support from Carrow Abbey who held the benefice of St Julian's Church. Most solitaries also received gifts of money or in kind from those who came to see them, and often, as in the case of Julian, they were the beneficiaries of wills – sometimes of royal wills.[57]

The upshot was that sometimes they had more than they themselves needed. They were warned, however, not to become alms-houses. Although it was assumed that an anchoress would keep no more than was essential for her own needs, she was to give away anything extra through the church or the priest, not to individuals who came begging to her window.

> Her cell is not to be besieged by beggars, nor by orphans and widows crying for alms.
> But who, you ask, can prevent them?
> Sit still, and say nothing, wait. When they realize that you have nothing, that they will get nothing from you, they will soon grow tired and depart.[58]

This is not, of course, because the anchoress hoards money or property of any kind; she is 'to guard her poverty so jealously that she always has just a little less than lawful necessity might allow her',[59] in food, clothing, and everything else. But by channelling any excess through the priest or the church she preserves her cell from becoming a place where people might use a spiritual pretext to seek a material hand-out; she also protected herself from burglary. It was an age of beggars, many out of real need, some for less credible motives; and there was no social security system to help the unfortunate. If an anchoress once began to allow her compassion to lead her into direct alms-giving, laudable though it might be, there would be no end to it and her life of prayer would be severely disrupted.

This, in fact, was the real austerity for the anchoress, the sacrifice that bit deepest, linked as it was to the commitment to a life of solitude and confinement. An anchoress was cut off from human contact, apart from her domestics, except insofar as she spoke to her confessor or to those who came seeking counsel. Such isolation could lead some anchoresses to extreme loneliness and desolation, and sometimes to utter boredom. On the other hand, perhaps even worse, the solitary life could be sought out not by people who sincerely wanted to live a life of prayer and devotion to God, but simply people who wanted to live alone because they did not like other people and could not get along in society. It could be a haven for the neurotic and it could drive sane people mad.

For this reason, the later Middle Ages developed a careful screening procedure: not just anyone was allowed to become an anchoress. Those who felt called to this vocation were examined by the bishop or his representative, and only after he was satisfied of the genuineness of the calling would he allow the enclosure to take place.[60] This seems to have had the desired effect, because as already noted there is little evidence of scandal, madness, or failure to fulfil the vocation; and many seem to have found the lifestyle agreeable enough to persevere to a ripe old age. It would be fascinating to know how the bishop conducted his examination. The mind boggles at the thought of Henry Despenser, *episcopus martius*, examining Julian to discern whether she was truly a woman of prayer – whose shoe latchet he was hardly worthy to unloose. One hopes that at least on this occasion he appointed a delegate.

Because of the relentless solitude of the anchoress' life, the window to the world offered great temptation. Only her own discipline ordered the way she spent her time; if she allowed herself to do so, she could become the recipient of all the town gossip. Aelred satirizes the recluse who in fact is nothing but a bag of tales:

> At her window will be seated some garrulous old gossip pouring idle tales into her ears, feeding her with scandal and gossip; describing in detail the face, appearance and mannerisms of now this priest, now that monk or clerck; describing too the frivolous behaviour of a young girl; the free and easy ways of a widow who thinks what she likes is right; the cunning ways of a wife who cuckolds her husband while she gratifies her passions. The recluse all the while is dissolved in laughter, loud peals of laughter ...[61]

But one need not be such a wanton anchoress to fall into gossip. A woman to whom many would come to unburden their consciences and to seek counsel about personal matters would be the recipient of many confidences, and since many of the people would no doubt come from the same town, much of the information could easily be interlinked. Even a deeply devoted anchoress would have to exercise great discretion not to betray these confidences in the giving of counsel. And an anchoress who was feeling lonely and in need of someone to talk to – as anyone would from time to time – could easily be tempted to keep people interested by occasionally letting slip some morsel of information about her fellows. This would of course be a travesty of what the life of an anchoress was intended to be; but it would be a totally understandable travesty nonetheless. It is interesting to notice how fully Julian preserves confidences: she tells us nothing of anyone who came to her, and it is only from Margery Kempe, not from Julian, that we hear of Margery's visit and the counsel she received.

Nevertheless, although these temptations would be a part of her life, taken all in all the anchoress, though strictly enclosed and devoted to a life of prayer, seems to have had sufficient safeguards to prevent it from becoming intolerable. There was austerity, but not such extreme deprivation that the physical or psychological strain would itself become a distraction. The anchoress, after all, was not to be a seven day wonder of ascetical heroics, but a life-long witness of dedication to prayer and holiness. Thus although discipline must be strict, it must also be moderate. This moderation is emphasized in all the documents we have.[62]

Perhaps this emphasis was partly in response to harsh measures which some anchorites and anchoresses in previous centuries had tended to adopt for themselves. Wulfric of Haselbury in the eleventh century had worn a hair shirt, over which he wore a complete coat of mail to remind himself that he was engaged in a spiritual battle. Each night, before going to a bed made deliberately uncomfortable by constructing it out of intertwining rough branches, he immersed himself in a bath of cold water for as long as it took to recite the whole Psalter.[63] Yet his biographer portrays him as a sane and balanced man with a delightful sense of humour and, as already noted, a great reputation for wisdom and sanctity.

Nevertheless, by the time of Julian, and already in Aelred and the *Ancrene Riwle*, this sort of practice was forbidden, largely on the grounds that it was seen as counter-productive. The fourteenth-century author of the *Cloud of Unknowing* cautions the solitary to whom he is writing not to confuse spiritual exercises with bodily asceticism: those who 'turn their bodily sense inwards on themselves' and strain against nature may very well see visions and hear voices, but they will be illusions, attributable to the devil via their own foolishness.[64] In modern terminology we might say that anyone who violently represses his or her physicality is a prime candidate for neurotic fantasies and religious hallucinations: the author of the *Cloud*, along with many other medieval spiritual directors, knew this very well long before Freud re-emphasized it for modern consciousness. The *Cloud* warns his contemplative reader,

> Insofar as you can, never be the cause of your physical weakness. For it is true what I say: this work demands a great tranquillity, and a clean bill of health as well in body as in soul. So for the love of God, govern yourself wisely in body and in soul, and keep in good health as much as possible.[65]

The Life of an Anchoress

The author of the *Ancrene Riwle* offers the same cautions, and indeed suggests to the three anchoresses to whom he is writing that

> your meat and your drink have seemed to me less than I would have it. Fast no day upon bread and water except ye have leave.[66]

Yet this last comment should give us pause. For although the writer is concerned that they have adequate food and warm clothing, 'adequate' must be taken in context, and not by twentieth-century standards. We have already seen that they *do* have leave, indeed they are expressly required, to fast on bread and water every Friday: not many of us would need to be cautioned against too frequent repetition of this on other days! Nor would these further commands be necessary:

> Wear no iron, nor haircloth, nor hedge-hog skins; and do not beat yourselves therewith, nor with a scourge of leather thongs, nor leaded; and do not with holly nor with briars cause yourselves to bleed without leave of your confessor; and do not, at one time, use too many flagellations.[67]

How many is too many? This 'counsel of moderation' clearly takes for granted that *some* flagellation, as also some extra fasting, will properly be permitted.[68]

In the same spirit, Aelred of Rievaulx pours scorn on those who are more concerned not to deprive their body than for the development of their soul:

> We are all wise, all prudent, all discreet. We sniff war from afar and are in such dread of bodily disease before it makes itself felt that we take no notice of the spiritual sickness which is already troubling us – as if the flame of lust were easier to bear than the complaints of the stomach; as if it were not much better to avoid the wantonness of the flesh by continual weakness than to be brought into subjection to it by health and strength.[69]

The rest of his book makes it clear that Aelred is not advocating ill health or indeed ascetical extremes, but he leaves us in no doubt about the priorities should one be required to make a choice between physical and spiritual well-being.

The very fact that these people, while taking some ascetical measures for granted, find it necessary to caution their recluses against excesses, shows that it was common to see ascetical measures as necessary for spiritual progress. One of the reasons for this was that they believed that spiritual growth could take place only when the bodily appetites were kept in control. But even more importantly, they felt that actual physical pain was helpful to them in identifying with the suffering of Jesus.[70] It is interesting to see how Julian takes up and modifies each of these themes in her own teaching on spiritual growth, born out of the most extreme physical suffering in her severe illness, which was an answer to her prayer to share in the bodily suffering of her Lord.[71]

It cannot be over emphasized, however, that although practices which would seem extreme in the twentieth century were taken for granted by solitaries of the time, the austerities were not undertaken to score points in a competition of rigour, but rather were to be used, as with all the rest of the rules, only insofar as they fostered spiritual development. Bernard of Clairvaux, a primary influence on Aelred and himself a firm upholder of stringent ascetical measures, stressed the primacy of the internal over the external:

> If it happened that one or the other element must be left aside, it is better that it be the material. For, just as the soul is more important than the body, so spiritual practices are more fruitful than material ones.[72]

This was taken up pointedly by the author of the *Ancrene Riwle*, who emphasized that all the anchoress' practices had as a single aim the development of love for God; otherwise they were worthless. He modifies the words of St Paul in 1 Corinthians 13 to make them say,

> though I inflicted upon my body all the pains, and all the sufferings that a body could endure; and though I gave poor men all that I had; unless I had therewith love to God and to all men, in him and for him, it were all lost.[73]

And lest there be any doubt, he adds,

> They who love most shall be most blessed, not they who lead the most austere life, for love outweigheth this.[74]

In order to develop that love, a framework of prayer was created, which was to provide the context for the inner life of devotion for the anchoress. Aelred sketches the outline of the recluse's day. The schedule of prayer is similar to that of a convent or monastery, with seven set times daily: Matins sometime after midnight, Lauds just before dawn, followed by Prime, Terce about 9.0 a.m., Sext at noon, None about 3.0 p.m., Vespers in the early evening, and Compline at bedtime. The cathedral clock had been functioning in Norwich since 1325, and Julian would have been able to regulate herself by it. At these times, fixed prayers were to be used: the *Ancrene Riwle* specifies a demanding routine of psalms, paternosters, aves, and other vocal prayers, as well as the position the anchoress is to take – sitting, standing, kneeling, making the sign of the cross – as she says them. Yet these are meant only to set the context for her own prayer, which was to take place, according to Aelred, especially between Prime and Terce, and before Vespers. 'Prayer' here would include spiritual reading and meditation, and if the times were faithfully observed, it would allow for a great deal of spiritual study and reflection upon which Julian drew so much in seeking to understand the revelations.

To make all this possible, it would be necessary to specify times of silence, both from the domestics and in terms of the people who come to see her, so that there could be long periods without interruption. Therefore Aelred lays down the times when the anchoress is to give instruction to her domestics and talk with them, and also when she is to receive visitors.[75] Apart from these times, silence is to be observed. During some seasons of the year, particularly Lent, talking is to be cut to a minimum, so that she can give her attention wholly to God. She is not at this time to receive visitors at all unless it is someone who has come 'unexpectedly from a distance': the rules always have a human touch. The whole point of all this silence is to foster the quietness of heart that can listen to the quiet voice of God without distraction from outward things. The noise and commotion of the world would press in on the medieval town dweller as insistently as it does today, for people lived closely together and there would rarely be the protective barrier of impersonality which the modern city has fostered. The recluse is to develop stillness, internal as well as external; and although entry into the anchorhold is a large step in the right direction, it is still possible to fritter away the time even in an anchorhold chatting with domestics and with visitors who come for counsel and stay for gossip. The *Ancrene Riwle*, having spoken with irony about anchoresses who are 'great talkers', enjoins silence upon them by means of a homely example: the anchoress is not to be like the hen, which cackles as soon as it has laid an egg.

> And what does she get by it? Straightway comes the chough and robs her of her eggs and devours all that of which she should have brought forth live birds. And just so the wicked chough, the devil, beareth away from the cackling anchoresses, and swalloweth up, all the good they have brought forth, and which ought, as birds, to bear them up toward heaven, if it had not been cackled.[76]

Long periods of unbroken contemplation would require a foundation of much silence, which, beginning with outward things, would enable the development of an attentive spirit.

Yet these long times for prayer, day after day, could have the undesirable effect of turning the whole enterprise into an utterly tedious existence, engendering nothing so much as boredom. It is noteworthy that Julian, though she does not usually enter into discussion of specific sins, does speak pointedly of impatience, which she equates with sloth; and says that we are inclined to these by 'spiritual blindness and bodily heaviness'.[77] The arduousness of the anchoress' life would not consist so much of bodily austerities as of this steady long-term discipline of spirit not to give way to impatience or boredom in the life of prayer, and thus to become slothful in inner longing for

God, even though the external routine of prayers might be maintained. Her chief temptation might well be the very subtle one of simply losing sight of the purpose of her enclosure, so that instead of finding prayer a deepening communion with God it became a tedious routine. From this, temptations to gossip or even to unchastity could quickly follow.

To help cope with the tedium of the life-style, the rules offer practical advice. The anchoress

> must take care that prolonged prayer does not engender a distaste for prayer; it is more profitable to pray often and briefly than for too long at one time, unless of course it be prolonged without one's knowing it, by the inspiration of devotion. Avoid imposing on yourself the recitation of a fixed number of psalms as an obligation; when the psalms attract you use them, but when they become a burden change to reading; when reading palls rouse yourself to prayer; when wearied of them all take to manual labour. By this healthy alternation you will refresh your spirit and banish spiritual weariness.[78]

It would be a great mistake to think of anchoresses as women of such depth of prayer that temptations to boredom and utter distaste for the whole venture would never come upon them. While it is true that many of them did become women of great spiritual stature, they did not start out that way; their growth in prayer came precisely by refusing to be defeated by the torpor and sense of pointlessness that inevitably afflicted them from time to time.

The mental and spiritual alertness necessary to continue in this way without losing the sense of longing for God and collapsing into a dull and pointless existence would be very considerable. It would scarcely be compatible with the ascetical practice we find in some of the desert fathers of trying to sleep as little as possible. The author of the *Ancrene Riwle* recommends plenty of sleep. It would be necessary to go to bed very early in order to be ready to rise in the small hours of the morning to say Matins and then proceed with personal prayer until nearly dawn; if this practice was to be sustained, a siesta during the day would also be necessary. And these rests are not to be used for reading or meditating or even prayer:

> In bed, as far as you can, neither do anything nor think, but sleep.[79]

Although all the cares of the world might come to her window, the anchoress was to foster such quietness of heart and tranquillity of mind that this counsel could be complied with.

On the one hand, the reclusive life has sometimes been treated with awe as itself saintly. On the other hand, it has been portrayed as utterly selfish. The thought of a woman voluntarily adopting a life of seclusion, and vowing not to come out of her enclosure until death, dedicating herself to prayer and holiness of life, might seem heroic to

the point of impossibility in the twentieth century. Yet by the
standards of the time, the anchoress' life might have seemed enviable
to some. She was after all normally assured of food, clothing, and
decent accommodation, usually without having to toil for it. She had
domestic staff to attend to her daily wants, and unless she undermined
it by scandalous behaviour, she was assured of a high reputation. In
return for all this, she was expected simply to live quietly in her
enclosure, pray for the town and its inhabitants, and be willing to listen
to people and counsel them at fixed hours in the week. She did not have
to take responsibility for her own financial or domestic affairs, or
associate with people whom she found difficult. Some people of her
time and since could well see the anchoritic life as luxury and self-
indulgence.

The charge of self-indulgence could bite much more deeply than the
physical level. It was not just that anchoresses did not have to labour as
others did. More telling was the charge that they were so intent on their
own salvation that they devoted their entire lives to its attainment
rather than ministering to the needs of their fellow human beings.
Gerald of Wales expressed his objections in a letter to Archbishop
Stephen Langton in 1215: he contrasts ecclesiastical prelates with hermits and anchorites, much to the disadvantage of the latter:

> The former feed, the latter two are fed. The former restore, with heavy
> interest, the talent entrusted by God: the latter, in a way, conceal the talent
> entrusted – intent on little more than their own salvation ... Though there-
> fore the contemplative life be securer and much more tranquil, as you know,
> far more useful is that (life) which is active – far more strenuous also and
> glorious: many does it perfect for salvation: much gain is produced by it for
> Christ.[80]

These reflections of Gerald of Wales may have been prompted by less
worthy motives than the ostensible concern for the Kingdom of God;
nevertheless, his remarks are worth pondering. It might be thought that
the solitaries of the Middle Ages were so selfishly preoccupied with
their own soul that they would cheerfully let the rest of the world go to
hell while they basked in their communion with God. None of them
would have been happy about that way of putting it, of course, but it is
the implication of the charges of Gerald of Wales. The Christian ideal of
perfection is the love of God alone; for the anchoritic life this appears to
imply the 'renunciation of every form of human love in the quest for the
vision of God', so that any human relationship of social concern de-
tracts from the 'one thing needful'. According to John Passmore, this
means that 'anchoritism ... carries egocentric Christianity to its
extreme point'.[81] And this, in turn, seems to have moved a vast distance
from the healing and teaching ministry of the compassionate Christ.

It is of course true that the anchoritic life-style, like any other, could become sheer self-seeking and spiritual self-indulgence. Yet it must be recognized that that was not the intent. Presumably part of the bishop's examination of a candidate was an effort to determine whether or not this was the candidate's motive. The physical enclosure was not intended to be a way of shutting out concern for others but a way of focusing it. It is clear from her book that Julian identified deeply with the suffering and brokenness of humanity, refusing to accept even the experience of God himself as a substitute for an answer to her urgent questioning about why all of this should be necessary. The life of prayer which the anchoress led was not prayer only on her own behalf. She sought holiness of life and communion with God in order to be able to intercede more effectively for others.

The anchoritic life stands for a rejection of the assumption that praying for someone in difficulty is less demanding than actually doing something to alleviate the situation. Of course, this could also sometimes be the case: 'If a brother or sister is ill-clad and in lack of daily food, and one of you says to him, "Go in peace, be warmed and filled", without giving them the things needed for the body, what does it profit?'[82] But the fundamental belief of anyone committed to a life of intercession is that prayer is not a substitute for involvement, it is a method of involvement. If this was the platform from which an anchoress began, then sustained intercessory prayer would be 'doing something' in the most effective way possible. Thus judging the anchoritic life by its own presuppositions cannot generate a verdict of selfishness. Aelred summarized the extent of the anchoress's prayer:

> Embrace the whole world with the arms of your love and in that act at once consider and congratulate the good, contemplate and mourn over the wicked. In that act look upon the afflicted and the oppressed and feel compassion for them ... In that act call to mind the wretchedness of the poor, the groan of the orphans, the abandonment of widows, the gloom of the sorrowful, the needs of travellers, the prayers of virgins, the perils of those at sea, the temptations of monks, the responsibilities of prelates, the labours of those waging war. In your love take them all to your heart, weep over them, offer your prayers for them.[83]

The contemplative, who draws near to the compassionate heart of God, should thereby become the most compassionate of persons. This, indeed, will be a test of the genuineness of her prayers. It is the very opposite of egocentricity; it is a love which 'embraces the whole world'. It is the development of this unselfish love which requires the strict discipline of the anchoress, not an effort to lift herself to heaven by her own ascetical bootstraps. The theme of compassion and all-inclusive love becomes a major aspect of Julian's spirituality.

Also, as we have seen, the anchoress was available to offer care and

46

counsel to those who came to her window. Into her ears poured the sins and sorrows of the world around her. The people who came to her would hope for two things: her understanding and wisdom, and her continuing prayer for them after they had gone their way. Thus along with the obligation of preserving scrupulous confidentiality, the anchoress had the obligation of ensuring that her life of prayer and communion with God be such that the peace and love of God which she experienced, along with his holiness and mercy, could be communicated to those who came to her.

The ministry of an anchoress could be compared in some respects with that of a modern psychotherapist or professional counsellor. She would not go out seeking people in their problems, but would be available to them when they had sufficient motivation to seek her out. Nor would she 'do' anything about the problems of the people who came to her, any more than a psychotherapist would intervene in the financial or legal or marital affairs of those who came to talk about them. Instead she would offer her time and her understanding and her prayer, listening with patience and acceptance to the tales of sin and sadness and brokenness, and helping the person to find a path of healing.

To be able to listen effectively and sympathetically in this way without allowing her own preoccupations to determine what she heard would require much inner quietness and discipline, the ability to be fully available to listen, without being mentally involved with other concerns. It would also take a great deal of grip on herself for the anchoress not to yield to the sense of urgency and offer hasty 'solutions' which might give immediate relief, but would only cover over the wound instead of allowing the gentle though painful process of prolonged exposure and healing. Exposure of old wounds is painful and unpleasant, not only for the one who has been hurt, but also for the one who accepts the wounded. Considerable humility would be required of the anchoress to desist from applying remedies which, even if they were the right ones, could not help because they were imposed from the outside. The anchoress must not become 'little miss fix it', but rather the place where the love of God patiently takes to itself the pain of the world, and thereby brings lasting healing. From her writings it is clear that Julian must have pondered this deeply. She is as usual silent about how she applied it to her own availability as an anchoress to those who came to her; but part of what prompted her reflections on how wounds could be healed may well have come from her experience of opening her heart to receive the troubled people of her troubled time.

The suspicion that an anchoress does not engage in actively helping meet the needs of society carries with it an assumption about what those needs are: food, clothing, shelter, justice, freedom from oppression. It would be a very peculiar anchoress who denied the importance

47

of those needs, or disparaged the vocation of the men and women who work to alleviate human suffering wherever it occurs. But the anchoress herself had another vocation which stood for the conviction that there was also a spiritual hunger, a need for healing and fulfilment even when the material and social conditions of life are adequate. The unhappiness and brokenness of those who formed the wealthier classes of fourteenth-century society needed care and healing as surely as the poor needed shelter and the hungry needed food. Julian found in the experience of the love of God release from guilt and despair, and the resources for the healing of persons. It is this which makes her so significant not only for the poor but also for the affluent and broken society of our time. We will see this more fully as we turn to the visions she experienced and the prayer which formed a context for them.

Notes to Chapter Three

1. For background to the desert fathers, see Rowan Williams, *The Wound of Knowledge* (Darton, Longman & Todd, London, 1979), Ch. 5; Derwas Chitty, *The Desert a City* (Blackwell, Oxford, 1966); Thomas M. Gannon and George Traub, *The Desert and the City: An Interpretation of the History of Christian Spirituality* (Collier-MacMillan, London, 1969), pp.17–50.
2. Medieval hagiography often modelled itself on Athanasius' vastly influential *Life of St Anthony*, the hero of the desert tradition; and spiritual giants caught up in political and ecclesiastical turmoil sighed for withdrawal and solitude: cf. Bernard of Clairvaux' letter to the Carthusians, *Epistle 250* (PL 182 col. 451). New monasteries, especially Cistercian and Carthusian, regularly referred to themselves as desert wildernesses, and did, often, establish themselves in relatively remote areas, cf. E. Margaret Thompson, *The Carthusian Order in England* (SPCK, London, 1930); Peter F. Anson, *The Call of the Desert* (SPCK, London, 1961).
3. cf. Simon Tugwell, 'Monastic Rules in the West', in his *Ways of Imperfection*, Ch. 7 (Darton, Longman & Todd, London, 1984); Jean Leclercq, Part One in *The Spirituality of the Middle Ages* (volume II of *A History of Christian Spirituality*, by Louis Bouyer, Jean Leclercq and François Vandenbroucke, (Seabury, New York, and Burns Oates, London, 1968).
4. cf. Rotha Mary Clay, *The Hermits and Anchorites of England* (Methuen, London, 1914; rpt. Singing Tree Press, Detroit, 1968), p.xvii.
5. Grimlaic, *Regulae Solitariorum* (PL 103 cols. 575–664); cited in Francis D. S. Darwin, *The English Medieval Recluse* (SPCK, London, 1944), p.9.
6. cf. Linda Georgianna, *The Solitary Self: Individuality in the Ancrene Wisse* (Harvard University Press, Cambridge, Mass., and London, 1981) esp. Ch. 2.
7. Wulfric of Haselbury, p.50.
8. Richard II also consulted with and made his confession to an anchorite at Westminster Abbey on 13 June, 1381, before setting out to confront Wat Tyler at Smithfield, cf. Darwin, p.40.
9. *The Book of Margery Kempe*, ed. W. Butler-Bowden (Oxford University Press, Oxford and New York, 1944), pp.54–6; cf. Maureen Fries, 'Margery

Kempe', in Paul Szarmach, ed., *An Introduction to the Medieval Mystics of Europe* (State University of New York Press, Albany, 1984), pp. 217–35.

10. Aelred of Rievaulx, *De vita eremitica ad sororem liber* (PL 32 cols. 1451–74), incorrectly placed among St Augustine's works; also called *Regula ad sororem, De institutione inclusarum.* English tr., 'A Rule of Life for a Recluse', I.1, in *Treatises and the Pastoral Prayer* Cistercian Fathers Series: Number Two (Cistercian Publications, Kalamazoo, Michigan, 1971), hereafter RR. As Georgianna points out, however, Aelred somewhat loses sight of the positive final reason in the rest of his book (p. 44).
11. LT 2; see below, pp. 89–103.
12. PL 103 cols. 575–664.
13. For an account of the date and authorship of the *Ancrene Riwle*, sometimes called the *Ancrene Wisse*, see E. J. Dobson, *The Origins of the Ancrene Wisse* (Clarendon Press, Oxford, 1976).
14. For an illuminating account of the *Ancrene Riwle* as antirule, see 'Self and Religious Rules', in Georgianna, pp. 1–31.
15. For a typical example of its praise, cf. *The Cloud of Unknowing* I, Classics of Western Spirituality (Paulist Press, New York, with SPCK, London, 1981).
16. *The Ancrene Riwle* VIII, ed. James Morton (Chatto and Windus, London, and John W. Luce, Boston, 1907), pp. 314–15. Hereafter AR.
17. RR 31, p. 85; cf. *Cloud* XVI–XXI.
18. AR I, p. 35.
19. RR 26, pp. 72–4.
20. cf. Wulfric of Haselbury, p. xxx.
21. RR 4.
22. AR VIII.
23. AR VIII, p. 324.
24. See above, p. 21.
25. LT 75. The phrase here translated, 'it is proper to his divinity to be loved', is 'it longyth to his godhed to be lovyd'. 'Godhed' could be translated 'goodness' (following S2), as Clifton Wolters does. This makes better sense of the passage, and is an even closer parallel to AR.
26. RR 14, p. 62; cf. AR VI, p. 286.
27. Darwin, p. 10.
28. Though exceptions were sometimes made in cases of dire necessity such as severe illness or extreme old age; cf. Dunn in Sayer, p. 23.
29. Darwin, Ch. 6; cf. Clay, Appendix A, pp. 193–8; also pp. 94–6.
30. cf. Georgianna, pp. 4–6.
31. AR VIII, p. 317.
32. AR VIII, p. 316.
33. RR 3, p. 47.
34. AR VIII, p. 319.
35. RR 4, p. 49.
36. Aelred Squire, *Aelred of Rievaulx: A Study* (SPCK, London, 1969), p. 120.
37. RR 5, p. 51.
38. RR 2, p. 47.
39. Darwin, Ch. 7; cf. Christopher J. Holdsworth, 'Christina of Markyate', in Derek Baker, ed., *Medieval Women* (Ecclesiastical History Society, Blackwell, Oxford, 1978).
40. RR 6, p. 51.
41. cf. AR II.2, p. 53.

42. RR 7, pp.52–3; AR II.2, pp.53–4.
43. AR II.2, p.54; cf. Wulfric of Haselbury, p.xxxix.
44. AR II.1, pp.40–1.
45. AR II.3, p.72.
46. Georgianna, pp.50–78.
47. AR IV, p.137; cf. Janet Grayson, *Structure and Imagery in Ancrene Wisse* (University Press of New England, Hanover, New Hampshire, 1974), pp.83–94.
48. See below, Ch. 9.
49. RR 13, p.60; cf. Rule of St Benedict 39.4 and 40.2; AR VIII, p.313.
50. AR VIII, p.313.
51. AR VIII, p.312; RR 12 and 13, pp.60–1.
52. AR VIII, pp.319–20.
53. AR VIII p.317.
54. RR 4, p.48.
55. AR VIII, p.318.
56. See also Robert W. Ackerman and Roger Dahood, ed. and tr., *Ancrene Riwle: Introduction and Part I*, Medieval and Renaissance Texts and Studies vol. 31 (Binghamton, New York, 1984), pp.14–16.
57. Darwin, Ch. 5.
58. RR 4, p.48; cf. AR VIII, pp.314–15.
59. RR 13, p.60.
60. The would-be solitary also sometimes had to serve a probationary year; cf. Grimlaic, *Regula Solitariorum*.
61. RR 2, p.46; cf. AR II.3, p.67.
62. In this, of course, they are following the Rule of St Benedict.
63. Wulfric of Haselbury, p.xlii.
64. *Cloud* LII.
65. *Cloud* XLI; cf. Walter Hilton, *The Scale of Perfection*, I.75.
66. AR VIII, p.314.
67. AR VIII, pp.317–18.
68. Georgianna, in her helpful discussion of the emphasis on the interiority of the *Ancrene Riwle*, does not sufficiently take this into account.
69. RR 22, p.69.
70. cf. Ackerman and Dahood, p.9; also 'The Discipline', in *New Catholic Encyclopedia*, 4. 895.
71. See below, Ch.4 and Ch.9.
72. *St Bernard's Apologia to Abbot William*, nn.13f. in Cistercian Fathers Series I vol. I, pp.49f.; quoted in Aelred RR, p.44.
73. AR VII, p.291.
74. AR VII, p.293.
75. RR 9, p.54.
76. AR II, p.52.
77. LT 73.
78. RR 10, pp.55–6.
79. AR I, p.37.
80. Quoted in Darwin, pp.83–4.
81. John Passmore, *The Perfectibility of Man* (Duckworth, London, 1970), pp.120–1.
82. James 2. 15–16 RSV.
83. RR 28, pp.77–8.

PART TWO

Julian's Spirituality

4 Julian's Prayers

When Julian was thirty years old, she became seriously ill, and it was in the context of that illness that she received the vivid and dramatic visions of the passion of Christ. These visions can easily be treated as though they were the focus of her spirituality. In one sense, of course, they were; for they were the stimulus of her profound theological reflection which she developed in the Long Text. Yet in another sense, the visions themselves can be appreciated only by looking both forward and backward from them: forward to Julian's development of their significance, and backward to the context in which they took place in Julian's own spiritual pilgrimage. Vivid and unexpected as they were, the visions were rooted in a life of prayer. Only because of this could such experiences have the depth of significance which Julian discerned in them. In this chapter, therefore, we will concentrate on Julian's prayer which provides the context for her visions and subsequent reflection upon them, before turning to the visions themselves in Chapter 5.

It is, as already noted, not clear whether Julian's growth in prayer had occurred in an anchoritic setting prior to the visions; but in any case, she discloses that she had been a devout person from an early age.[1] In her youth she had prayed specifically for three things. Her first prayer was for an understanding of the passion of Christ, not merely at an intellectual level, but at a level of personal participation. Secondly, she prayed for a physical illness so severe that she herself and everyone around her would think that she was dying. Her third prayer was for 'three wounds': true contrition, loving compassion, and the longing of the will for God.[2] She herself recognizes these prayers as somewhat unusual, and offers further explanation of them.

In the case of her first prayer for 'mynd of the passion', she says that although she already had some feeling for the passion of Christ, she wished she could have witnessed his crucifixion and death as did 'Magdalen . . . and others who were Christ's lovers'.[3] The reason for this desire was that she wished she might have participated in his suffering, as others did who loved him while they watched him die.

Julian's longing to witness and participate in the suffering and death of Christ can be partly understood in terms of a shift of medieval thinking about God and salvation. In earlier times, God had often been portrayed in rather remote terms; and Christ was the majestic Lord sent from this remote God to conquer the devil. This picture gradually changed to an awareness of the generously loving Father who sent his Son to bring humankind to salvation.[4] Interconnected with this was a strong interest in the human dimensions of the life of Christ, and in particular his suffering and death.

In earlier medieval times, Christ had often been thought of as the conquering hero, mounting the cross in triumph: *Christus Victor*. This is vividly portrayed in the art of the Anglo-Saxon and Roman-esque period, where Christ on the cross is presented as a noble figure, his body straight and his head crowned. Literature similarly reveals this conception. In *The Dream of the Rood*, written in the eighth century, Christ is a young warrior whose ascent of the cross is his victory; and although there are darker notes of agony, the theme of triumph predominates.[5] A common metaphor reinforced by artistic representations was that of the cross as a banner, leading to conquest.[6]

This understanding, however, gave way before Julian's time to a more humanistic one, perhaps reinforced by the recurrent waves of human misery that washed over the later medieval period. Gothic art pictures Jesus not as a hero but as a twisted, tormented sufferer, head bowed or turned to one side in visible agony, and observed by his mother and disciple in obvious grief and distress.[7] At about the same time the motif of the Pietà, the virgin mourning over her dead Son, became familiar as a 'tragic counterpart' to the long popular Madonna and Child: the Pietà of the period often has an exaggerated realism in the agony of Mary and the rigidity and thinness of Jesus' limbs. As one art historian puts it, its purpose was

> to arouse so overwhelming a sense of horror and pity that the beholder will identify his own feelings completely with those of the grief-stricken Mother of God.[8]

The same sense of pity was roused by the lyrics of the time, which became affective meditations on the passion of Christ: in some of them, Christ describes his sufferings to the reader, while in others, the reader is cast in the role of someone observing Christ's agonies and sadly describing what he or she sees.[9] And Langland in *Piers Plow-man* presents quite a different understanding of Christ from that of the eighth-century *Rood*: Christ's victory in the harrowing of hell comes precisely by way of his incarnation and identification with suffering humanity.

'Consummatum est', quod Crist, and comsed for to swone,
Pitousliche and pale, as prisoun that deyeth.

('It is finished', said Christ, and began to swoon,
Piteously and pale, as a prisoner dying.)[10]

Such meditation on the suffering of Jesus, and efforts toward identification with it, had deep roots in Scripture and Christian tradition. It formed a basis for the Pauline theology of the death and resurrection of Christ as the effective basis for the healing transformation of life: the identification is strongly expressed in the prayer of St Paul,

... that I may know him, and the power of his resurrection, and may share in his sufferings, becoming like him in his death, that if possible I may attain the resurrection from the dead.[11]

This desire to share in the sufferings of Christ is in accordance with Jesus' own sayings as presented by the gospel writers. St Matthew describes Jesus' efforts to communicate his impending suffering and death to his disciples, and their uncomprehending attempts to dissuade him, to which Jesus replies:

If any man would come after me, let him deny himself and take up his cross and follow me.[12]

In the early Church, the cross did not represent merely some slightly unpleasant aspect of life, but ignominious execution. To take up one's cross was an invitation to identify so fully with Christ that martyrdom would be a likely consequence.

It is no wonder that as the list of martyrs lengthened, the Church pondered not only the death of Christ but also the significance of their own identification with it, in life as well as in death. They found in the cross a way of understanding their own martyrdom, but also their dying to brokenness and sin, and their new life of healing and freedom and integration.[13] They spoke of themselves, accordingly, as crucified with Christ and thus made truly alive; and came to see this as true in a spiritual sense whether or not the physical martyrdom and its resurrection might also await them.

I have been crucified with Christ; it is no longer I who live, but Christ who lives in me; and the life I now live in the flesh, I live by faith in the Son of God, who loved me and gave himself for me.[14]

As the period of martyrdom receded and the Church entered an era of respectability and strength, new models were needed to express their theology and spirituality, and the emphasis on the suffering humanity of Christ was displaced by triumphalist images. From the time of Anselm, however, there was a resurgence of awareness of the human dimension of Christ, and monastic spirituality took this up in its loving meditation on all the aspects of Jesus' early life.[15] Bernard of Clairvaux and William of St Thierry helped to promote this affective devotion, recognizing the importance of the humanity of Jesus for the development of the spiritual life.[16] This had found its way into English spirituality strikingly in the writings of Julian's older contemporary, Richard Rolle, particularly in his *Meditations on the Passion*;[17] and Walter Hilton in a sane and balanced way presented the necessity and method of 'seeking Jesus' as the first means of bringing about transformation of life in the path toward union with God.[18] There were variations on the theme among these and other writers; and it would be a mistake to suppose either that they all said exactly the same thing or that Julian took over their teachings without modification; it will be necessary to examine some of the differences in due course. It is important to see, however, that her desire for identification with the passion of Christ was consonant with the theological direction of the time.

The way in which this theological current became part of the spirituality of the time warrants special attention. As it develops in the prayers of Anselm, there is a considerable imaginative ingredient. His prayer involved dialogue with Christ; but also with some of his disciples and other holy men and women: Saints John the Baptist, Peter, Paul, Mary Magdalene, Benedict, and others. He wrote his prayers in the form of rhythmic prose, intending them for the benefit of others besides himself; and gives emphasis to his longing for recollection of the passion.

> Why, O my soul, were you not there
> to be pierced by a sword of bitter sorrow
> when you could not bear
> the piercing of the side of your Saviour with a lance?
> Why could you not bear to see
> the nails violate the hands and feet of your Creator?
> Why did you not see with horror
> the blood that poured out of the side of your Redeemer?[19]

The very things which will be the significant ingredients of Julian's visions, Anselm presents to himself in his prayers, recognizing the terrible privilege it was to be a witness of those dreadful events, and prays,

> Will you not make it up to me for not seeing
> the blessed incorruption of your flesh,
> for not having kissed the place of the wounds
> where the nails pierced,
> for not having sprinkled with tears of joy
> the scars that prove the truth of your body?[20]

This imaginative ingredient was fostered by the practice of spiritual reading in the monasteries. A passage of Scripture would be selected and read or listened to, probably several times over. But 'reading' for them did not mean a cursory survey of the words on the page, or even a detailed but wholly intellectual assimilation of its contents. Reading involved 'the participation of the whole body and the whole mind';[21] so that the readers entered into the text, meditated upon it, and thereby thought not only of what was written but also of their own response to it. This concept of totally involved reading was fundamental to the Benedictine tradition, and through them to the whole monastic and spiritual culture of the Middle Ages, much reinforced by the Cistercian renewal. As they understood it,

> To meditate is to read a text and to learn it 'by heart' in the fullest sense of this expression, that is, with one's whole being: with the body, since the mouth pronounced it, with the memory which fixes it, with the intelligence which understands its meaning and with the will which desires to put it into practice.[22]

This sort of imaginative meditation was specifically encouraged for anchoresses in Aelred's letter to his sister. She is to begin her thoughts with the beginning of the gospel story.

> First enter the room of blessed Mary and with her read the books which prophesy the virginal birth and the coming of Christ. Wait there for the arrival of the angel, so that you may see him as he comes in, hear him as he utters his greeting, and so, filled with amazement and rapt out of yourself, greet your most sweet Lady together with the angel.[23]

Aelred then leads her through each aspect of the nativity: she is to join the shepherd's vigil, ponder the Magi, and accompany the holy family in their flight to Egypt. Next she is to participate imaginatively in the events of Jesus' adult life, accompanying him in the solitude of the temptations in the desert, putting herself in the place of the adulterous woman, joining the crowd in the house where the paralytic was let down through the roof, listening to his teaching, and so through the whole gospel account. At last she is to be a witness of all the events of the passion, which Aelred presents to her in vivid detail:

> Follow him ... to the courtyard of the High Priest and bathe with your tears his most beautiful face which they are covering with spittle ... Mark well how he stands before the governor: his head bent, his eyes cast down, his face serene, saying little, ready for insults and scourging. I know you can bear it no longer, that you will not be able to look on while his most sweet back is torn with whips, his face struck, his majestic head crowned with thorns, that right hand which made heaven and earth mocked with a reed.[24]

She follows him to Calvary and the quietness of the tomb, identifying sometimes with him, sometimes with a disciple or one of the women, until finally she experiences with them the triumph of the resurrection and lingers in the delight of his glorified presence. Pondering the life of Jesus was meant to make that life her own, partly in the sense of her entering into past events, but also in the sense of bringing those events into her present context, so that all of life could be lived in the light of Christ.

Walter Hilton, in his book written to an anchoress in the fourteenth century, makes explicit the purpose of this sort of meditation. The goal was to become existentially aware of the love and goodness of God in Christ; and in order to reach this goal, compassionate entry into the passion of Christ was considered a crucial means.

> Your mind is suddenly detached from all worldly and material things, and you seem to see Jesus in your soul as he appeared on earth; you see him taken by the Jews and bound as a thief, beaten and despised, scourged and condemned to death; with what humility he carried the cross on his shoulders, and with what cruelty he was nailed to it. You see, too, the crown of thorns upon his head and the sharp spear that pierced him to the heart, and at this sight you feel your heart moved to such great compassion and pity for your Lord Jesus, that you mourn and weep and cry out with all the power of your body and soul, marvelling at the goodness and love, the patience and humility of your Lord, that he would for so sinful a wretch as you are suffer such great pain. And nevertheless you feel so much the great goodness and mercy of our Lord that your heart overflows and you shed many sweet tears. And you have great confidence in the forgiveness of your sins and the salvation of your soul by virtue of his precious passion.[25]

When prayer took on these dimensions, it would have become a very different thing from a few ill-considered petitions. Julian's request to share in the passion of Christ was, in the context of her time, a request to develop the sympathetic entry into his death which would increase her love for him and awareness of his goodness, and would facilitate her salvation and the transformation of her life. The quietness of an anchorhold and its purpose of life-transforming devotion to God would be a context highly favourable to the development of such prayer and the translation of it into daily life. Julian's reflective meditation on the parable of the lord and the servant[26] is an illustration of the way in which she made use of imaginative prayer.

Nevertheless, although it becomes clear that Julian's desire for participation in the passion has roots in the spirituality and history reaching back through Aelred and Anselm to St Paul and the gospel writers, she is asking for rather more than they did. Her prayer is not only for deeper imaginative empathy with the passion, but for an actual

> bodily sight, in which I might have more knowledge of our Saviour's bodily pains, and of the compassion of our Lady and of all his true lovers who were living at that time and saw his pains, for I would have been one of them and have suffered with them.[27]

She is asking for a vision, an actual experience of the passion, not just a meditative entry into it.

This is rather surprising. The spiritual literature of the period is greatly cautious about visions and ecstasies and other such mystical phenomena: these can be brought about as easily by the angels of darkness as by the angels of light, warns Walter Hilton, and they are never to be trusted or dwelt upon for their own sake.[28] The author of the *Cloud of Unknowing* is scathing about self-induced phenomena, likening people who seek such experiences to 'sheep suffering from the brain disease', fully aware that eruptions of the unconscious may be much closer akin to madness than to holiness.[29]

Julian's request for a vision, however, is not a desire for mystical ecstasy, nor does she confuse mystical phenomena with sanctity. Rather, she states that her request was made as a means to an end: she wanted this vision in order that she might be able to identify more fully with Christ's sufferings and be in unity with those who deeply loved him. To make her position even clearer, she specifies that she wanted no other visions or special revelations: she was not seeking these phenomena for themselves, but only as an entry for her into the passion of Christ and its costly transformation of life, so that her subsequent life would be more closely identified with the values represented by the dying Christ as her love and sympathetic understanding of him increased.

Julian's second prayer demonstrates the depth of seriousness of her request. At first sight her prayer for a physical illness to the point of death seems even more dubious than her request for a vision. Perhaps it seemed unusual to Julian too, for she makes a point of mentioning that it came to her mind without her seeking it, as a free gift from God.[30] And again, she offers an explanation for her desire:

> I intended this because I wanted to be purged by God's mercy, and afterwards live more to his glory because of this sickness.[31]

The 'dress rehearsal' for her actual death was intended to have an impact on her life thereafter.

Medieval spirituality had a strong sense of the importance of coming to terms with death, rather than pretending that it was somehow unreal: no doubt the successive waves of the Black Death re-emphasized the fragility of life and unpredictability of its end. Emphasis on preparation for death was partly because a good death was considered to have implications for the after-life, shortening or eliminating the time to be spent in purgatory: this was part of the reason why the suddenness of death during the plague years had so great a psychological impact, since people had no time to prepare themselves and many died unshriven. Julian, however, goes beyond this in her thinking. She shows an awareness of how the remembrance of death and a recognition of its immanence can cut through the layers of trivia in which life can be blanketed, so that the individual is thereby freed to attend to things of lasting significance. A salutary effect of the awareness of death is its ability to eliminate as unimportant things which had previously preoccupied the mind, and its inculcation of the resolve to live whatever life may remain according to truer values. This is what Julian is asking in her desire to be 'purged': not that the sickness itself has any magically purifying effect but that it focuses the mind and heart on what has been chosen as the all important centre of life, namely the passion of Christ, and thereby strengthens the resolution to 'afterwards live more to his glory'.

This prayer, therefore, can be seen as consistent with Julian's first request. In both, her intention is that her life be purged not just of evil but of the unimportant, and be focused on the love of God manifested in Christ. Whether or not she was in the anchorhold at this time, she was certainly expressing the aspirations of the anchoritic life. Her willingness to undergo severe illness in order to make these ideals take concrete form in her life rather than remain mere pious abstractions shows the seriousness of her purpose.

The word 'recollection' is a happy choice in translating Julian's phrase in which she expresses her desire to 'haue the more true mynd in the passion of Christ'. As the term 'recollection' is used in spiritual writings, it does not mean simply memory. Rather it means, literally, to be re-collected, collected again. In other words, all the thoughts and ideas and distractions are brought back again to a central focus, a focus that has been deliberately chosen to be the centre of life. Instead of being distracted by each thing as it comes along, so that life is lived in many directions at once without reference to a unifying centre, the practice of recollection is the practice of drawing all things quietly back for measurement against that which is of ultimate importance, so that life and activity are integrated rather than haphazard. From this focal point, things regain their proper perspective, restored to true proportion if they had assumed a larger or smaller significance than they warranted. Julian, desiring 'mynd in the passion', is seeking this as the central focus of her life, the standard against which all else should be measured. In her view, it is in the light of the suffering and compassionate Christ that the worth of other things and actions can be correctly assessed. By comparison with his unselfish integrity things which might otherwise have assumed a false importance would fall back to their proper size, while attitudes of humility, generosity, and compassion, which could have been left out of account, are seen in their real worth.

Although Julian's request for a vision of the passion and for a severe illness are unusual, therefore, she does not fit the popular modern picture of a mystic longing for raptures and ecstasies and unusual experiences for their own sake. Furthermore, her desire for unity with God in Christ is not an escape from social responsibility. In the Christ-centredness of her spirituality she sought identification with his self-giving love: a compassion which extended to all of humanity. And although at this point in her text it is left implicit, in asking for severe physical illness she is surely also seeking greater solidarity with suffering humanity, identifying simultaneously with the suffering of Christ and of humankind, and thus able to mediate his compassion. The extent of her concern for her fellow-Christians becomes more and more apparent as her book proceeds; from the outset, she is willing to develop experiential empathy with their sufferings, thereby sharing with them as Christ shared. Julian was aware that identification with Christ must include identification with those for whom he suffered, and hence with their suffering; her prayer for illness represented a willingness to share the pains of the dying in such a way that her understanding and compassion for them would increase and she would be purged of any self-centredness in her responses.

Thus, in spite of their strangeness to modern conceptions, solid common sense pervades these prayers. Julian was not praying for visions for their own sake, or for strange spiritual or physical occurrences to gratify a religious mania. She was praying, rather, for greater integration, compassion, and generosity; and it seemed to her that these means would enable her to develop them. Nevertheless, she herself recognized that such means are most unusual, and that she might have been misguided in requesting them, so she added,

> Lord, you know what I want, if it be your will that I have it, and if it be not your will, good Lord, do not be displeased, for I want nothing that you do not want.[32]

If the revelation of his passion and the onset of physical illness would not have the desired effect of deepening her spiritual integrity and would be contrary to the will of the Lord, then she did not want them at all: again, it is obvious how fully they were seen as means to an end, and not desired for their own sake. Having come to that position, Julian states that she ceased to dwell upon these requests: they passed from her mind. We need not take this to mean that she forgot all about them, but rather that they no longer occupied her attention or mental energy, analogous to the way in which a puzzle, once resolved, can be remembered without engagement.

The third petition, however, was a different matter. For this she continued to pray, steadily, urgently, and without condition, certain that it must be correct to do so. Her third prayer had been to receive 'three wounds': true contrition, loving compassion, and longing of her will for God. In the Short Text we are told that Julian was moved to this request by hearing the story of St Cecilia, a martyr of the second or third century who was much venerated in the Middle Ages and about whom was constructed many an apocryphal tale. The story Julian had heard was of how St Cecilia had suffered death by receiving three wounds to her neck with a sword. Just how it came about that these three wounds to her neck were transfigured in Julian's mind to become the profound desires of which she tells us is left undisclosed: it is tempting to speculate that it might have been through the preaching of Adam Easton.[33] In any case, it is hardly accidental that it was a martyr, one who was willing to identify with the suffering Christ even to the point of giving up her own life, who became a model for Julian.

The idea of the soul receiving wounds in relationship to God had a long history in Christian spirituality, and Julian took it up in a profound development in which several diverse strands were woven together in a rich new harmony. One of the ways in which spiritual writers had used the concept of wounding was in the erotic imagery frequently used to describe the experiences of the love of God. Because this seemed appropriate language, there was a predilection for commenting on the Song of Songs, the Hebrew love poem which they interpreted allegorically in terms of the love and mystical union between the soul and her divine spouse, a love which heals as it wounds.[34] Thus for instance Origen spoke of those who begin to turn their attention to spiritual things as falling in love with their true heavenly bridegroom rather than with an adulterer or a seducer, and says,

> Indeed, the soul is led by a heavenly love and desire when once the beauty and glory of the Word of God has been perceived, he falls in love with his splendour and by this he receives some dart or wound of love ... he will receive from him the saving wound and will burn with the blessed fire of his love.[35]

When Bernard of Clairvaux, in his *Sermons on the Song of Songs*, took up this theme of the penetration of the divine love, he set it in terms of the hardness of the heart, which the piercing of the Bridegroom-Word must soften by means at once painful and pleasurable.

> He is life and power, and as soon as he enters in, he awakens my slumbering soul; he stirs and soothes and pierces my heart, for before it was hard as stone, and diseased.[36]

The love of God is costly and painful in its wounding quality, yet it is the wound of love, and total consummation as the soul becomes receptive rather than resistant to its penetration.

This use of explicitly erotic metaphor, together with the idea of union with God as a mystical marriage, found frequent expression also in the Rhineland and the Low Countries in the thirteenth century. It was especially prominent among Dominican nuns influenced by Eckhart and his followers Tauler and Suso, and also among the Béguines,[37] some of whom developed the connection between the wounding penetration of love and the wounds of the crucified Lover.[38] Mechthild of Magdeburg, for instance, who was originally a Béguine and later entered a convent, explicitly used the theme of erotic wounding and its healing to express the surrender of the soul to the love of God manifested in the wounded Christ:

> Whosoever shall be sore wounded by love
> Will never become whole
> Save he embrace the self-same love
> Which wounded him.[39]

It is as usual impossible to prove that there is any direct historical link between these various writers of the *Brautmystik* tradition and Julian; but the themes have much in common. The influence of Bernard and the Cistercians was of course ubiquitous in fourteenth-century England; and the impact of the Rhineland and the Low Countries on East Anglia during this period when England was at war with France is incalculable.

It might be tempting to us in a post-Freudian age to dismiss the erotic imagery as a predictable but neurotic consequence of sexual repression and guilt in a period which tended to consider chastity a necessary element of sanctity. There are, indeed, bizarre cases, as for instance the self-preoccupied Margery Kempe bewailing her lost virginity (she had borne her husband fourteen children before talking him into a reluctant acceptance of continence) because this made her unfit for espousal to the heavenly Bridegroom. She then had an experience of the Lord speaking to her, reassuring her that this sin has been forgiven, and saying,

> I have told thee beforetime that thou art a singular lover ... And forasmuch as thou art a maiden in thy soul, I shall take thee by the one hand in Heaven, and my Mother by the other hand, and so shalt thou dance in Heaven with other holy maidens and virgins, for I may call thee dearly bought, and mine own dearworthy darling ...[40]

But this was an exception. Indeed, as one studies the use of erotic language among medieval mystics, what is astonishing is how freely they use these sexual images in a sane and balanced way to express their experience of God. In an age of suspicion of sexuality, such usage indicates considerable liberation of spirit and personal integration, as we shall see further in the discussion of Julian's attitude to creation and the physical body.[41]

The theme of sexual wounding as a mystical image was taken to its height by John of the Cross two centuries later; but the ideas he expressed were the same as those crucial to Julian:

> O living flame of love,
> How tenderly you wound
> And sear my soul's most inward centre!
> ... O cautery that heals!
> O consummating wound!
> O soothing hand! O touch so fine and light
> That savours of eternity
> And satisfies all dues!
> Slaying, you have converted death to life.[42]

Julian, like John of the Cross in this passage, combined the strand of erotic mysticism with the sharing of the wounds of Christ in his death, and found in those wounds the marks of his victory: the metaphor becomes extended for her in her pondering of how oneness with Christ in his suffering turns the wounds of human suffering into honours.[43]

A further dimension of the metaphor developed in medieval spirituality as a result of pondering long on the words of St Paul:

> Henceforth let no man trouble me; for I bear on my body the marks of Jesus.[44]

These wounds of the dying Lord were wounds accepted by his followers in solidarity with him, not simply for their own spirituality but for the sins and sorrows of the world. Perhaps the most outstanding medieval example of this total identification with Christ in his compassion for the outcasts of human society was Francis of Assisi, who tried to take literally the gospel injunction to sell all and follow Christ in his ministry to others. Against the wealthy and powerful monastic orders which purported to be the representatives of Christ on earth, Francis and his followers tried to live in deliberate imitation of the Christ who walked among the poor, sharing their poverty and simplicity, bringing them healing and hope. The theme of solidarity with Christ was thus interwoven with the theme of solidarity with suffering humankind; and identification with the passion of Christ was neither a morbid desire for suffering nor a selfish preoccupation with personal holiness but rather an acceptance of the cost of total and redemptive self-giving. In the case of Francis, this identification with Christ was seen to be so complete and carried forward with such integrity that his followers spoke of his receiving the stigmata – the wounds of Jesus on the cross in Francis' own hands and feet and side. Whatever one makes of this in historical terms, it at least points to the extent to which Francis was perceived as being at one with Christ in his total self-giving love.

Julian's willingness to suffer physical illness in her identification with Christ's passion and with suffering humanity points to the same sort of solidarity with his wounds that Francis had demonstrated. Again, we cannot know that when Julian prayed for recollection of the passion and sought for the three wounds, she necessarily had Francis in mind.[45] However the ideal of identification both with Christ himself and with those for whom Christ suffered, for which Francis stood, had become part of the thinking of those serious about spirituality in the recognition that genuine love, the penetration of the love of God into the heart and into the world, cannot evade the pain of his passion.

Yet another strand must be recognized in the theme of wounding, however, namely the sense in which the wounds of Christ belong uniquely to him and cannot be shared by his followers, since it was precisely for his followers that he bore them:

> He was wounded for our transgressions, he was bruised for our iniquities . . . and with his stripes we are healed.[46]

A prayer for sharing in the wounds of Christ, though at one level appropriate as a prayer to share in the salvation of humankind by becoming increasingly a channel of his self-giving love, would become inappropriate unless it were also remembered that at another level no human being can be identified with the Saviour, because all men and women are among the very ones who stand in need of the salvation which his love brings.

Julian recognized that the heart which could come to share the wounds of Christ in his passion and in his solidarity with sufferers must be a heart pierced by Christ to repentance and contrition and sincere longing for God, accepting his love not only as something to be given to others but as a personal whole-making. She thereby developed a trend of medieval spirituality in its movement away from external forms of contrition and penance toward internal compunction for sin and acceptance of divine mercy. An earlier penitential system had viewed sin primarily as an offence against a just God, to whom strict satisfaction had to be made; rule books were drawn up which listed the penances deemed adequate for particular sins. Penances were often payments of money, or ascetic practices for specified periods of time.[47] With the shift of emphasis already noted from a stern, aloof God to the loving Father of Jesus Christ, however, sin was recognized to be an affront to his love, which could therefore not be rectified by merely external penances: interior contrition and sorrow were also needed to restore the relationship.[48] Even to be truly penitent, turning to God in acceptance of his mercy and love rather than concentrating on the sin or guilt or shame was recognized to require a reorientation well beyond human capability. Unless the love of God penetrated and softened the heart, it would remain cold and indifferent, defensive in its hurt, open neither to God nor to humankind.

Sometimes this awareness was expressed by assimilating the imagery of the wounds of the dying Christ with the wounds inflicted by the Word or Spirit of God, which is

> living and active, sharper than any two-edged sword, piercing to the division of soul and spirit, of joints and marrow, and discerning the thoughts and intentions of the heart.[49]

There could be no dissembling before this steadily penetrating light, yet its entry would always be the illumination of love, and in seeking out the 'thoughts and intentions of the heart' it would soften the defensive hardness and gradually make reorientation possible. Anselm had placed great stress on how this wounding love was the means of true contrition and longing for God.[50] In his Prayer to St Mary Magdalene he said,

> Ask urgently that I may have
> the love that pierces the heart; tears that are humble;
> desire for the homeland of heaven;
> impatience with this earthly exile;
> searing repentance; and a dread of torments of eternity.[51]

This desire for contrition and compassion was explicitly taken up into the thinking of those who used erotic imagery. Bernard in his *Sermons on the Song of Songs* uses the love poem's mention of ointments with which the bride attracts her lover as an opportunity to enlarge on the very same attitudes which Anselm had seen as wounds, only increasing the emphasis on social concern. He says,

> I have been discussing two ointments with you: one of contrition, that takes account of numerous sins, the other of devotion, that embodied numerous benefits ... The first one is known to carry a sting, because the bitter remembrance of sins incites compunction and causes pain, whereas the second is soothing, it brings consolation through a knowledge of God's goodness and so assuages pain. But there is another ointment, far excelling these two, to which I give the name loving-kindness, because the elements that go to its making are the needs of the poor, the anxieties of the oppressed, the worries of those who are sad, the sins of wrong-doers, and finally, the manifold misfortunes of people of all classes who endure affliction, even if they are our enemies.[52]

Although there are differences of detail, this list is similar to that given by Aelred to his anchoress sister as a reminder for prayer.[53]

In Julian, we find that the order is changed, and the whole is transposed from the key of nuptial mysticism to that of sharing in the wounds of Christ, but none of the elements are lost in her prayer for contrition, compassion, and the longing of the will for God. The synthesis she effects demonstrates the depth and originality of her own thought, even while rooting it within the rich soil of medieval Catholic

spirituality. The erotic imagery is subdued, but there is a deep awareness of the penetrating and wounding love of God which heals even as
it sears. Yet the other strands of compassion with the wounds of
humankind, and of awareness of the love of God in the wounds of
Christ on our behalf, are also prominent in her consideration of his
suffering. It thus becomes clear that the spiritual life for Julian is not a
matter of visions and ecstasies, whether or not these occur, but of
steady growth in love for God, and thus in healing of persons. The
identification with the suffering Christ and union with him in love for
humankind would be a pious idealism suitable only for short bursts of
religious ardour but not compatible with the realities and irritations of
everyday life, were there not also a thorough and progressive transformation of the self in total conversion toward God. The wounds for
which Julian prayed are the means which she sees of such conversion.
An individual is led to contrition by the Holy Spirit, and in the confession of his or her sins, finds grief in having 'befouled God's fair
image',[54] and accepts both the penances imposed by the confessor, and
the sicknesses and sorrows sent by God, not as punishment, but as
means to true repentance.

> And also God in his special grace visits whom he will with such great
> contrition, and also with compassion and true longing for him, that they are
> suddenly delivered from sin and from pain, and taken up into bliss and
> made equal with the saints. By contrition we are made clean, by compassion
> we are made ready, and by true longing for God we are made worthy. These
> are three means, as I understand, through which all souls come to heaven,
> those, that is to say, who have been sinners on earth and will be saved.[55]

As Julian's prayers were answered and she reflected upon the meaning
of her experiences, this eventually resulted in nothing short of a
complete theology, in which the love of God manifested in the
wounded Christ becomes the salvation of humankind. And 'salvation'
as Julian understood it must include not only eternal destiny but
human healing and fulfilment and delight. Accordingly, there must be
a response to the shattering questions of why God allows sin and suffering, which Julian also considers in relation to the theme of the
wounds. She reflects upon how human brokenness is met by God's
healing love, so that those very wounds inflicted upon individuals by
others or by their own hand become the means of finding healing and
wholeness which results in a mature joy which unbruised innocence
could never have known.

But this is to anticipate. It is unlikely that when Julian prayed for the
three wounds she had worked out her theology of how wounds are
turned into honours. She wanted simply to grow in love of Christ in
identification with his suffering, thus combining in her desire the longing for union and the sharing of Christ's pains. It becomes clear from

considering the three wounds for which she prayed that they are the underlying meaning of her other prayers as well. The first wound, true contrition and genuine repentance for sin, is ultimately more than a matter of feeling sorry about wrongs done, and more even than sincerely trying to do better. Contrition, rather, is as Anselm had seen, a matter of turning from focus on the self to focus on God in Christ as the centre from whom all thought and action flow. Thus it makes a unity with Julian's prayer for 'mynde of the passion', the spirit of recollection; and whether or not it was the will of God that she be granted the vision which she desired of him, she could be in no doubt that it was his will that her life be centred in him.

Historical precedents apart, it was no accident that she called this a wound. True contrition, a determined and humble turning to God, would require a determined and humble refusal to set up oneself and one's selfish moods and preoccupations as the central point of reference in life. If the focus for recollection is the passion of Christ, then it cannot at the same time be personal pleasure or gratification; and the abandonment of self as the centre of reference cannot but be painful. Julian believed, in common with the spiritual teaching of the Church, that ultimately this is the path of greatest personal integration, fulfilment, and joy, because we are made, as Augustine had said, to find our rest in God.[56] But this does not make it easy: the model, after all, is the Christ who suffers.

The second wound which Julian requested, loving compassion, is again parallel to her earlier prayer, especially in its identification with the compassionate Christ. Her depth of sharing in his pity for the sinner, whom he wished not to rebuke but rather to help and heal, must have made her a sensitive counsellor to the troubled men and women who would have found their way to an anchoress's window. She would have had too strong a will to integrity to gloss over with cheap comfort the problems which people brought to her; nevertheless she would have been in touch with that comfort which, though costly, would answer their needs.

The two wounds of contrition and compassion are more closely linked than might at first appear. Compassion requires genuine care for the other, not a pretence which underneath is really seeking something for oneself: love or attention or regard. Thus to be truly compassionate it is necessary to be detached from one's own inner preoccupations. But that, as was already discussed, is just what contrition is. Contrition means steadily turning away from self-orientation to attend to God; it is this which liberates a man or woman from compulsions and self-regarding motives so that real care for others becomes possible. The paradigm, once again, is the dying Christ, whose love did not withdraw from the cost, and who thereby manifested what the compassion of God is like. Julian is right to call compassion, like contrition, a wound: there is no room here for sentimentality.

The third of the three wounds for which she continues in urgent prayer is 'the wound of longing with my will for God', and this is the summation of all the other requests.[57] Julian sought single-mindedness, asking that she be helped not to fluctuate in her orientation to God. She had clearly recognized that emotional desire for God comes and goes – a recognition which was reinforced during the course of her visions[58] – and thus emphasized that the longing is to be a matter of the will, a consistent choice of God and the values of the crucified Christ, whether any ardour of feeling accompanies it or not. This longing or desire of the will, as contrasted with the emotions, had been stressed by Walter Hilton:

> Indeed I would rather have a true and pure desire of Jesus in my heart, though with very little spiritual enlightenment, than practise all the bodily mortification of all men living, enjoy visions and revelations of angels, or experience the most pleasing effects in my bodily senses, if they were without this desire.[59]

Neither Hilton nor Julian disparages the emotions: both teach that God can bring healing to the emotions along with the rest of the personality. But both are cautious about domination by the emotions. In Julian's experience, deliberate orientation of her whole self to God comes into severe conflict with her personal feelings, when she is given a choice between spiritual consolation or continued painful probing for spiritual truth and integrity. She is invited to 'look up to heaven' away from the suffering Christ, and 'there was nothing between the cross and heaven which could have grieved me'. But to turn away from Christ meant renouncing the identification with his suffering love as her heaven, her supreme value; and though she admits that her flesh cringes, she refuses to reject him, even for spiritual delights.

The immediate result is a sense of regret, for it means that she continues to suffer, and she has a hearty dislike of suffering. She then perceives that 'reluctance and deliberate choice are in opposition to one another, and I experienced them both at the same time'. But let her emotions and her flesh be as reluctant as they will, her choice is fixed, as she 'powerfully, wisely, and deliberately chose Jesus for my heaven'.[60] She does not waste time castigating her fluctuating emotions, nor does she think that God in any way blames her for them. But neither does she allow them to dominate her will.

Julian's account of her prayers and the theme of wounding indicates a recurrent paradox of Christian spirituality: the emphasis on deliberate free choice and yet also the recognition that even the longing of the will for God is itself a divine gift. Left to human devices, the will is at best divided, reflecting the fragmentation of the human soul. The unification of the will, and with it the healing of the emotions, is needed for the integration of personality; and this is seen by Julian to flow from anchoring in the love of God manifested in the passion of Christ. It will be a recurring theme.

As Julian probed it, she came to see that not only were contrition, compassion, and the longing of the will for God themselves gifts, even the desire for them was a gift, received 'by the grace of God and the teaching of Holy Church'.[61] On the other hand, it was the sort of desire which could only be had by one who already had a very considerable integrity and singleness of heart. Unless one had already fixed on God as the standard by whom all other interests and desires were to be measured, recognizing him as the supreme good not just in an abstract theoretical sense but in the practical sense of bringing all one's thoughts and goals and actions to the illumination of the Spirit of God which 'pierces to the division of joints and marrow' one would scarcely pray for contrition. Yet if this choice had already been made, why should it continue to be necessary to pray for a longing of the will for God?

Julian's knowledge of human psychology recognizes that such a question is shallow. She is only too well aware that human beings live only very falteringly by that which they acknowledge in their better moments to be their highest good. Her prayer is a prayer for greater integrity: more unity or wholeness between her deepest recognition and her lifestyle, rather than the fragmentation of a life that fleetingly glimpses its true goal but cannot properly orientate itself towards that goal. It is true that one has already come a considerable distance in being able to recognize the goal at all, let alone to be able to see it in the profound terms of wounds – the severe grace of God which purges to purify and which crucifies to redeem and fulfil. But she does not make the mistake of supposing that having caught this glimpse of her highest good, or even of having an ever clearer awareness of it, is equivalent to having actually achieved it. It is the paradox of reciprocity which is found throughout Christian spirituality: truly to desire purity of heart one must already have such purity; yet the more purity of heart and singleness of intention is developed, the more one recognizes its indispensability and thus the depth of need for it to be more fully developed. And if total purity were achieved by the grace of God, that would be the equivalent to complete integration and human wholeness in full relationship to God: the beatific vision.

Notes to Chapter Four

1. LT 14.
2. LT 2.

Julian's Prayers

3. ST 1.
4. cf. R. W. Southern, 'From Epic to Romance', in his *The Making of the Middle Ages* (Yale University Press, New Haven and London, 1953).
5. cf. J. A. W. Bennett, *Poetry of the Passion* (London 1982).
6. Jaroslav Pelikan, *The Growth of Medieval Theology (600–1300), The Christian Tradition: A History of the Development of Doctrine*, vol. 3 (The University of Chicago Press, Chicago and London, 1978), p. 132.
7. cf. M. Rickert, *Painting in Britain: The Middle Ages*, (London, 1954) Plates 30 and 43.
8. H. W. Janson, *History of Art* (Prentice-Hall, Englewood Cliffs, N.J., and Henry N. Abrams, New York, 1969 edn), pp. 257–8, cf. fig. 408.
9. Rosemary Woolf, *The English Religious Lyric in the Middle Ages* (Clarendon, Oxford, 1968), pp. 19–20; cf. Douglas Gray, *Themes and Images in the Medieval English Religious Lyric* (Routledge & Kegan Paul, London and Boston, 1972), pp. 122–45.
10. Langland, 'Harrowing of Hell', in *Piers Plowman*, lines 58–9, in Boris Ford, p. 424. Modernization mine.
11. Phil. 3. 10–11 RSV.
12. Matt. 16.24 RSV; cf. Luke 9. 18–27.
13. cf. Ignatius of Antioch's *Epistle to the Romans*; and, for the development of the idea of 'green martyrdom' – the idea of the living identification with the death of Christ even though no blood might be shed – see Origen's *Exhortation to Martyrdom*.
14. Gal. 2.20 RSV.
15. Anselm's epoch-making *Cur Deus Homo* was significant in redirecting theological thinking to the humanity of Christ, and his prayers and meditations show its implications for his affective spirituality.
16. cf. Bernard's *Sermons on the Song of Songs*, which are full of emphasis on the humanity of Christ, the Name of Jesus, meditation on the sufferings of Christ, etc.; also William of St Thierry in his vastly influential *Golden Epistle to the Carthusians of Mont Dieu* (long attributed to Bernard) recommended daily meditation on the passion and redemption of Christ.
17. cf. Mary Felicitas Madigan I B V M, *The Passio Domini Theme in the Works of Richard Rolle: His Personal Contribution in its Religious, Cultural and Literary Context*, Elizabethan and Renaissance Studies, ed. James Hogg, Salzburg Studies in English Literature (Institut Für Englische Sprache und Literatur, Universität Salzburg, 1978).
18. Walter Hilton, *The Scale of Perfection*, tr. Gerard Sitwell, O S B (Burns Oates, London, 1953), Bk. I Chaps. 46–54.
19. cf. Sr Benedicta Ward, tr., *The Prayers and Meditations of St Anselm* (Penguin, Harmondsworth, Middlesex, 1973), p. 95.
20. ibid., p. 97.
21. Jean Leclercq, *The Love of Learning and the Desire for God* (ET SPCK, London, and Fordham University Press, New York, 1961), p. 19.
22. ibid., pp. 21–2; cf. Ward, Introduction, pp. 43–6.
23. RR 29, p. 80.
24. RR 31, pp. 88–9.
25. Walter Hilton, Bk. I Ch. 35; cf. S. S. Hussey, 'Walter Hilton: Traditionalist?', in Marion Glasscoe, ed., *The Medieval Mystical Tradition in England*, Papers read at the Exeter Symposium, July 1980, Exeter Medieval English Texts and Studies, General Editor: M. J. Swanton (University of Exeter 1980).

26. LT 51; see below, pp. 191–201.
27. LT 2.
28. Walter Hilton Bk. I. Chaps. 10–11.
29. *The Cloud of Unknowing* L 111.
30. ST 1 and LT 2. The critical edition makes clear what the translation leaves ambiguous, namely that it was the desire for the illness, not just the accompanying contrition, which is the unsought gift in question.
31. LT 2.
32. LT 2.
33. See above p. 17.
34. I agree with Evelyn Underhill when she comments that they used the Song of Songs because they wished to use erotic imagery; they did not use erotic imagery merely because they felt constrained to interpret the Song of Songs. *Mysticism* (London, 1911), p. 137.
35. 'Prologue to the Commentary on the Song of Songs', in Rowan A. Greer, tr., *Origen* (Classics of Western Spirituality, Paulist Press, New York, and SPCK, London, 1979), p. 223.
36. Bernard of Clairvaux, Sermon on the Song of Songs 74.6 (Cistercian Fathers Series: No. 40, Cistercian Publications, Kalamazoo, Michigan, 1980), p. 91.
37. David Knowles and Dimitri Obolensky, *The Christian Centuries Vol. II: The Middle Ages* (Darton, Longman & Todd, London, and Paulist Press, New York, 1969), Chaps. 20 and 30.
38. cf. Hadewijch, *The Complete Works* (Classics of Western Spirituality, SPCK, London, and Paulist Press, N.Y. 1980) Letter 6. p. 63; Vision 1, p. 269 Poem 5, pp. 328–9; Valerie Lagorio, 'The Medieval Continental Women Mystics', in Szarmach.
39. Mechthild of Magdeburg, *The Flowing Light of the Godhead* II.14, ET Lucy Menzies, *The Revelations of Mechthild of Magdeburg* (Longmans, Green, London and New York, 1953), p. 40.
40. W. Butler-Bowden, ed., *The Book of Margery Kempe*, ch. 22 (Life and Letters Series No. 103, Jonathan Cape, London and Toronto, 1936), p. 350. But for a view that argues for Margery's sanity, see Maureen Fries, 'Margery Kempe', in Szarmach, pp. 217–35.
41. See below, pp. 142–6.
42. John of the Cross, 'The Living Flame of Love', ET Lynda Nicholson in Gerald Brenan, *St John of the Cross: His Life and Poetry* (Cambridge University Press, London and New York, 1973), p. 163.
43. cf. LT 38 and 39; see below, Chapter 10.
44. Gal. 6.17 RSV.
45. She certainly might have. The first friars had come to England in 1224 and become established in Oxford. Under Robert Grosseteste, Oxford became a centre for Franciscan learning which in turn sent teachers to convents in various places in England, among which Norwich was significant. cf. A. G. Little, 'The First Hundred Years of the Franciscan School at Oxford', in Walter Seton, ed., *St Francis of Assisi 1226–1926: Essays in Commemoration* (University of London Press, London, 1926), pp 165–90.
46. Isaiah 53.5 RSV.
47. cf. Burchard of Worms penitentiary included in the Decretum Bk 19, PL 140 cols. 000 950; cf. John T. McNeill, *A History of the Cure of Souls* (Harper & Row, New York, 1951).

48. For a useful discussion of this, see Linda Georgianna, 'Self and the Sacrament of Confession', pp. 79–119 in her *The Solitary Self*.
49. Hebrews 4.12 RSV.
50. cf. Sr Benedicta Ward, '"Faith Seeking Understanding" Anselm of Canterbury and Julian of Norwich', in *Julian of Norwich* (Fairacres Publication No. 28), pp. 27–9.
51. Anselm in Ward (Penguin), p. 202; cf. Introduction pp. 53–6.
52. Bernard of Clairvaux, Sermon 12 in Kilian Walsh, tr., *The Works of Bernard of Clairvaux vol. II; On the Song of Songs I*, Cistercian Fathers Series: No. 4 (Cistercian Publications, Kalamazoo, Michigan, 1977), p. 77.
53. See above, p. 46.
54. LT 39.
55. ibid.
56. Augustine of Hippo, Confessions I.1 (tr. John K. Ryan, *The Confessions of St Augustine* (Image, Doubleday, N.Y., 1960).
57. cf. Jean Leclercq, *The Love of Learning and the Desire for God*, pp. 83–6.
58. LT 15.
59. Walter Hilton, *Scale of Perfection*, Bk. I Ch. 46.
60. LT 19.
61. LT 39.

5 Julian's Visions

'Blessed are the pure in heart, for they shall see God.'[1] The examination of the actual nature of Julian's visions as she described them requires awareness of the formative period – probably years – during which she prayed for deeper purity and singleness of heart. Such prayer would be meaningless unless she simultaneously tried to fashion her life in accordance with it, whether in an anchorhold or not. Her preoccupation was not with the prayers for a direct vision of Christ's passion and for a severe bodily illness, but she says that she continued to pray urgently and without qualification for the three wounds.

Then, when she was 'thirty and a half years old', one of her prayers was unexpectedly answered: she became seriously ill to the point of death. She received the last rites of the Church, and progressively weakened, lingering for two more days and nights. On the third night, it appeared that the end was approaching. Those who were with her shared her belief that she could not survive long, and sent for a priest to be present in her dying moments. The priest brought with him a crucifix, which he placed before her eyes so that she could gaze upon it to the end. She thought that she was very near death. She says that she agreed to fasten her eyes on the cross as the priest suggested, because when the end came she would be able to gaze straight ahead of her longer than she would have been able to look upwards to heaven as she seems at first to have intended.[2]

What her illness was is unknown; some have speculated that it may have been cardiac failure;[3] others that it was botulism.[4] Significantly, she is not interested in describing its details, except insofar as they are pertinent to the revelations which soon occurred. As Paul Molinari has pointed out, this is strong evidence, if it were needed, for Julian's sanity: anyone who suffers from neuroses which develop into self-induced illness would take the opportunity Julian here has to enlarge on the sickness and draw attention to every detail.[5]

Julian, however, is much more interested in how various aspects of her experience parallel those of the passion of Christ. The way in which she presents them reinforces her earlier comment that she was already to some extent 'mindful of the passion': like Christ, she is thirty years old when she enters into suffering; she suffers for three days and nights; her prayer echoes his Gethsemane resolution that 'not my will but thine be done'; and she notices the hours at which the various experiences occur in a possible reminiscence of the hours of Christ on the cross.[6] The allusions are not laboured, however. Where they occur, they might be the result of the absorption of the Scriptures which allowed the medieval writers, especially those in the monastic tradition, to incorporate it into all their thinking, even at a subconscious level.[7]

Julian says that as her sight began to fail, she could see only the crucifix which had been placed before her. Her body had for some time felt to her 'dead from the middle downwards' and now the upper part also seemed to be 'beginning to die'. Her hands fell down, and her head, which had been propped up, 'lolled to one side'.[8] Her breath became short and painful. And then, at the very moment when she believed she was on the point of death,

> suddenly in that moment all my pain left me, and I was as sound, particularly in the upper part of my body, as ever I was before or since.[9]

She did not take this to be actual physical healing, but rather a miraculous deliverance by God from the pain she was suffering so that her dying would be eased. She continued to expect that she would not live. Those around her apparently shared this view: her mother at one point reached out to close her eyes, thinking that she had actually died.[10]

It was in this state of proximity to death that her earlier prayer was recalled to her mind, the desire that she might have an experience of the passion of Christ, suffering with him and identifying with his pains 'with compassion which would lead to longing for God'. In this context it becomes apparent that her desire was at the farthest remove from idle curiosity about idiosyncratic experiences or mystical phenomena: the whole object, as far as Julian was concerned, was to relate her own extreme suffering to the passion of Christ. And in the purity of her intention, her prayer was answered.

> Suddenly I saw the red blood trickling down from under the crown, all hot, flowing freely and copiously, a living stream, just as it seemed to me that it was at the time when the crown of thorns was thrust down upon his blessed head.[11]

There follows a series of remarkably vivid visual and auditory phenomena in which, with her eyes fixed *in extremis* on the crucifix, she has both 'corporeal' vision of the suffering and dying Christ, and 'spiritual sight' and understanding of the teachings which he conveyed to her. She says that after a time she saw in the face of the crucifix a part of Christ's passion: contempt, spitting to defoul his body, buffeting of his blessed face, and many woes and pains, more than I can tell; and his colour often changed, and all his blessed face was for a time caked with dry blood.[12]

All this while the bleeding persisted, 'until I had seen and understood many things';[13] she described this in vivid analogies:

> The drops were round like pellets as the blood issued, they were round like herring's scales as they spread, they were like raindrops off a house's eaves, so many that they could not be counted.[14]

Then she began to see the body itself bleeding, where Christ had been scourged, as before she had seen the bleeding of his head from the crown of thorns.[15] Presently she observed him approaching death, just as she herself had done:

> I saw his sweet face as it were dry and bloodless, with the pallor of dying, then more dead, pale and languishing, then the pallor turning blue and then more blue, as death took more hold upon his flesh ... This was a grievous change to watch, this deep dying, and the nose shrivelled and dried up as I saw.[16]

Having seen all this, Julian fully expected to see Jesus expire, perhaps believing that she herself would die when this occurred. Suddenly, as she continued to gaze at the crucifix, she saw a change in Christ parallel to her own miraculous recovery. His appearance became joyful, and he began to teach her by speaking to her, combining visions with locutions. The Lord looked down at his wounded side, and to the right of the cross where Julian supposed that his mother stood during the passion.[17] Julian says that at that point she expected to see Mary 'in bodily likeness', but instead she received a spiritual vision of her: a comment which reveals that Julian kept a clear distinction between bodily and spiritual vision, so that when she says that she saw something with bodily vision, we have to take it that she means what she says, and is not talking about spiritual illumination or her own imagination.[18]

All her visions took place within the context of gazing at the crucifix (apart from one that occurred during sleep) but they were not all visions of the crucifixion. At one point she was shown 'something small, no bigger than a hazel-nut, lying in the palm of my hand';[19] this formed the basis for her theology of creation. At another time,

> My understanding was let down into the bottom of the sea, and there I saw green hills and valleys, with the appearance of moss strewn with seaweed and gravel;[20]

from this she comes to understand the security of someone who is protected by God. She has an extended vision of a Lord and a servant, whose meaning she pondered for fifteen years or more, until it became

76

the key to her theology of the incarnation, and with it her understanding of the problem of evil and human transformation into wholeness.[21]

Not all the visions were pleasant, however. She recounts that after some time she fell asleep, and in her sleep it seemed that the devil was trying to strangle her: in the nightmare he had all the hideous characteristics of the medieval idea of him. When she awoke, the people with her moistened her temples so that she felt a little better.

> And then a little smoke came in at the door, with great heat and a foul stench. I said: Blessed be the Lord! Is everything on fire here? And I thought that it must be actual fire, which would have burned us to death. I asked those who were with me if they were conscious of any stench. They said no, they were not. I said: Blessed be God! For then I knew that it was the devil who had come to assail me.[22]

This physical experience which she took to be the devil continued for a considerable time, characterized by a foul smell, oppressive heat, and chattering and muttering in her ears.[23] Some of the vivid experiences, therefore, involved other physical senses besides vision, and not all the experiences were directly related to the crucifix held before her eyes.

The question that arises here as in any consideration of mystical visions is why they should be taken seriously as coming from God or as having spiritual significance. How, for instance, would all these intense experiences differ from hallucination or indeed from drug-induced phenomena? Julian was after all extremely ill, and when the previous intensity of her life and prayer are taken into account, it becomes plausible to suppose that she might have been susceptible to unusual hallucinations of a religious variety. It is not unreasonable to suppose that she might have been given such herbs or drugs as were available to medieval medicine to ease her pain; and those familiar with the effects of hallucinogenic drugs know that intense and varied sensations, especially of colour but also of sound and smell, can occur; and if there is a focus for the eyes, as the crucifix was for Julian, all manner of strange things may appear to happen to it. Because the experiences she was having – the changes of colour, the voices, the heat, the smells – are not dissimilar to drug-induced experiences or other sorts of hallucinations, the question arises why they should be taken seriously, or invested with a religious significance.

It is worth noticing that at one stage Julian herself asked that question. After the visions of Christ on the cross had ceased, she had a recurrence of her physical distress, though she now no longer believed that she would die. For her, this was all the worse, because, having experienced the consolation of God's love and now having it taken from her, she longed to be released from this life so that she might abide in his loving presence forever. As she lay in this state of physical and mental suffering, a 'man of religion' came to ask how she was.

> And I said that during the day I had been raving. And he laughed aloud and heartily. And I said: the cross that stood at the foot of my bed bled profusely; and when I said this, the religious I was speaking to became very serious and surprised.[24]

The fact that the priest took her seriously and refused to treat her visions as hallucinations brought Julian up short, so that she became very much ashamed of herself for calling her experiences ravings, and wished to make her confession. She felt unable to do so, however, apparently feeling that the priest would not accept that she was telling the truth – a condition for the practice of confession:[25]

> But I could not tell it to any priest, for I thought: How could a priest believe me, when I, by saying that I had been raving, showed that I did not believe our Lord God?[26]

She felt that she had been thoroughly ungrateful and inconstant so to trivialize the experiences which she had had.

Looking at this from the perspective of the late twentieth century, we might wonder whether she was right about this. On what grounds did the priest take her seriously rather than agree that she might have been hallucinating? No further information is given about him, but it is likely that a 'man of religion', that is a monk or friar, who was welcome to come and see Julian at a time of such severe illness would have been one who knew her previous life of prayer at least in general terms, and would himself be devout. This, however, does not resolve the question, acute for us today, which may also be phrased in more general terms: What is the value, if any, of religious experiences such as these?

The first response must be a negative one. The value of these intense experiences cannot lie in their sensory content taken on its own, because in this respect there is no significant difference between them and hallucinations, drug-induced or otherwise. Mystical experiences convey a strong sense of certainty, and have often been taken, even by serious writers, to be in themselves evidence for their own authenticity.[27] Since sensations of this kind can arise from a variety of causes, however, it is inadequate to suppose that their intensity and the psychological certainty which they generate is itself evidence that they come from God or that they reveal religious truth.[28]

Nor will it do to say that although in some cases voices and visions can be accounted for by drugs or readily explicable hallucinations, there are other cases where such accounts are not available, and in these latter instances God is the source of the experiences. This point of view would in the first place undermine taking Julian's experiences as from God, because in her case an alternative explanation for hallucination is readily available: she was after all *in extremis*. More generally, it would be a mistake to attribute to God only that for which no causal explanation is yet available. The science of psychology is in its infancy; as it grows, much more development is to be expected in the sorts of accounts available for hallucinations and kindred experiences. If God is to be considered the cause only of those things which are not otherwise accounted for, then this amounts to a psychological version of the 'god of the gaps' theory which has already been discredited at the level of the physical sciences. For it would mean, on the one hand, that as understanding develops and gaps become smaller, God is squeezed out; and on the other, that God is barred from working within and through the ordinary causal sequence, having been relegated to that which is outside it. Any divine intervention would then be like a spanner in the works, an unnatural and disruptive occurrence, rather than the continuous action of God within his world and within human lives.[29]

This is not to say that the vivid sensory content of Julian's experiences did not come from God or have religious significance, but only that taken on their own they cannot themselves be the guarantee of such significance. Nor would Julian herself have supposed they could. Profound though their psychological impact undoubtedly was, to Julian these 'bodily visions' were least in importance in her overall account. She says,

> All the blessed teaching of our Lord God was shown to me in three parts ... that is to say by bodily vision, and by words formed in my understanding, and by spiritual vision. About the bodily vision I have said as I saw, as truly as I am able. And about the words formed, I have repeated them just as our Lord revealed them to me. And about the spiritual vision, I have told a part, but I never can tell it in full ...[30]

It is clear that Julian believes that to have proper understanding, these three will have to be interpreted together. The bodily visions would be of small importance without the spiritual understanding which was also experienced; they could never be isolated from it and still retain their meaning.[31] It would be quite foreign to Julian's thinking to make the sensory content of the visions the basis upon which the whole account is to be judged. For her it is the other way around: the spiritual insight and its effect upon her subsequent life are what is important; the bodily visions were a gracious psychological aid, sent to her in answer to her prayer that she might be more mindful of the passion of Christ.

What then was the real test of the experiences according to Julian? In her view, ultimately the point of it all was increasing love for God.

About this she is emphatic: the revelations in themselves do not single her out as special, but are given for the good of all her fellow-Christians, not to prove to them by the fact of her vivid experiences that God exists or that religious doctrines are true, but to help them by her spiritual insights to proceed more deeply into the love of God.

> I am not good because of the revelations, but only if I love God better; and inasmuch as you love God better, it is more to you than to me. I do not say this to those who are wise, because they know it well. But I say it to you who are simple, to give you comfort and strength; for we are all one in love, for truly it was not revealed to me that God loves me better than the humblest soul who is in a state of grace. For I am sure that there are many who never had revelations or visions, but only the common teaching of Holy Church, who love God better than I.[32]

Julian's attitude toward the mystical phenomena, then, is one of gratitude to God; her wretchedness when she temporarily dismissed them as raving was because of her ingratitude in so doing. This gratitude, however, was based on the recognition that what is truly important is not the fact of the experiences themselves, but the deepened love of God which results from them and the insights communicated with them. This is the basis of her insistence that the visions were not given for her own private benefit: they were given for all her fellow Christians. She never suggests that other people ought to try to have visions, or pray for them, or seek them in any way; the visions were like the receptacle for the spiritual treasure, given to all through her.

> And you who hear and see this vision and this teaching, which is from Jesus Christ for the edification of your souls, it is God's will and my wish that you accept it with as much joy and delight as if Jesus had shown it to you as he did to me ... And so it is my desire that it should be to every man the same profit that I asked for myself ... for it is common and general, just as we are all one; and I am sure that I saw it for the profit of many others.[33]

Julian shows some embarrassment at being the one to communicate such teaching, because she is 'a woman, ignorant, weak and frail'. Yet she cannot allow the unconventionality of a woman teaching stop her from passing on what she has seen, for she is convinced that it was not given for her profit alone. This is why she takes such pains to ponder it. We see in the difference between the Short Text and the Long Text a significant coming to terms with her intellectual ability[34] as well as her femininity, to the extent of thinking of God in feminine as well as masculine terms.[35] This is also why, in spite of the odour of heresy surrounding writing in the vernacular, she risks possible association in ecclesiastical minds with the Lollards, for she is not writing only for the learned, but for all her fellow-Christians. If she were to stop herself from communicating her insights, she would be disobedient; whereas she is hopeful that if she faithfully conveys it, the content of it will so lead its readers to the love of Christ that they will quickly forget about Julian and the fact that she is female in their contemplation of Jesus and his manifestation of the love of God.

> But it is truly love which moves me to tell it to you, for I want God to be known and my fellow Christians to prosper, as I hope to prosper myself, by hating sin more and loving God more. But because I am a woman, ought I therefore to believe that I should not tell you of the goodness of God, when I saw at the same time that it is his will to be known?[36]

The seriousness with which she took the imperative to communicate what she had seen is indicated by her sustained efforts to understand the revelations so that she could write the expanded version. It was important enough for all her fellow-Christians that it deserved her best efforts over twenty years, during which time she integrated the insights of her experience with biblical and monastic spirituality the better to convey what she took to be 'our Lord's meaning'. The fruit of this meditation will become more apparent in subsequent sections: what is important here is that her writing down of the revelations was no momentary impulse. For her own sake, for the sake of her fellow-Christians, and for the sake of the truth itself, this could be no casual exercise. It demanded all her effort and learning and love.

There must have been a great self-sacrificial will-to-integrity underlying her willingness, as a medieval woman in the time of the Peasants' Revolt and the Lollards, to probe and study and think through her experiences before finally writing the Long Text. One can hardly suppose that she received much encouragement from her bishop, Despenser, and it was probably prudent not to advertise her visions before him. One wonders how carefully her secret was guarded. Margery Kempe, in her account of her visit to Julian, makes no mention of Julian's visions: was this because she did not know about them, or was it rather because Margery was more interested in talking about her own experiences than in recounting someone else's? Whatever we speculate here, one thing is clear. Julian's whole aim had been, as was clear from her prayers, to increase in true contrition, loving compassion, and a longing of the will for God. These are the context as well as the measure of her experiences. It is certain, therefore, that although Julian valued the visions, they were to her secondary to the much more important matter of ongoing experience, and this was to be seen not in terms of strange phenomena but in terms of her overall relationship to God as measured by the three wounds.

For Julian, therefore, there is a sense in which religious experience preceded and indeed was the necessary condition for religious experiences. It was the developing relationship with God as evidenced by her three prayers which made the religious experiences – the visions – possible. By this I do not mean simply that had she not already been a devout woman God would not have given her the visions, though of course this may be true as well. But more strongly, if she had not prayed as she did – if these prayers had not expressed the longings of her heart – she would not have understood the visions as she did, no matter how vivid the sensations might have been. It is the context of devotion and longing for God which makes her receptive not only to the visions themselves, but also to the spiritual insights she received.

This was not, however, simply a passive piety. Julian's longing for God was an active longing, wanting enlightenment and understanding, and doing whatever lay in her power towards it. This is obvious from the fact that she entered an anchorhold – hardly a casual act on her part. It can also be seen from the way in which she persisted in her probing questions about sin, not content to accept the consolation of the visions as long as she was aware of the sufferings of others. Someone more self-centred might have been overwhelmed by the visions, emotionally submerged in the intensity of God's love, so that the intellect went into passive abeyance. Julian, by contrast, kept her wits about her, and when she was assured of the love of God, boldly asked him to explain why, if he is so loving, he ever allowed sin. And when in response she was told that 'all will be well', her reply was, in effect, 'It doesn't look at all well to me!'

> But in this I stood, contemplating it generally, darkly and mournfully, saying in intention to our God with very great fear: Ah, good Lord, how could all things be well, because of the great harm which has come through sin to your creatures? And here I wished, so far as I dared, for some plainer explanation through which I might be at ease about this matter.[37]

She did receive a response to this request, but it took her another twenty years to understand it! What her final resolution was of the problem of evil and suffering will be examined in Chapter Nine. The point here is her active involvement in the experiences themselves, her faith seeking understanding, and seeking it always in accordance with her overriding commitment of longing of the will for God. She did not take the visions themselves as definitive, but continued to probe them for deeper enlightenment for herself and her fellow-Christians, reflecting on them in the light of Scripture and the 'teaching of Holy Church', including the theology and spirituality available to her.

The example of Julian in this relationship between her overriding religious framework and the particular experiences she had points to a more general understanding of the reciprocity between context and mystical experience. Recent philosophical writing on mysticism has sometimes held that mystical experiences like voices and visions are decisive events which carry complete conviction and which would by themselves bring about religious commitment or conversion: the case of Saul on the Damascus Road in the biblical story might be cited here, where the vision of the risen Christ was enough to change him from a Pharisee persecuting the Christians to a Christian believer and apostle. On the other side, it is urged that the context is already determinative of the experience.[38] Thus in medieval Europe people had visions of the Virgin Mary, but not of Ṣiva dancing: this was because they already had a religious conceptual structure in which the Virgin Mary played a significant part, and in which visions of her were, if not common, at least within the realm of accepted possibility. Indeed if, *per imposs-ibile*, someone in medieval Europe did have a vision of Ṣiva dancing, he or she would simply not have known what it was, and would therefore probably not have attached any religious significance to it at all (unless in terms of the demonic), let alone have become a convert to Hinduism. As for the case of Saul, this can be explained by the fact that he was already thoroughly familiar with Christianity, and his dramatic conversion was a matter of coming to terms in his life and consciousness with something he had already been subconsciously aware of for some time and was violently repressing in his persecution of the Church.

Thus the argument is between those who see the experiences as determinative of the beliefs on the one hand, and those who see the framework of belief as determinative of the experiences on the other. The example of Julian shows, however, that in her case at least the two are reciprocal. There is an enduring context of devotion and commitment to God, seeking greater recollection and compassion: without this, the visions, if they had occurred at all, would not have carried the significance which she was able to find in them. But reciprocally, the visions are for Julian revelations of divine love, and greatly increase her perception of the dimensions of that love. That, indeed, is why she took all the trouble to ponder them and write the two versions of them. She believed that they contained important teaching, not only for herself but for others as well.

It is now possible to return to the previous question: to what extent can Julian's experiences be taken seriously as evidence for the truth of religious claims? In a sense, that question is explored through the whole book, and cannot be answered until its conclusion. But a preliminary response can be sketched at this point. First, negatively, one-off odd experiences, whether visions, voices, or other mystical phenomena, cannot in themselves justify religious beliefs, no matter how psychologically compelling they are. They do not differ in kind from hallucinations or drug-induced experiences, and taken on their own they would at best reveal something about the psychology of the percipient, not give evidence about an external source of the experiences, let alone prove the existence of God or the truth of religious doctrines.

But, on the other hand, experiences like Julian's are misunderstood if they are taken as psychological phenomena occurring in isolation. They take place in the context of a lifestyle of belief and devotion, and serve in turn to deepen that lifestyle. Now, that lifestyle is itself based crucially upon the premise of religious belief, and is incomprehensible without it. What must be examined, therefore, is not the extent to which the visions taken on their own justify religious beliefs, but rather the extent to which the lifestyle as a whole lends credence to the premises upon which it is based, and the experiences which play a part in it. This is a far less straightforward investigation, requiring the weighing not only of the phenomena of the visions and voices, but, far more importantly, the spiritual insights and interpretation derived from them. We need to seek to understand them for ourselves, and decide whether they are true and worthwhile.

But this, of course, cannot be done in as detached a manner as one can weigh up the evidential value of mystical phenomena. For if we are seeking to understand and assess what Julian presents as spiritual insight, then to whatever extent we find it valid or profound, to that extent we will ourselves be illuminated and challenged by it. Even to begin the exercise requires a certain sympathy: if one could make nothing of the aim of recollection – measuring life and attitudes by the standard of the passion of Christ – then it would be impossible even to consider seriously the rest of Julian's teaching.

This in turn means that the pseudo-ideal of objective neutrality is both useless and impossible in this investigation. That does not of course mean that rationality and critical assessment are to be abandoned (Julian would have been appalled at the suggestion!) so that one rubber stamps the end from the beginning in a rush of mystical enthusiasm. It does mean, however, that we cannot pretend to be uninvolved. It will be from within our own experience that we will have to decide on the spiritual value of Julian's insights; and this means that we will have to become aware of what our own experience is: its depths and its shallows. As we probe her teaching, we find that we are ourselves being probed. What begins in an effort to understand her culminates in an effort to understand ourselves. As with any great art or literature or spiritual writing, critical assessment turns the challenge back upon the challenger, and the measure with which we mete is measured to us again. Indeed, it could not be otherwise. We cannot in consistency find something of value and at the same time refuse to be evaluated by it. This, although not a neutral way of proceeding, is surely the only honest way: a willingness to submit ourselves to the same moral and religious assessment to which we submit others.

It would be disingenuous to pretend that Julian's teaching could be explored with detached neutrality, any more than that ultimate moral or religious decisions could be made without subjective involvement. Rather, in the exposition of her teaching, we find ourselves exposed; and it is only after an encounter of our integrity with her own that we will be able properly to assimilate the value of her life-style and the teaching which her experiences brought to her. As she herself emphasized,

> I am not good because of the revelations, but only if I love God better; and inasmuch as you love God better, it is more to you than to me.[39]

Notes to Chapter Five

1. Matt. 5.8.
2. ST 2.
3. C & W, p. 69.
4. James T. McIlwain, 'The "Bodelye Syeknes" of Julian of Norwich', in *Journal of Medieval History* vol. X. No. 3 (Sept. 1984), pp. 167–80.
5. Paul Molinari s J, *Julian of Norwich: The Teaching of a 14th Century English Mystic* (Longmans, Green, London and New York, 1958), pp. 28–9. This is contrary to the opinion of R. H. Thouless that Julian's visions were hallucinations showing precarious mental balance, or C. Pepler's comment that she suffered from 'acute neurosis induced perhaps by an over-enthusiastic life of penance and solitude'. Fuller justification of the claim of her sanity will emerge as this chapter progresses. R. H. Thouless, *The Lady Julian: A Psychological Study* (London 1924), p. 25; Conrad Pepler OP, *The English Religious Heritage* (London 1958), p. 312.
6. cf. LT 2, 3, 65, etc.; C & W, p. 287 n34.
7. cf. Jean Leclercq, pp. 89–96.
8. ST 2.
9. ibid.
10. ST 10.
11. ST 4.
12. ST 7.
13. LT 7.
14. ibid.
15. ST 8.
16. ST 10.
17. ST 13.
18. cf. Molinari, pp. 33–49; the distinction derives from Augustine, *De Genesi ad literam*, xii. vii.
19. LT 5.
20. LT 10.
21. LT 51; see below, Chapter 9.
22. ST 22.
23. McIlwain discusses how these phenomena could have been associated with her illness.

24. ST 21; cf. LT 66.
25. C & W, p.633 n5.
26. LT 66.
27. cf. William James, *The Varieties of Religious Experience* (Fontana, Collins, Glasgow, 1977), p.408; first published 1902.
28. C. B. Martin, *Religious Belief* (Cornell University Press, Ithaca, New York, 1959), Ch. 5.
29. cf. Patrick Sherry, *Spirit, Saints, and Immortality* (Macmillan, London, 1984), pp.42–3; also pp.10–30.
30. ST 23.
31. Note that she says that the spiritual understanding was *revealed*, it was not simply her inference or conjecture on the basis of the visions.
32. LT 9. Note the unself-centred contrast with Margery Kempe, cited above, p.63, who seeks to show herself special, 'singular', in God's sight.
33. ST 6.
34. cf. Tugwell, pp.188–9.
35. LT 57–63; see below, pp.115–24.
36. ST 6.
37. LT 29.
38. For a detailed presentation of these views, cf. Steven Katz, 'Language, Epistemology and Mysticism', in his, ed., *Mysticism and Philosophical Analysis* (Sheldon Press, London, 1978).
39. LT 9.

PART THREE

Julian's Theology of Integration

6 'Love was his meaning': Julian's Theological Method

The reciprocity between Julian's experiences and her background in the framework of the teaching of 'Holy Church' emerges more clearly in an examination of her method of theological development. In this section we will consider Julian's theological method, and then investigate how its application led her to understand the doctrines of creation, the Trinity, and human personhood. This will provide the necessary background to explore, in subsequent chapters, her conception of the Trinity and of ourselves, and how her understanding of the incarnation and its efficacy for the healing of persons resolves for her the problems of sin and human suffering.

None of this is divorced, for Julian, from her visions of the crucified Christ. In her initial summary of the sixteen showings, she says,

> This is a revelation of love which Jesus Christ, our endless bliss, made in sixteen showings, of which the first is about his precious crowning of thorns; and in this was contained and specified the blessed Trinity, with the Incarnation and the union between God and man's soul, with many fair revelations and teachings of endless wisdom and love, in which all the revelations which follow are founded and connected.[1]

Although it is possible for her to list the revelations separately, none of them stand on their own without reference to each other and especially to the first one which is fundamental to them all. This becomes apparent also in her theological explorations of their meaning, in which she cannot proceed in a straightforward linear pattern, but is constantly referring back to what has gone before, adding touches or qualifications, and in the Long Text making significant additions of substance which are a product of her many years' prayerful reflection on the experiences.

One result of this is that, in spite of its clarity and simplicity of expression, her book in its final form is astonishingly complex, when taken as a whole rather than read simply for its edifying passages taken out of context. She has worked through her material with great care and precision; the result requires similar care, going back to reconsider earlier passages in the light of later ones. A single linear reading (or even several) cannot take the place of patient study: this is solid meat and requires a great deal of theological chewing. At the beginning of the Long Text Julian sets out the sixteen visions in order, briefly mentioning the contents of each. For a study of her theology and spirituality, however, it is necessary to move back and forth through the interconnections of her teaching, rather than expound the visions consecutively: as we proceed, we will see how the profound integration of her style makes this non-linear approach helpful.

Unfortunately not very much has been written about Julian's theology[2] (as contrasted with articles about her spirituality, or extracts of her writings for spiritual reading); and it has even sometimes been dismissed as the uncertain if sincere meanderings of an ecstatic visionary, with 'the accent ... on the psychological aspects of ... experiences, with no great stress laid on theological foundations or moral presuppositions'.[3]

Those who have taken the trouble to look closely, however, are of a very different opinion; and gradually the depth and profundity of Julian's theology is being recognized. Thomas Merton, after a study of Julian, ranked her with the greatest of all theologians;[4] unfortunately he died before he could write about her in any detail. Julian has waited for recognition for many centuries; her understanding of the relationship between God and the world, and its implications for the healing of persons and confrontation with the problems of evil and suffering, as well as her theology of the motherhood of God, attracts particular attention in our own time.

An implication of her recognition that all she was taught is grounded in the first revelation is that all of her theology ultimately finds its focus in the passion of Christ. Whatever she has to say about creation, the Trinity, the incarnation, or any other topic about which the scholastically oriented theologians of her time were engaging in learned disputations must ultimately be measured by the standard of the cross. This is not to imply any belittling of the scholastics on her part, even implicitly. She would have been the last to minimize the importance of careful thought and presentation, and her Long Text is meticulous in its organization, with careful backward and forward references, and profound in its depth. Even though her methodology is different from that of the scholastics, her intellect is no less penetrating. But in her own thinking, theological investigation started from and was centred in the passion of Christ as it had been given to her in her own experience.

This central focus had the effect of unifying the various dimensions of Julian's life and thought. As already discussed, she desired from her youth up to develop recollection of the passion: she wanted her daily living to be measured by the standard of Christ, so that he became the focus of her existence to whom every thought and action and decision could be 'collected again' to be seen in its true perspective. It was this which led her to the anchorhold where she felt that this aim could, for her, be more fully realized. Her visions, too, were in a very literal sense centred on the passion: the crucifix was their actual physical focus, and her extraordinary experiences were all connected with it (except for the nightmare about the red-headed devil). Thus it is no surprise to find that her theological reflection is grounded squarely in the passion of Christ. Julian is an outstanding example of an integrated theologian, for whom daily life and religious experience and theological reflection are all aspects of the same whole.

What, then, according to Julian, is this 'standard of the cross'? How, concretely, does one begin to measure a life or a religious experience or for that matter a theological doctrine by it? To be able to make a response here, it is necessary to have an understanding of the cross, an interpretation of its meaning which will then provide a focus in which to see other things. Julian recognizes this need, and from the first chapter to the last her book vibrates with the gently insistent theme: 'Love was his meaning.' In the statement of the first revelation already quoted, she did not say that she had had a revelation of the passion of Christ; she says, 'This is a revelation of *love* which Jesus Christ ... made in sixteen showings ...' Though there were sixteen visions or showings of it, there was in the basic sense only one revelation, and that was the revelation of love. The book is filled with references to love, and is in one sense nothing more (and nothing less) than an exposition of its meaning. And at the very end, Julian states that even then she continued to ponder the experiences, for though at some levels she did understand them, in other ways she was still puzzled and wanted to understand more deeply.

> And from the time that it was revealed, I desired many times to know in what was our Lord's meaning. And fifteen years after and more, I was answered in spiritual understanding, and it was said: What, do you wish to know your Lord's meaning in this thing? Know it well, love was his meaning. Who reveals it to you? Love. What did he reveal to you? Love. Why does he reveal it to you? For love. Remain in this, and you will know more of the same. But you will never know different, without end.[5]

It might at first be thought that this is the substitution of a subjective emotion for the objective standard of the passion of Christ. How can one say simultaneously that the cross of Christ is the measure of theological understanding and yet that the cross itself must be interpreted? Is it not the measure after all? Closer reading, however, shows that there is no confusion in Julian's mind. The passion itself is understood as love, as the supreme manifestation of the love of God. But this in turn brings with it a revision of the common understanding of what love means. It is true that love is the measure; but this is not just any sentimental idea of love. The passion of Christ offers a principle for understanding what love really is; it is the standard by which love itself must be measured. What we have here is not a circle, as might at first appear, but reciprocity. As there is growth in understanding of the passion of Christ, more and more of the dimensions of love can be seen; and that in turn facilitates the interpretation and assimilation of the passion at still deeper levels. Put in the abstract, this reciprocity is less striking than we will see it to be as we see how Julian finds that the dimensions of the love of God revealed in the passion of Christ modify and make practical some of the traditional Christian doctrines and attitudes, particularly in terms of the problems of sin and suffering, and healing from their wounds.

The emphasis on practicality is important to Julian, though not in any trendy sense of immediate 'relevance'. The theological reciprocity we have just noted parallels the practical reciprocity between her subjective commitment to a life of prayer and the objective experiences of the visions. What the showings reveal is the love of God in its various dimensions, but it is a love revealed not to one who does not care or who disparages the love of God, but to one who already reciprocates it. There can be no doubt about the sincerity and intensity of Julian's experience of the love of God for her, or about her loving and generous response. And she believed them to be interconnected. Although she had an acute intellect, and did not desist from using it both within the course of the visions when she asked God for further explanations as well as afterwards when she pondered the revelation, this is not an intellect which had been disengaged from the rest of her personality. It would have been utterly foreign to her thinking to ask for reasons for belief which would satisfy her intellect before allowing her emotions to become involved, or before allowing for any implications for the pattern of her life. Rather, she was willing to shape her life in such a way that faith had some room in which to seek understanding, including, presumably, the solitude and silence necessary for such a search; and she realized that it would be a search in which all her powers would have to be engaged. There is no indication that she expected further understanding to come upon her in blinding flashes or in additional visions; the understanding was to come in years of prayerful pondering. It was only in living by what she already understood that she could hope to come to understand more deeply.

Any other procedure would divide personhood against itself; and Julian, in her life as well as in her teaching, could be called the theologian of integration. This has important implications for her understanding of human whole-making. Her account of human wholeness is rooted in her understanding of God, because human personhood as she understands it is a reflection of divine wholeness. The love of God which is the 'meaning' of the experiences is not one aspect or characteristic of God among others. Love is a way of describing every attribute of God, all his activities. Love is not something that God does alongside other things; all his actions and all his being is integrated in love, because 'God is love',[6] or, as Julian expounds it in a rich passage to which we shall return,

> Truth sees God, and wisdom contemplates God, and of these two comes the third, and that is marvellous delight in God, which is love ... For God is endless supreme truth, endless supreme wisdom, endless love uncreated; and a man's soul is a creature in God which has the same properties created.[7]

Because all these properties are united in God, they are also to be reunited in fragmented human persons who were created and restored in the image of God. Yet this unification of all God's attributes in love is the most difficult to assimilate at the level where it can be of practical help to us.

> He wants us in all things to have our contemplation and our delight in love. And it is about this knowledge that we are most blind, for some of us believe that God is almighty and may do everything, and that he is all wisdom and can do everything, but that he is all love and will do everything, there we fail. And it is this ignorance which most hinders God's lovers ...[8]

Julian argues that this ignorance of the love of God is paralleled by an ignorance of our own souls as created and restored in that love, so that we become depressed and fragmented, divided against ourselves. Thus, according to Julian, to come to know ourselves, we must come to know God,

> For our soul is so deeply grounded in God and so endlessly treasured that we cannot come to knowledge of it until we first have knowledge of God, who is the Creator to whom it is united ... We must necessarily be in longing and in penance until the time when we are led so deeply into God that we verily and truly know our own soul; and as I saw certainly that our good Lord himself leads us into this high depth, in the same love with which he redeemed us, by mercy and grace, through the power of his blessed passion.[9]

True theology leads to true psychology and to wholeness of personhood, and vice versa.

But more than this is needed if we are to come to understand specific theological doctrines, without which all talk of integration of theology and life is rose-tinted fantasy. What are the criteria by which a doctrine can be understood and evaluated? Julian offers three:

> The first is the use of man's natural reason. The second is the common teaching of Holy Church. The third is the inward grace-giving operation of the Holy Spirit; and these three are all from one God.[10]

Because they are all from one God, these three, although different, are all in harmony with one another. Julian puts this in very strong terms as she continues:

> God is the foundation of our natural reason; and God is the teaching of Holy Church, and God is the Holy Spirit, and they are all different gifts, and he wants us to have great regard for them, and accord ourselves to them.[11]

None of these are automatic or function independently of human effort and responsiveness; nevertheless they are the means which God has given whereby Julian believes that it is possible to come to knowledge of Christian truth. Although it is true that God far transcends our thinking and imagining, they can give us 'as it were an ABC' of the knowledge of God which will be known in its fulness only in heaven.

Julian here differs somewhat from the apophatic tradition which taught that it is impossible to know what God is, and that at most we can come to understand what God is not. This tradition had received a strong impetus from the writings of the Pseudo-Dionysius, a sixth-century Greek spiritual writer who for many centuries was universally thought to have been the disciple of St Paul himself, and not recognized as 'pseudo' until modern times. His works had been made available to the Latin West in the ninth century through the translations of John Scotus Erigena; and his thinking was deeply influential through, for instance, the immensely popular *Golden Epistle* of William of St Thierry, whose thought was enriched by Greek spiritual writings. Some of Julian's contemporaries in medieval England, especially the anonymous author of *The Cloud of Unknowing*, had also been much affected by the Pseudo-Dionysius, particularly in his teaching on the inadequacy of any intellectual concepts in theological development. The *Cloud* author writes to his young solitary:

> But now you put me a question and say, 'How might I think of him in himself, and what is he?' And to this I can only answer thus: 'I have no idea' ... For a man may, by grace, have the fulness of knowledge of all other creatures and their works, yes, and of the works of God's own self ... But no man can think of God himself.[12]

Julian, however, has a different emphasis. Although she would agree with the author of the *Cloud* that a detached intellect cannot grasp the essence of God, she does believe that by means of natural reason, Christian teaching, and the inner experience of the Holy Spirit, we can have, though never exhaustive knowledge of God, at least that kindergarten ABC variety of real communion with him which is the preliminary to the fulness of knowledge which she believes awaits us when we see him face to face.

The difference from the *Cloud*, however, is more a matter of what is to be understood by natural reason than a dispute about the possibility of a relationship with God while still on earth. The *Cloud* author had drawn a contrast between reason and love, saying that since his reason cannot in principle know God as he is in himself,

> it is my wish to leave everything that I can think of and choose for my love the thing that I cannot think. Because he can certainly be loved, but not thought. He can be taken and held by love but not by thought.[13]

If 'thought' here means the calculating intellect, separated from love, then Julian would certainly agree. But she refuses to drive a wedge between thought and love, reason and feeling. In her view there would be little to choose between unthinking emotion and cold ratiocination. Either one would be a travesty because it would fragment human nature and therefore lead to a distorted relationship with God.[14]

When Julian speaks of 'natural reason' as one of the things that makes knowledge of God possible, she is not voicing a mere pious optimism. The phrase in Middle English is 'oure kyndly reson'. 'Kyndly' here does not mean kind or friendly, but rather that which belongs to our kind, humankind. Reason is 'kyndly': that is, it is specifically and naturally human, rooted in our nature: this is what makes 'natural reason' a legitimate translation. But we would be mistaken if we were to take 'natural' here as somehow contrasted to or in opposition to 'spiritual', as it is in the Authorized Version of the Bible when it translates St Paul to say, 'The natural man receiveth not the things of the Spirit of God . . .'[15] 'Oure kyndly reson' is the reason which distinguishes humankind; it is therefore part of what makes us special on the face of the earth, and is integrated with our whole natural selfhood.

When Julian recognized this, she says that she contemplated it

> greatly marvelling at the sight and the feeling of the sweet harmony, that our reason is in God, understanding that this is the highest gift that we have received, and its foundation is in nature.[16]

Nor does this passage contradict the one quoted above where she said that its foundation is in God, because for Julian *all* of nature is grounded in God. As we will see in Chapter Eight, nature is not to be thought of in negative terms in contrast to God; rather, he is its loving creator, preserver, and restorer, and is himself everything that is good. And this is most specifically true of natural reason:

> Our reason is founded in God, who is nature's substance.[17]

Julian, therefore, lends no support to the camp that holds that ignorance is akin to holiness, or that spirituality requires a mortification of our mental powers. Mindlessness is not what we are made for. Although the experience of God can call preconceived ideas into question, and is certainly incompatible with intellectual arrogance, it requires full human response, mentally as in every other way. Julian herself, as we saw, made that response very generously as she sought understanding of what she experienced. She would have agreed with the patristic saying: 'Holy simplicity is good, but holy knowledge is better!'[18] Her book rings with such phrases as, 'God desires us to know';[19] God 'wishes that we desire to know';[20] 'Our Lord wants us to have true understanding.'[21]

Julian's approach here is in close conformity with that of Thomas Aquinas in his introduction to the *Summa Theologiae*, though as usual there is no way of being certain that there was a direct link between them. Aquinas was concerned to show the legitimacy of a full engagement of the intellect in the things of God. Human reason, created by God, is to be used in the understanding of doctrine, always seeking the enlightenment of divine grace. However,

> Since ... grace does not destroy nature, but perfects it, natural reason should minister to faith as the natural inclination of the will ministers to charity.[22]

Julian extends this (and Aquinas would surely approve) to the understanding not only of Christian teaching, but also of experience.

There is therefore no case in Julian for resting on religious experience or even on received doctrine without personal mental application which investigates the meaning and truth of doctrinal or devotional claims. Julian's search for understanding involved probing of what was given, whether it seemed mysterious or mundane, until she had extracted its meaning in sufficiently concrete terms for it to be meaningful in a practical sense. When the Lord told her that 'All shall be well', she questioned him and pondered his answer until she had something which she could live by in times of suffering, and something that could be offered for the enlightenment and comfort of others. God has not given us our 'kyndly reson' so that we may bask in pious abstractions.

Nevertheless, this search for understanding is the search for faith and cannot be separated from it, for just as our natural reason is founded in God, so also, Julian emphasizes, 'God is the teaching of Holy Church.'[23] She takes some trouble to stress her allegiance and submission to the teaching of the Church, despite the not altogether holy state that it was in during her time. Yet Julian cannot have been unaware of the contemporary ecclesiastical mess. What did she mean, therefore, by this emphasis?

Perhaps her stress on the word 'teaching' is not accidental. Julian goes so far as to say that the content of the Church's teaching is identical with Christ himself,[24] she speaks with approval of its laws,[25] and submits herself to its teachings even when she does not understand how her experiences square with them.[26] She is at pains to say that the special experiences she has had have given her no advantage over those who love God without visions but simply according to the 'common teaching of Holy Church',[27] and makes it plain that even in her own case, this teaching preceded the showings and is the basis on which they are to be understood. It constitutes, in short, the whole framework of her life and thought.

> But in everything I believe as Holy Church preaches and teaches. For the faith of Holy Church, which I had before I had understanding, and which, as I hope by the grace of God, I intend to preserve whole and to practise, was always in my sight, and I wished and intended never to accept anything which might be contrary to it.[28]

Might there be a trace of sadness here? Julian affirms not only the teaching of the Church but also her own intention to practise it: surely she was only too aware of the Church's increasingly bad odour among those who participated in the Peasants' Revolt because many in ecclesiastical ranks were less concerned than they might have been about actually practising the teaching of the Church. She is emphatic in her assertions that she wishes to do as the Church *teaches*; in that very assertion she may have been distancing herself from what the Church in her time actually did, and placing herself instead in the teaching and practice of the patristic and monastic tradition.

Only once does she venture a comment on the current state of the Church, and that is to express compassion for fellow-Christians, for she sees that

> Holy Church will be shaken in sorrow and anguish and tribulation in this world as men shake a cloth in the wind.[29]

The Lord reveals to her that the reason for this tribulation is not punishment, but to liberate his people from 'the harm which they might have from the pomps and the pride and the vainglory' to which they are exposed in this life:

> For he says, I shall completely break down in you your empty affections and your vicious pride, and then I shall gather you and make you meek and mild, pure and holy through union with me.[30]

Vocabulary such as this, stressing God's breaking and destroying action, is very rare indeed in Julian's writing; it cannot be insignificant. In the context, she follows this passage immediately by pursuing her questioning of the Lord as to why he allowed so much harm to come to humankind through sin. Though she does not make the connection explicit, it is plausible to suppose that the sin she has most in mind at this juncture is the 'pomp and pride and vainglory' that she has just been considering, and that some of the chief offenders are those who call themselves after Christ's name.

Julian, therefore, aligns herself with the teaching of the Church in spite of her sorrow at its current practice. This teaching was made her own in two interrelated forms, Scripture and tradition, especially the tradition of monastic theology and spirituality which drank deeply from patristic springs, and was fed continuously by study of Scripture.

> Our faith is founded on God's word, and it belongs to our faith that we believe that God's word will be preserved in all things.[31]

Julian's love for the Bible would have been evident even if she had not given this straightforward statement of it. She makes frequent references to biblical characters, especially those directly involved with Christ in the Gospels, like Pilate, Mary Magdalene, and Mary his mother. Sometimes her comments involve more than just mentioning their names; there is a quotation of something they said to illustrate her own point. One interesting example of this occurs when she is allowed to swing violently back and forth between a sense of total safety and consolation in God's presence, and the sense of utter abandonment:

> And in the time of joy I could have said with St Paul: Nothing shall separate me from the love of Christ; and in the pain I could have said with St Peter: Lord, save me, I am perishing.[32]

In all probability Julian had heard accounts of these biblical men and women in the popular preaching of her time, and seen portrayals of them in the paintings and sculpture of the many churches and the cathedral in Norwich.

However, Scripture becomes part of the texture of Julian's thought far beyond simple reference to biblical characters. She incorporates its phrases and allusions to it into her writing to such an extent that there is no gap between her own language and quotation. Colledge and Walsh believe that she was already familiar with the Latin Vulgate Bible when she wrote the Short Text, and that she incorporated it increasingly into her meditation on the showings so that when she wrote the Long Text twenty years later it was fully integrated into her presentation, which often used phrases translated directly from the Vulgate as part of her own sentences.[33] In her discussion of the parable of the Lord and the servant, for example, occurs the following sentence:

> For all mankind which will be saved by the sweet Incarnation of the Passion of Christ, all is Christ's humanity, for he is the head, and we are his members, to which members the day and the time are unknown when every passing woe and sorrow will have an end, and every joy and bliss will be fulfilled, which day and time all the company of heaven longs and desires to see.[34]

In this single sentence there are clear references to the Pauline phrases about Christ as the head of the Church and we as his members (Eph. 5.23, 30; 1 Cor. 12.27), the uncertainty of the time of the end of the age

(Mark 13.1–2), and the cessation of all sorrow and pain (Rev. 21.4). Besides these there are allusions to other Scriptures though these are not so precisely definable. Colledge and Walsh suggest Heb. 10.5–8; Eph. 4.12–13; 2 Cor. 5.17; and John 8.56;[35] but other alternatives would be possible. The exact references are not as important as the fact that Scripture has been made so much Julian's own that she thinks and writes in its terms without distinction between quotation and her own words.

In this she is similar to other writers in the tradition of monastic spirituality. Bernard of Clairvaux, for instance, in his *Sermons on the Song of Songs*, presents his own original thought and experience in vocabulary which is a tissue of biblical quotation and allusion. So also to a slightly lesser extent does Aelred; and both of them, with many others in the monastic tradition, are walking in Augustine's footsteps. The ability to do this, to think one's thoughts in scriptural language, was part of the fruit of the *lectio divina*, learning the Scriptures 'by heart' not only in the sense of committing them to memory, though that was included, but also becoming so immersed in them that they were part of the atmosphere of thought and speech. I suggested earlier that one's background and intellectual framework forms the perspective for any experience, vitally affecting what the experience will be, as well as its subsequent interpretation. Julian's immersion in Scripture and particularly in the accounts of the passion of Christ was crucial to her religious experience and her understanding of it. It is this which forms a vital element of her loyalty to Holy Church.

Nevertheless the many quotations and half-quotations from the Scriptures, important though they are, are not as significant as her absorption in biblical theology, especially the thought of St Paul and St John.[36] Of course, quotation and theology are not unrelated; but the catena of quotations would not by itself demonstrate loyalty to the Scriptures or the Church unless these were in line with basic doctrines: as the old proverb has it, even the devil can quote Scripture to his purpose. Her reliance on biblical teaching is evident, for example, in her accounts of creation and of the theme of humankind bearing the image of God, as we shall see later. But nowhere is her use of Pauline theology so profound as in her discussion of the parable of the Lord and the servant, where the servant is at once Adam, all mankind, and Christ the second Adam, who by taking human flesh manifests the love of God and thereby brings salvation and help to men and women who have 'fallen into a ditch' and are bruised and muddied. Because of the new possibilities of wholeness and fulfilment revealed in the passion of Christ, it is possible to come to thankfulness for the wounding and brokenness which alone made the maturing response to the love of God a reality. Julian, however, immediately voices a caution: this must not be taken as an excuse for continuing to wallow in the ditch.

> If any man or woman be moved by folly to say or to think 'If this be true, then it would be well to sin so as to have the greater reward, or else to think sin less important', beware of this impulse, for truly, should it come, it is untrue and from the fiend.[37]

And this is again a close following of the wording of St Paul:

> What shall we say then? Are we to continue in sin that grace may abound? By no means![38]

Biblical doctrine and biblical terminology are thus woven together to provide the key to Julian's understanding of her revelations. The results of this method will become more apparent in succeeding chapters; but we can see already the extent to which her 'kyndly reson' is interacting with her loyalty to the teaching of the Church in Scripture for creative interpretation of its message of human wholeness.

This teaching of the Church was mediated to her by many centuries of Christian meditation and practice, not least of which was the sacramental dimension. Julian affirms her adherence to the seven sacraments as these had been developed in medieval theology,[39] and, as we would expect given her single-minded devotion to the passion of Christ, draws special attention to the sacrament of his Body and Blood.

> Jesus can feed us with himself, and does, most courteously and most tenderly, with the blessed sacrament, which is the precious food of true life; and with all the sweet sacraments he sustains us most mercifully and graciously, and so he meant in these blessed words, where he said: I am he whom Holy Church preaches and teaches to you. That is to say: All the health and life of the sacraments, all the power and grace of my word, all the goodness which is ordained in Holy Church for you, I am he.[40]

Julian thus stands in direct opposition to those who would say that mystical experience makes for uneasy alliance with the Church, if by 'Church' is meant Scripture and sacrament and Christian doctrine.[41] Her life-style and teaching are indeed a resounding protest against the corrupt practices of the Church in her time: how, for instance, would the purveyors of indulgences in aid of the Norwich Crusade have responded to the statement just quoted? But her protest is not against the Church as such; on the contrary, she seeks to draw it back to its focus in the love of God in Christ. She desires for the Church the same spirit of recollection that she desires for herself; and she is able to make a distinction between the empirical Church which is soiled and corrupt and the Church as God sees it, which, as the Body of Christ, is as pure and precious in the sight of God as Christ is himself.

For one single person may often be broken ... but the entire body of Holy Church was never broken, nor ever will be without end. And therefore it is a certain thing, and good and gracious to will, meekly, fervently, to be fastened and united to our mother Holy Church, who is Christ Jesus.[42]

Some might initially suspect that Julian was writing with premonitions of the smoke from the Lollard pit in her nostrils, and found it prudent to state her loyalty to the Church frequently even if her actual teaching and experience made an uneasy alliance with it. But we have by now seen enough of Julian to discredit that suspicion on two counts. The first is that she was not lacking in courage: her prayer for severe illness and her willingness to embrace the anchoritic life are sufficient evidence of her fortitude. In any case, her life and writings, even (perhaps especially) in her affirmation of solidarity with Holy Church, are a standing protest against the unholiness of the empirical Church, a protest quite sufficient to besmirch her in the eyes of the ecclesiastical hierarchy of her time, which would quite rightly feel challenged by her. Secondly, we have seen that the Church, Scripture, and the sacraments are so interwoven into her theology that it would be impossible to separate her experience and teaching from her loyalty to it. The Church is the Body of Christ in whom we are grounded: to do violence to the Church would in Julian's thinking be to do violence to ourselves. We will see later how her distinction between the empirical Church and the Church as it is in God's eyes offers a parallel to the wounded and sinful life we now live and the way that we are looked upon as pure and perfect in the sight of God.[43] Julian's account of the Church, therefore, is integral to her total theological understanding: it is not token loyalty to avoid a heresy hunt.

Her strong allegiance to the Church is all the more striking because there are parts of its teaching which she admits she finds difficult to reconcile with her own experience. In such a case, when it is recognized that there seems to be discrepancy between one's own experience and the teaching of the Church, affirmation of the Church's teaching carries considerable weight. There are several levels of this in Julian's case. The least problematic are instances in which the Church's teaching, while going *beyond* her own experience or understanding, is nevertheless compatible with it. Chief among Julian's perplexities here is how it is possible to retain both the revelation which she had had that God will make all things well, and the belief in hell, the devil, and damnation. The latter she found to be part of the teaching of the Church which could not be jettisoned without violating Christian tradition; but if there will indeed be people 'eternally condemned to hell, as Holy Church teaches me to believe', it is impossible for Julian to see how it could possibly be true that 'every kind of thing should be well'.[44] Although she accepted the scriptural assurance that things

101

which are impossible with man are possible with God,[45] she continues
to be very puzzled about it. She emphasizes that her firm intention was
to abide by what she had been taught, though it was in unresolved
tension with her own experience.

> And yet in this I desired, so far as I dared, that I might have had some sight of
> hell and of purgatory; but it was not my intention to make trial of anything
> which belongs to our faith, for I believed steadfastly that hell and purgatory
> exist for the same ends as Holy Church teaches. But my intention was to
> have seen for instruction in everything which belongs to my faith, whereby I
> could live more to God's glory and to my profit.[46]

In spite of the purity of her intention, however, this desire was not
granted. Instead, she is reminded of one of the previous revelations in
which she had seen that evil would finally be overcome. On reviewing
the teaching she had received in the revelations, she finds that they
concern themselves primarily with the goodness and love of God, not
with evil and judgement, and this is not changed in spite of her request
for fuller understanding.

By this unresolved puzzlement, however, she is taught something
else. By the very fact that she remains in ignorance, she is shown how
important it is to pay careful attention to what God does reveal,
knowing that this is for our profit, rather than being distracted from it
using the excuse that we have not understood something else. On this
basis she is able to make a distinction between two kinds of mystery.
The first is the 'great mystery' (which remains hidden for the present)
of all that will happen hereafter.[47] But the second is mystery not
because God is keeping something from us, but because we are too
ignorant or blind or lazy to penetrate the teaching of the Church.
Having recognized this, Julian makes a strong plea for diligence in the
study of Christian teaching, for it is in this way, not in voices or visions
but by prayerful thought and labour, that God is more fully known.

> He is the foundation, he is the substance, he is the teacher, he is the end, he
> is the reward for which every loving soul labours; and this is known and
> will be known to every soul to whom the Holy Spirit declares this. And I
> truly hope that all who seek in this way will prosper, for they are seeking
> God.[48]

The reason for the importance of adherence to the teaching of the
Church is that it is through prayerful, patient reflection and participation in its sacraments, Scriptures, and theological traditions that God
is known. This is much more important than idiosyncratic experiences
which may or may not be given. Therefore when the Church teaches
something which goes beyond what has been experienced, the
teaching is to retain its normative place, not out of veneration for dead
dogma, but because its total framework provides the context in which

God himself can be known. But that of course does *not* mean that its doctrine can never be reconsidered: a mind as lively as Julian's would never acquiesce to that.

Loyalty to Christian teaching is much more difficult when that teaching goes not simply *beyond* experience but *contrary* to it, as at one crucial point it seems to do for Julian. In the experiences she had, she was shown that God is totally loving and compassionate; there is no wrath or blame or judgement of any kind against us in him. Yet she is acutely aware that the Church *does* pass judgement on sinners, and that this recognition of sinfulness is an important step in reconciliation. She is therefore torn between this teaching that sinners do justly deserve blame and punishment, and her experience that a perfectly just God does not blame sinners in any way.

> This then was my desire, that I might see in God in what way the judgment of Holy Church here on earth is true in his sight, and how it pertains to me to know it truly, whereby they might both be reconciled as might be glory to God and the right way for me.[49]

The reward for this desire was the parable of the Lord and the servant which we will explore later – and which took Julian fifteen years of prayerful labour to untangle!

This is an indication of the stature of Julian. In a situation of apparently irreconcilable teachings, she holds to both sides of the tension until by patient diligence she wins through to integration. We might have thought that it would be easier for her to be so overwhelmed by God's attitude of unblaming compassion that she would dismiss the teaching of the Church as inadequate, setting up her own spirituality as the criterion by which Christian teaching should be assessed. She would not have been the only one to do so. Alternatively, she might have rejected her own experience because it was at variance with Christian doctrine: measured against received teaching, she might have felt that her insights were not worthy to be taken seriously.

Yet she could jettison neither the one nor the other without doing violence to herself. The teaching of the Church was not for Julian a batch of discrete doctrines amongst which she could pick and choose those that suited her; it was rather a holistic framework which made knowledge of God possible by his revelation of himself in word and sacrament. So she could not abandon a doctrine here or a precept there. Nor could she contemplate rejecting the whole. Her life was lived within the context of Christian faith and worship; it is unrealistic to suppose that Julian could have conceived of any other possibility of meaningful life than in relation to the Church. By this I of course do not mean that Julian could contemplate only what is sometimes called 'religious life': she could have been or become a laywoman. But she could not have become an atheist. Yet if she could not have rejected the teaching of the Church without uprooting her soul, neither could she cut off the most significant experiences of her life. The magnitude of the conflict and of her will to integrity is evident in the effort she took labouring for fifteen years to come to understanding. She would settle for neither undevotional theology nor for untheological devotion. Her persistence is, as we shall see, rewarded in her final understanding of how persons are healed when their wounds, judged by the Church, are opened to the penetrating love of Christ, who, because he is Mother as well as Father, restores the child within us and brings us to joyful maturity in himself.

Her practice here shows the extent to which her appreciation of the teaching of the Church was shaped by monastic spirituality, which never left personal experience out of account. Dom Jean Leclercq has drawn an insightful contrast between the method of theology in the monastic tradition and the method used by the schoolmen. Both drew upon patristic and scriptural writings and the teaching of the Church; and both emphasized the use of natural reason as Julian also did. But, contrary to scholastic practice,

> what individualizes monastic thought is a certain dependence on experience. Scholastic theology, on the other hand, puts experience aside. It can subsequently hark back to experience, observe that it agrees with its own reasonings, and that it can even receive nourishment from them; but its reflection is not rooted in experience and is not necessarily directed toward it. It is placed, deliberately, on the plane of metaphysics; it is impersonal and universal.[50]

There were good reasons why the schoolmen adopted this approach, and no reason to suppose that Julian did not respect them. Indeed, in at least one passage she seems to affirm that she accepts what they say even when it does not form part of her own experience:

> I believe and understand the ministration of holy angels, as scholars tell, but it was not revealed to me; for God himself is ... all that we need.[51]

We need not doubt that she means what she says here, but perhaps she may have smiled a little while saying it, remembering the useless debates about angelology for which the scholastics were notorious.[52] It may be that my interpretation here reads too much into the word translated 'scholars': Middle English has 'clarkes', and although this could well refer to the scholastics proper, it might only mean 'learned men'. In any case, while Julian was hardly one to belittle learning, her own approach was consistently like that of the monastic tradition, where learning and experience were integrated, and where reading was not simply the assimilation of information and ideas, but was itself prayer, *lectio divina*.

Thus for Julian it is experience, which, though not allowed to break loose from its moorings in natural reason and the teaching of the Church to fly away into fantasy land, nevertheless breathes life into scholarship and dogma. Julian attributes spiritual experience directly to the 'inward grace-giving operation of the Holy Spirit'.[53] Although it is to be kept within the framework of rationality and doctrine it is to be treasured as the gift of God himself. By 'experience' Julian does not mean only the sort of experiences she had in the revelations, unusual visions and words from God, though these would be included. She means, rather, the day by day experience of the love and comfort and enlightenment of God, which enables us to make steady unspectacular progress in knowing ourselves and responding to the love of God which liberates us to respond in turn to others. Experience in this sense is both a basis from which we better understand doctrine, and a practical consequence of that understanding, as we discover in our daily lives the truth of God's love and delight.

> For it is God's will that we have true delight with him in our salvation, and in it he wants us to be greatly comforted and strengthened, and so joyfully he wishes our souls to be occupied with his grace.[54]

As an anchoress Julian devoted herself to quiet learning to know and delight in God, finding peace that was not the resolution of all tensions but rather was the integration of them in the wholeness of her response to God. It was this wholeness and peace coming from delight in God and in herself, that must have made her attractive and helpful to those who came for counsel, as it still makes her attractive to us who know her only through her book.

Openness to experience is also, however, openness to its darker sides: depression, despair, fear, self-rejection. From the way that Julian writes about these, it is clear that she had to come to terms with them in her own life. She does not ignore them; instead, she offers insight about how these can be progressively transformed to become part of a creatively integrated personality. Yet in this life the transformation is never complete; we are always prone to recurrence of sin and the sense of desolation.

> And when we have fallen through weakness or blindness, then our courteous Lord, teaching us, moves us and protects us. And then he wants us to see our wretchedness and meekly to acknowledge it; but he does not want us to remain there, or to be much occupied in self-accusation, nor does he want us to be too full of our own misery ... And he hastens to bring us to him, for we are his joy and his delight, and he is the remedy of our life.[55]

It is this steady will to live in response to the love of God which makes for the right use of our natural reason and the teaching of the Church. It motivates study, not out of a desire for cleverness but as a means to develop enlightened holiness of life. It is clear that for Julian the teaching of the Church was not a static quantity which could not be investigated or reinterpreted. Rather, reason and experience are in reciprocity with its teaching, and all three are modified by the love of God revealed in the cross of Christ. Though Julian respects Christian doctrine, she feels at liberty to probe and reinterpret it, in some cases bringing out dimensions that, though not at variance with it, had not been fully recognized before her time, and give a new perspective. A significant example of this, as we shall see, is her teaching of the motherhood of God.

But what is of greatest importance is that the three dimensions helping toward knowledge of God do not become disintegrated from one another, but that they 'work continually, all together'.[56] They are all rooted in God: he is the foundation of Holy Church which is his gift of mercy because it is his revelation of himself in word and sacrament, and he is the foundation of our experience which is the grace of the Holy Spirit. These means to the knowledge of God are therefore rooted in the Trinity, and as such are dimensions of unity. The way Julian applies this to the understanding of what God is and how he offers his own integration to humankind will occupy us in the following chapters.

Notes to Chapter Six

1. LT 1.
2. One important exception is Pelphrey's *Love Was His Meaning*; unfortunately this book is not readily available.
3. Thus Dom François Vandenbroucke in *A History of Christian Spirituality Volume II, The Spirituality of the Middle Ages* by Jean Leclercq, François Vandenbroucke, and Louis Bouyer (Burns & Oates, London, and Desclée, New York, 1968), pp. 425–6.
4. *Conjectures of a Guilty Bystander* (Doubleday, Garden City, New York, 1966), pp. 191–2; cf. his 'The English Mystics', in *Mystics and Zen Masters* (Farrar, Straus & Giroux, New York, 1967), p. 140.
5. LT 86.
6. 1 John 4.16.
7. LT 44.
8. LT 73.
9. LT 56.
10. LT 80.
11. ibid.
12. *The Cloud of Unknowing* VI.
13. ibid.
14. Arguably, the *Cloud* author could at least in part agree, since 'love' for him is not a subjective emotion but the focal point of the whole individual, whose 'dart of longing love' tries to pierce the cloud of unknowing, and is

sometimes met by a ray of divine illumination. Apophatic theology encourages mindlessness no more than Julian does.

15. 1 Cor. 2.14 AV.
16. LT 83.
17. LT 56.
18. PL 168, col 1218, quoted in Leclercq, *The Love of Learning and the Desire for God*, p. 253.
19. LT 53.
20. LT 46.
21. LT 42.
22. Thomas Aquinas, *Summa Theologiae*, I.1 Q1, a 8, ad 2.
23. LT 80.
24. LT 26, 61.
25. LT 73.
26. LT 32.
27. LT 9.
28. ibid.
29. LT 28.
30. ibid.
31. LT 32.
32. LT 15.
33. C & W, pp. 43–7; cf. E. Colledge and J. Walsh, 'Editing Julian of Norwich's *Revelations*', in *Medieval Studies* 38 (1976), pp. 404–27. Not all scholars agree with this specific point, but there is no dispute about the extent to which Scripture is part of the fabric of her thinking.
34. LT 51, p. 276.
35. C & W, pp. 537–8, notes 254–9.
36. cf. Sr Mary Paul, 'Julian of Norwich and the Bible', pp. 11–23 (Fairacres Publication No. 28).
37. LT 40.
38. Rom. 6.1–2.
39. LT 57.
40. LT 60.
41. cf. Walter Terence Stace, *Mysticism and Philosophy*, pp. 234–5.
42. LT 61; cf. LT 34.
43. See below, pp. 137–49.
44. LT 32.
45. LT 32; cf. Matt. 19.26; Luke 1.37.
46. LT 33.
47. See below, pp. 173–80.
48. LT 34.
49. LT 45.
50. Leclercq, pp. 278–9.
51. LT 80.
52. cf. Jaroslav Pelikan, *The Growth of Medieval Theology: The Christian Tradition: A History of the Development of Doctrine Vol. III* (University of Chicago Press, Chicago and London, 1978), pp. 293–303.
53. ibid.
54. LT 23.
55. LT 79.
56. LT 80.

7 The Trinity: Attributes of Love

Julian's integrated theological method enables her to develop profound insight into the doctrine of the Trinity. She is careful to take the framework of her understanding from the teachings of Holy Church, and stands squarely in the Augustinian tradition, as we shall see.[1] Yet it does not remain for her an abstract dogma: it is a matter of Julian's immediate personal experience, as well as intense application of her 'kyndly reson'. Although it is a mystery, for Julian a mystery is not to be thought of as utter unintelligibility, so that further thought or discussion are useless. For Julian a mystery is more like a very deep well than like an impenetrable barrier, a well whose waters are continuously springing up: the more that is drawn from it, the more remains to be drawn. We can never exhaust the mystery of the divine Trinity, but we can continually refresh ourselves in contemplation of it.

Julian's reflections on the Trinity begin with the first vision. As she gazed on the crucifix in her dying moments, and unexpectedly saw the blood running down from under the crown of thorns,

> in the same revelation, suddenly the Trinity filled my heart full of the greatest joy, and I understood that it will be so in heaven without end to all who will come there. For the Trinity is God, God is the Trinity. The Trinity is our maker, the Trinity is our protector, the Trinity is our everlasting lover, the Trinity is our endless joy and our bliss, by our Lord Jesus Christ and in our Lord Jesus Christ.[2]

It is interesting to note that this passage does not appear in the Short Text; indeed, one of the significant differences between the two versions is that there is much more discussion of the Trinity in the Long Text than in the Short. As Julian pondered the content of her visions for over twenty years, and probably also studied patristic and medieval theology, this was one of the doctrines which came very much more to the fore, so that by the time she wrote the Long Text Julian had become profoundly trinitarian in her thought patterns.

Even in the Short Text, however, where the doctrine receives only passing mention, her starting point is, as always, the love of God: from this all his other attributes, and indeed the Trinity itself, are to be understood.

The Trinity: Attributes of Love

> Though the persons of the blessed Trinity be all alike in their attributes, it was their love which was most shown to me, and that it is closest to us all . . . For of all the attributes of the blessed Trinity, it is God's will that we have most confidence in his delight and his love.[3]

The reason for this is, characteristically, not some metaphysical necessity. It is rather that in our spiritual struggle, the power and wisdom and majesty of God might overwhelm us, and contemplation of them might discourage us, making us fear and despair rather than trust him, unless we were aware that this majesty was the majesty of love. But

> love makes power and wisdom very humble to us; for just as by God's courtesy he forgets our sin from the time that we repent, just so does he wish us to forget our sins and all our depression and all our doubtful fears.[4]

For Julian, theology is at one with the practical psychology of spiritual growth. We find here a threefold integration: the integrated theological method discussed in the previous chapter, the integration of theology with psychology which we will examine in more detail in the rest of this section, and the integration of the personality as these insights are applied to practical spiritual growth, as we shall see in subsequent chapters of the book. This threefold integration is itself theologically grounded, for it is theologically reasonable to suppose that if God's intent and desire for us is development in psychological and spiritual wholeness, which is also increasing union with him, then the revelation of divine reality will foster this spiritual goal and not be at variance with it.

This is brought out even more forcefully by Julian's teaching that the Trinity is not to be understood as a dogma on its own, but in the light of the incarnation. Jesus himself, as she sees him bleeding on the cross, is the source of her understanding of the Trinity. Thus she explains that, though in one sense each of her visions was of the dying Jesus, in another sense each of her visions was of the Trinity:

> And this was revealed in the first vision and in them all, for where Jesus appears the blessed Trinity is understood, as I see it.[5]

It is true to say that Julian's theology is christocentric, if by this is meant that a true understanding of Christ gives a true understanding of all other doctrines. In him divine and human nature are united; in him human wholeness is perfected, and in him the entire Trinity is comprehended.[6] This christocentricity, however, would be misunderstood if it were taken that other theological doctrines were unimportant. It is not that they are unimportant; it is rather that they are so important that they ought not to be considered independently from the incarnation which provides for them the proper focus. Not only Julian's life, but also her theological thinking, are grounded in the continuous practice of recollection, 'taking every thought captive to obey Christ'.[7]

At first sight, the notion that the Trinity is contained in Christ is a puzzling one. If Christ is himself one member of the Trinity, how can it all be contained or comprehended in him? A comparison to *The Cloud of Unknowing* helps to make this more clear. The author of *The Cloud* teaches that within the practice of contemplative prayer, all other things must be put aside under the 'cloud of forgetting'; this includes all theological doctrines, all meditation on the saints and on the joys of heaven, and so on. He explicitly includes in the things which must be forgotten during this prayer all thoughts of Christ and his passion. Consideration of these will only lead to meditation on one's own sinful wretchedness, and from there to the conditions of one's life, and soon all concentration will be gone.[8] The *Cloud* author is of course not saying that thinking about Christ is a bad thing. Yet

> no matter how much you were to weep and sorrow for your sins, or for the passion of Christ, or be ever so mindful of the joys of heaven, what would it profit you? Certainly it would be of great good, great help, great gain, great grace. But in comparison with that blind impulse of love, there is little it can or may do.[9]

God cannot be known perfectly through any of his manifestations, important though they are; only by the 'sharp dart of longing love' can he be truly 'taken and held'.[10]

How different this emphasis is from that of Julian can be seen by recalling the vision in which she tells us that she felt herself invited to turn away from the suffering and dying Christ, and the empathetic suffering which that entailed for her, and to look up instead to heaven to God the Father. But Julian refused.

> No, I cannot, for you are my heaven. I said this because I did not want to look up, for I would rather have remained in that pain until Judgment Day than have come to heaven any other way than by him ... Thus I chose Jesus for my heaven, whom I saw only in pain at that time.[11]

For the author of *The Cloud*, Jesus is, though certainly God incarnate, nevertheless a manifestation of God's essence rather than that essence itself: the distinction is a Neoplatonic one filtered through the Pseudo-Dionysius and Hugo de Balma, from whom the author of *The Cloud* drew much of his thought.[12] But for Julian, Jesus as God incarnate is *Deus veritas*; there is no coming to the Father independently of him.[13] As God incarnate, all the fulness of the Godhead dwells in him; he, therefore, is the revealer of God in every way, including, consequently, the Trinity itself. And since the revelation of God in Jesus is a manifestation of the totally self-giving suffering of love, this is also the most important fact about the Trinity.

It is in the context of this triune manifestation of love that Julian speaks of the attributes of the power, wisdom, and goodness of God, linking these respectively to the Father, the Son, and the Holy Spirit, even though all these aspects of divinity must always be understood from the standpoint of the experience of the love and suffering of Jesus the embodied Christ. These aspects of the Trinity Julian finds in all God's actions towards us. In the first place, the whole Trinity agreed and united in our creation and delights in it.

> And so in our making, God almighty is our loving Father, and God all wisdom is our loving Mother, with the love and goodness of the Holy Spirit, which is all one God, one Lord.[14]

But she immediately proceeds from consideration of our creation to thinking about our re-creation, our salvation and fulfilment, and in that context she articulates her Trinitarianism rather differently.

> In our almighty Father we have our protection and our bliss, as regards our natural substance, which is ours by our creation from without beginning; and in the second person, in knowledge and wisdom we have our perfection, as regards our sensuality, our restoration and salvation, for he is our Mother, brother and saviour; and in our good Lord the Holy Spirit we have our reward and our gift for our living and labour, endlessly surpassing all that we desire in his marvellous courtesy, out of his great plentiful grace.[15]

Here as elsewhere, Julian associates power particularly with the Father, wisdom with God the Son, and goodness with the Holy Spirit. Yet she of course recognizes that each of these attributes belongs to each of the persons of the undivided Trinity. To split them up is to create an artificial distinction, useful for our human understanding which grasps concepts by analysis into components, but mischievous if it leads us to suppose that the mystery of God can be separated. Thus immediately after the passage just quoted, Julian goes on to say,

> And our substance is in our Father, God almighty, and our substance is in our Mother, God all wisdom, and our substance is in our Lord God, the Holy Spirit, all goodness, for our substance is whole in each person of the Trinity, who is one God.[16]

In the context, Julian is making a point about the difference between our substantial and our sensual nature and how each relates to the Trinity; we will defer discussion of this to Chapter Eight. What is important here is the way in which she on the one hand characterizes the persons of the Trinity by the attributes of power, wisdom, and goodness, and yet simultaneously rejects the possibility of any division between them. Our substance is complete in each, and the Trinity is one God.

This characterization was a familiar one in the Augustinian

theological synthesis of the Middle Ages. Augustine in *De Trinitate* had discussed the divine Trinity in terms which set the parameters for subsequent theological thinking: the Father as power, majesty, and beauty, the Son as wisdom, the Holy Spirit as goodness and love. Yet Augustine, too, stressed that in the divine simplicity, each of these attributes belongs to the indivisible Trinity.[17] Throughout the Middle Ages, these characterizations and this qualification were the basis for thinking about the Trinity, both for scholastics such as Hugh of St Victor[18] and Thomas Aquinas[19] and for more devotional writers such as Richard Rolle,[20] to take only three examples from a whole catalogue of theologians.

Although this was true, however, and every serious Christian thinker felt it necessary to address the mystery of the Trinity, to the average Christian of Julian's time, as of our own, the doctrine of the Trinity was no doubt a puzzling item of Christian affirmation, not one whose significance for daily living and spirituality was at all obvious. What does it matter, after all, whether or how exactly God is three persons in one substance? Given that it is universally admitted that the doctrine is beyond human capacity to understand, why should so much effort be spent on speculation with regard to it? The time when wars were fought and empires divided over precise trinitarian formulation seems remote indeed (if in fact these were ever the real reasons as opposed to the stated reasons for conflict), and must have seemed just as remote to the ordinary Christian of fourteenth-century East Anglia. It is true that they would have encountered the doctrine of the Trinity, just as we do, every time they recited the Creed; also it was pictorially represented in the bright medieval paintings and sculpture which formed part of the fabric of churches and cathedrals. Often God the Father is portrayed as a majestic middle-aged man dressed in flowing robes sitting on a throne, the Son is between his knees or beneath him, sometimes pictured as a lamb, sometimes as a man hanging on a cross, and the Holy Spirit is a white dove hovering near or perched perhaps on the Father's hand or shoulder. If it were not for our sheer familiarity with this sort of visual representation of the Trinity, we would find it very odd indeed. How can this collection of images convey the idea of three divine persons in one substance? It is hard to imagine that someone uninitiated in Christian doctrine would conceptualize this pictorial representation in Christian trinitarian terms, no matter how aesthetically sensitive he or she might be.

Perhaps it was this that made intellectual formulation all the more necessary, so that aesthetic perception could be balanced by theological teaching. The method of procedure, however, was a very different one from what would be common today. Modern thinkers would tend to assess the doctrine of the Trinity (and other theological doctrines) by reference to epistemological criteria developed in other contexts, often empirical or scientific ones. The medievals, by contrast, measured an epistemological theory by how well it enabled them to understand received theological truth. Thus for example Anselm of Canterbury complained of Roscelin that, given the latter's nominalist epistemology, it would be impossible to understand the doctrine of the Trinity: Anselm considered this to be a *reductio ad absurdum* of nominalism.[21]

In spite of this difference of epistemological principle, however, scholastic writings on the Trinity, whatever the intentions of their authors, became increasingly difficult to understand. More significantly, it is hard to see how they could have any bearing on Christian spirituality. There is no reason to deny the personal sanctity of men like Thomas Aquinas, nor their theological and spiritual profundity. Yet although those who breathed the scholastic atmosphere might have found spiritual nourishment in the writings of the masters, it is unlikely that Julian's 'even Christians' would have found a passage such as this one taken from Thomas Aquinas' discussion of the Trinity in his *Summa Theologiae* helpful in stimulating their spiritual growth or developing their relationship to God in Christ:

> The many persons are the many subsisting relations really distinct from each other. But a real distinction between the divine relations can come only from relative opposition ...

Aquinas goes on to consider the relations of paternity and filiation, and how these connect with spiration, and ends the argument by saying,

> We must consequently admit that spiration belongs to the person of the Father and to the person of the Son, inasmuch as it has no relative opposition either to paternity or to filiation; and consequently that procession belongs to the other person who is called the person of the Holy Ghost ... Therefore only three persons exist in God, the Father, the Son, and the Holy Ghost.[22]

Careful scholarly articulation of doctrine is of great importance both in developing clearer understanding of it, and in defending it from sceptical attack; and the importance of Thomas Aquinas in both these areas can hardly be overestimated. Yet for the ordinary Christian, it is all too easy to miss the implications for Christian spirituality amid all this intellectual sophistication. Julian, while arguably being aware of scholarly teaching, and having great respect for it, wishes to focus explicitly on the aspects of the doctrine of the Trinity which have a bearing on the development of our spiritual wholeness in the love of God.

In one sense, Julian is here returning to Augustinian roots. In Augustine's presentation of the doctrine of the Trinity, it is the deep and reciprocal love of each divine Person for the others which is of greatest significance.[23] This was retained by many who followed in his steps; and as we have noted, it is the deep love of God which is most important also for Julian. Anselm, to whose teaching Julian's often bears resemblance, is one example among many who emphasized, like Augustine, the centrality of love. In his discussion of the Trinity, he says,

> But, while I am here considering with interest the individual properties and the common attributes of Father and Son, I find none in them more pleasing to contemplate than the feeling of mutual love ... That love is, then, the supreme Spirit. Hence if no creature, that is, if nothing other than the supreme Spirit, the Father and the Son, ever existed; nevertheless, Father and Son would love themselves and one another.[24]

In spite of Julian's agreement with Anselm on the centrality of love in the doctrine of the Trinity, however, how different is her presentation of it! For Anselm as for Augustine, this love is a love of the divine persons for one another; whereas in Julian it is experienced in personal terms as the love of God for herself and for all her fellow-Christians. Julian's teaching gently applies the love of God not only to the perfection of the divine beings, but to humankind in all our sin and suffering and wretchedness. This throws another light on her comment that the whole of the Trinity is comprehended in Christ. He, after all, is the one who makes incarnate this love of God, the one who brings the love of the divine Trinity into the experience of humankind.

Thus Julian takes the framework of Christian teaching on the Trinity, combines it with her own experience and with the profound exercise of her 'kyndly reson', and develops a doctrine of the richness of spiritual resources available to a Christian in his or her encounter with the love of God. That which had become for the scholastic philosophers a mystery in the sense of a paradox against which their greatest intellectual ingenuity must be found wanting became for Julian the mysteriously inexhaustible well from which can be drawn all that is needed for Christian living. God the Father is the almighty one who creates and preserves ourselves and our world in all our precious fragility. God the Son is the wisdom who makes us and restores us to God by wisely and courteously attracting us to himself. God the Holy Spirit is the goodness and comfort and delight necessary for our healing and fulfilment.

Not that Julian supposes that this account exhausts the meaning of the Trinity or of the attributes of God: God is far more than we can ever know. But precisely because of this, we cannot know or speak of God outside of our experience of him. We can only draw upon his revelation of himself to us in Christian tradition, in our own experience mediated by that tradition, and in our careful pondering of what we have received. As we do so, we encounter again and again the richness of his love and self-giving on our behalf. Even the fact that a great deal is kept secret from us is part of his love.

> For the great love which he has for us he reveals to us everything which is at the time to his glory and our profit. And those things which he now wants to keep secret he still in his great goodness reveals, but not openly.[25]

What Julian means by this is that some things are not for us to know now; they would not be of benefit to us at this stage. But at some future time, perhaps after this life, they will be available and good for us to know. They are like the contents of a sealed letter which is given to us and is ours to keep but which must not be opened until a specified date. That which is contained in it is ours, though we are not yet in full possession of it. It is promised to us for the appropriate time.[26] Thus Julian at once proceeds,

> In this revelation he wants us to believe and understand that we shall truly see it in his endless bliss. Then we ought to rejoice in him for everything which he reveals and for everything which he conceals ...[27]

The doctrine of the Trinity is revealed to us to help us in our spiritual integration and development, but not to resolve all intellectual puzzles that arise in our consideration of it. If the doctrine is little more than a form of words which has become a traditional part of the Christian Creed, then it has little spiritual value for us or for the Christians of the fourteenth century. Julian's approach, however, revitalizes the doctrine by connecting it with her own experience and making it the symbol of all the richness and resources of God. The precise metaphysical formulations can be left to their own appropriate contexts; Julian would not have thought that all the debates about the Trinity among the scholastics had to be settled one way rather than another for the doctrine to be spiritually rich. The resources of the power, wisdom, and goodness of God the Trinity have a bearing on each aspect of life, from our initial creation, through our purification, to our eventual perfection.

> Our Father wills, our Mother [Christ] works, our good Lord the Holy Spirit confirms. And therefore it is our part to love our God in whom we have our being, reverently thanking and praising him for our creation, mightily praying to our Mother for mercy and pity, and to our Lord the Holy Spirit for help and grace. For in these three is all our life.[28]

Jesus our Mother

In Julian's conception of the motherhood of God we find some of her most original and profound teaching, with special relevance to theological thinking in our own time. It is directly linked to Julian's

115

position that the Trinity is best understood in terms of love, and is a way of going more deeply into that doctrine. Yet her development of it also shows an interesting contrast to her development of the doctrine of the Trinity. In the latter case, as we have seen, Julian finds in the credal framework of the Church categories for rich understanding and inter-pretation of her own experience. Although she does not treat trinitarian dogma as a merely conceptual stance, but rather uses it to understand her own experience of the divine persons in her vision of the dying Jesus, the doctrine clearly is antecedent to and informs her experience. It is therefore an example of the reciprocity between framework and experience in which the framework takes the prece-dence, even though it does not remain unaffected by the experience.

In the case of her teaching on the motherhood of God, however, the ingredients of experience, natural reason, and the teaching of Holy Church, while all present, are combined in a rather different way. Unlike the doctrine of the Trinity, there was no formal doctrine of divine motherhood, although there were traces of the idea reaching well back before Julian's time.[29] Julian's experience, and her sustained reflection upon it, enabled her to take up these traces and develop them into an understanding of God which is of great significance for theological and spiritual wholeness.

Hints of the idea of divine motherhood can be found in the Scrip-tures. In the first chapter of Genesis, the image of the Spirit of God hovering over 'the face of the deep' is a maternal image, as of a hen hovering and brooding over her chicks. More explicit is the passage from Isaiah:

> Can a woman forget her sucking child,
> that she should have no compassion on the son of her womb?
> Even these may forget,
> yet I will not forget you.[30]

And St Paul, sometimes taken as an archetypal anti-feminist, contrasts the bondage to the law symbolized by Hagar and Mount Sinai with the freedom of Christ symbolized by the heavenly Jerusalem, and comments,

> But the Jerusalem above is free, and she is our mother ... So, brethren, we are not children of the slave but of the free woman.[31]

The early Christian Church was cautious in taking the ideas implicit here, however. Though there are maternal references, particularly in the Greek Fathers, and passing hints in Ambrose and Augustine, in general the theme is not important in early medieval texts.[32] The reason for this may have been that notions of femininity in God were a part of gnostic teaching; Valentinus, for example, spoke of a divine Dyad, a male and female principle, from which all else springs; and the use he made of this was strongly repudiated by Christian theologians.[33] It might well have been from the Gnostics that the *Zohar*, an important and widely pondered book of Jewish mystical literature published at the end of the thirteenth century but having much earlier roots, drew its ideas of divine motherhood.[34] Though it cannot be conclusively disproved, however, it is unlikely that Julian had any acquaintance with the *Zohar* or with earlier Gnosticism. In any case, her conception of divine motherhood is vastly different, resting on the ideas of a mother's patient and careful nurturing of her child rather than on notions of heavenly hierarchies, and bearing more resemblance to themes of affective spirituality found in twelfth-century Cistercian writings.

Various spiritual writers in the medieval period took up the idea of the divine motherhood, often using maternal metaphors to describe the abbot or instruct him in his duties, and then likening his care of monks to God's care for all his people. The *Regula Magistri* encouraged those who had authority over their brethren to exercise it as though they were both father and mother over those in their care.[35] This theme is taken up strongly by Cistercian writers, whose language moves from masculine to feminine and back without literary embarrassment.[36] Many instances could be cited, especially from Bernard of Clairvaux; typical is his letter to the newly elected Pope Eugenius III who had until recently been a monk under Bernard's jurisdiction:

> I urge you then, not as a master, but as a mother – quite simply as a loving mother. A fondly foolish one indeed, I may seem to be, but only to one who knows not love, who is a stranger to the strength of love ... Once you were flesh of my flesh, and you are not easily parted from me ...[37]

More interestingly in terms of Julian's use of the theme is the way in which mystical writers from at least the time of Anselm saw the passion of Christ in terms of motherhood. As a mother travails to bring forth her children, so Christ travails on the cross to give spiritual birth to those who would be called by his name. In Anselm's 'Prayer to St Paul' he reflects on the Pauline comment that Paul was like a nurse caring for his children in Christ; this leads Anselm to think of Jesus himself as mother, in a passage in which he combines biblical allusions to the feminine aspect of divinity.

> And you, Jesus, are you not also a mother?
> Are you not the mother who, like a hen,
> gathers her chickens under her wings?
> Truly, Lord, you are a mother;
> for both they who are in labour
> and they who are brought forth
> are accepted by you.

You have died more than they, that they may labour to bear.
It is by your death that they have been born,
for if you had not been in labour,
you could not have borne death;
and if you had not died, you would not have brought forth.
For, longing to bear sons into life,
you tasted of death,
and by dying you begot them ...
And you, my soul, dead in yourself,
run under the wings of Jesus your mother
and lament your griefs under his feathers.
Ask that your wounds may be healed
and that, comforted, you may live again ...
Mother [Jesus], know again your dead son [Anselm],
both by the sign of your cross and the voice of his confession.
Warm your chicken, give life to your dead man,
justify your sinner.
Let your terrified one be consoled by you;
and in your whole and unceasing grace
let him be refashioned by you.[38]

It is worth quoting Anselm at some length because, as we can see, many of his thoughts are close to those of Julian: the wounds which Jesus heals, the travail of Jesus in bringing us forth, the comfort and consolation of his tender motherlike love. It is as usual impossible to prove that Julian knew the Anselmian prayer, but given his enormous influence over monastic thinking generally and Benedictine thinking in particular in medieval England, and the association of Julian (in whatever capacity) with the Benedictines of Carrow Abbey and probably also the Cathedral priory, the likelihood must be strong.

Other sources are also possible. In the *Ancrene Riwle* Jesus is portrayed as the mother who reconciles her children to their angry father; and in the much circulated *Goad of Love*, Walter Hilton's translation of James of Milan's *Stimulus Amoris*, the idea is also present. Besides this, English Cistercians like Aelred had taken up the theme from their continental brethren; and it appears also in Dominican writings.[39]

Whatever the precise influences on Julian may have been, her presentation of the theme of the motherhood of God is uniquely her own, built up from her own experiences and her reflection upon them. It is noteworthy that the idea of divine motherhood never appears in the Short Text; it is only after long reflection and, no doubt, pondering the writings of others, that she comes to give this idea theological articulation as an aspect of her experience. She makes it clear that the ideas were present in the visions themselves; but she did not write them down until she had pondered them and saw their place in her overall understanding of divine love.

It is interesting that her first attribution of motherhood is not to Christ but to the Church. As we have noted, Cistercian writings of the preceding period had moved from thinking of the Abbot as Mother to Jesus as Mother: in Julian the Church is substituted for the Abbot. (Might this be a further reason to suppose that Julian was not a member of a convent?) She has been discussing 'hidden mysteries' which we cannot understand until God makes us worthy, and says,

> And with this I am well satisfied, waiting upon our Lord's will in this great marvel. And now I submit myself to my mother, Holy Church, as a simple child should.[40]

This statement would not in itself be striking. The idea that the Church was a mother had been extant since the time of the martyrs, and was a medieval commonplace;[41] and we have already seen how Julian considered the Church to be a protection against danger and error, and worthy of obedience and submission. The identification of Christ and the Church was also standard teaching; but it was Julian's depth of experience of this identification which allowed her to develop the move, touched upon but not expounded in depth by previous writers, from seeing the Church as 'Domina Mater Ecclesia' to the recognition of Christ as our Mother. For Julian, the Church is not something other than or independent of Christ; the Church is his Body. It is therefore a very short step from thinking of the Church as our Mother to thinking of Christ as Mother; and Julian takes that step.

> He [Christ] wants us to commit ourselves fervently to the faith of Holy Church, and find there our beloved Mother in consolation and true understanding, with all the company of the blessed ... And therefore it is a certain thing, and good and gracious to will, meekly and fervently, to be fastened and united to our mother Holy Church, *who is Christ Jesus.*[42]

Julian had referred to Christ as Mother in passages preceding the one just cited, so there is no way of being sure that this was the actual progression of her thought. Whatever the chronology, however, once she had begun to think in terms of divine motherhood, she developed the concept far beyond a sentimental one into one of great theological richness.

In the first place, she interweaves in her account of the divine motherhood the various strands of her doctrine of God; his creatorhood, his attributes, and his trinitarian nature. She says,

> And so in our making, God almighty is our loving Father, and God all wisdom is our loving Mother, with the love and the goodness of the Holy Spirit, which is all one God, one Lord.[43]

Divine fatherhood, therefore, is associated with the first person of the Trinity and with the attribute of power; divine motherhood with God the Son and with the characteristics of knowledge and wisdom, and divine lordship with the Holy Spirit and with all goodness; all these are involved in our 'making'.

But now she adds yet further dimensions. God the all powerful Father is the one who, having created our substantial nature, protects and cares for us; Christ shares our physicality and thereby redeems and saves us from death and destruction and restores us to ourselves and to God, and the Holy Spirit offers us fulfilment, both in terms of rewards for our efforts and in terms of the needs we have for comfort and strength and enlightenment to press on. It is worth quoting a long and rather complex passage which illustrates this.

> I contemplated the work of all the blessed Trinity, in which contemplation I saw and understood these three properties: the property of fatherhood, and the property of motherhood, and the property of lordship in one God. In our almighty Father we have our protection and bliss, as regards our natural substance, which is ours by creation from without beginning; and in the second person, in knowledge and wisdom we have our perfection, as regards our sensuality, our restoration and our salvation, for he is our Mother, brother and saviour; and in our good Lord the Holy Spirit we have our reward and our gift for our living and our labour, endlessly surpassing all that we desire in his marvellous courtesy, out of his plentiful grace.[44]

Here we see how the divine Trinity, which had been differentiated as Father, Mother and Lord, and has been characterized as power, wisdom and goodness, is now further developed as nature, mercy and grace, for our protection, restoration, and fulfilment. The extent to which Julian's thinking is permeated by a rich Trinitarianism becomes increasingly obvious, but, as already pointed out, this is no abstract divine ontology but connects at every point with Christian experience.

It is this combination of theological depth and carefully pondered experience, rather than pious sentiment (let alone any attempt to be feminist),[45] which we find in her teaching of God as Mother. As Julian considers the incarnation of the Christ who is hanging before her on the cross, she sees in it a double aspect of the most obvious dimension of motherhood, that of giving birth. In the first place, he took flesh in the womb of his mother for the purpose of being the saviour of the world, bringing humankind to a new birth. By being the Mother of Christ, Mary is in a sense the Mother of us all, since in Christ we are born again. Yet, more strictly, Julian sees Christ himself as our Mother.

> So our Lady is our mother, in whom we are all enclosed and born of her in Christ, for she who is mother of our saviour is mother of all who are saved in our saviour; and our saviour is our true Mother, in whom we are endlessly born and out of whom we shall never come.[46]

Secondly, however, Christ's formation of us is not only in this spiritual restoration; he has also brought us to birth in the primary sense by giving us life in the first place. Christ who is divine wisdom creates the world at the behest of the Father. This creation, insofar as it is creation of human beings, in turn has two aspects, the physical and the spiritual, or, as Julian prefers to put it, the sensual and the substantial. In each of these, Christ is Mother. We will look more closely at the implications of this double nature later on; put very roughly, Julian's view is that the sensual nature is our earthly empirical self, and the substantial nature is our spiritual essence or personhood. This latter is our true selfhood, and it was this which was originally created by God, and is held and protected by him. Our sensuality, that is our physical and empirical nature, though also created by God, has fallen into wretchedness and death through sin, and is thus in need of salvation and restoration.

Julian sees this salvation in terms of the incarnation of Christ which she considers as his unification with all humankind. She presents a parable which came to her in the revelations of a lord and a servant, who, in his eagerness to fulfil the will of the master, falls into a ditch and finds himself in a mess. We will consider this parable in detail in Chapter Nine; but we must note here that for Julian, the servant represents Adam, and in him all of humankind, yet at the same time it also represents Christ the second Adam, who cannot be detached from his solidarity with all men and women. In the terms of the parable the fall into the ditch represents simultaneously the sinfulness and wretchedness of the human condition and the descent of Christ to take flesh in human birth, in order to restore us in himself to our proper place at the right hand of the Lord. Our salvation is therefore not a salvation of our souls only. Our physicality, created by God, is also redeemed by him by Christ's incarnation. Our sensuality and our substantial nature have become separated through sin, thus losing their intended integrity; in modern terms we might say that we are alienated from our true selves. Christ, who is our Mother in our initial creation, therefore becomes our Mother in the new birth, by taking on our flesh, and through his death and resurrection bringing us life, reconciling us not only to God but to ourselves. Julian speaks, thus, of the reunification of our sensual and our substantial nature.

> The second person of the Trinity is our Mother in nature in our substantial creation, in whom we are founded and rooted, and he is our Mother of mercy in taking our sensuality ... and by the power of his Passion, his death and his Resurrection he unites us to our substance.[47]

Christ, therefore, is our Mother in this twofold sense of having done everything that is necessary – indeed everything that is possible – for our physical as well as our spiritual life. In the ninth revelation Julian heard Christ asking her whether she was well satisfied that he had suffered for her, and he assures her of the delight it was to him because of his love for her; he tells her that he would gladly suffer more if he could, out of sheer love.

> Then his meaning is this: How could it be that I should not do for love of you all that I am able? ... And for this love he said very sweetly this: If I could suffer more, I should suffer more ... It was done as honourably as Christ could do it, and here I saw the complete joy in Christ, for his joy would not have been complete if the deed could have been done any better than it was.[48]

Just as a mother is willing to endure pain and travail to whatever extent is necessary to bring forth a much longed-for child, so also Christ our Mother took upon himself the pains of death to bring us to spiritual birth. But Christ surpasses in generosity any human Mother, being willing to suffer even more than is necessary, out of his great delight in our salvation. Thus through Christ our Mother

> we are powerfully taken out of hell and out of the wretchedness on earth, and gloriously brought up into heaven, and blessedly united to our substance, increased in riches and nobility by all the power of Christ ...[49]

Furthermore, Julian sees Jesus as our Mother in nourishing us. As a mother lays her newborn child to her breast and encourages it to feed, so also Jesus gives his own Body and Blood for our spiritual sustenance. There was medieval precedent for equating the wounds of Jesus with the mother's breasts: Aelred, for example, had spoken of the wound in Jesus' side as the source from which the soul draws nurture.[50] Not only was this so, but also medieval medical theory held that the milk obtained from a mother's breasts was in fact processed blood; therefore the ideas of milk and blood can easily be interchanged.[51] Therefore Julian is able to interweave the work of motherhood with standard Christian teaching on the Eucharist:

> The mother can give her child to suck her milk, but our precious Mother Jesus can feed us with himself, and does, most courteously and most tenderly, with the blessed sacrament, which is the precious food of true life; and with all the sweet sacraments he sustains us most mercifully and graciously ...[52]

Yet there is a sense in which motherhood has only just begun when a child is born. The mother must then feed and foster the child, protect it from harm, teach and guide and where necessary chasten the child. She comforts the child in distress, and, although she may sometimes allow the child to fall or hurt itself for its own good, she is always careful that there is no real peril. She forgives the child's disobedience and corrects its recalcitrance, picking up the pieces of shattered toys or shattered illusions, and binding up hurts. Above all, she loves the child. All her activities are manifestations of that love, in which she rejoices and delights at the child's progress and takes pride in fostering its development.

Or does she? Julian is too much of a realist to accept this as an authentic picture of motherhood as most people actually experience it. The picture is a portrait of the mother of our dreams, the sort of mother we long for but few are fortunate enough to have had. It would be rare indeed for any actual mother to feel no resentment at all toward her baby for the misery and pain of pregnancy and birth and the hard work of looking after an infant, no matter how much the baby is loved and wanted. And not all children are wanted. When a child feels that its mother does not want it, that its needs are either not met at all or are met only grudgingly, without the joy and delight of its mother's love, the child quickly feels itself to be a nuisance or a nasty, unpleasant thing. Try as it may to please its mother, it can never rest while it feels unloved, and sinks into discouragement and self-despair. For a person who has felt like that about his or her mother, thinking of Christ as Mother may be as unhelpful as thinking of God as Father is to those whose fathers on earth have been tyrannical or ineffectual.

Julian is aware of all this. No mother on earth can fulfil our ideal of motherhood, and many do not or cannot try. Does this mean that there is no place for the ideal? Surely not; we do not abandon the concept of a perfect circle just because nobody can draw one, nor the ideal of moral integrity because nobody perfectly attains it. Julian points out, in fact, that the ideal of motherhood, unfulfillable as it is by a human mother, is nevertheless an accurate portrayal of Christ.

> This fair lovely word 'mother' is so sweet and so kind in itself that it cannot truly be said of anyone or to anyone except of him and to him who is the true Mother of life and of all things.[53]

Already before Julian, there had been reflection about the extent to which Jesus as Mother went far beyond the conception of earthly motherhood. A Carthusian prioress, Marguerite of Oingt, had written,

> Are you not my mother and more than my mother? The mother who bore me laboured in delivering me for one day or one night but you, my sweet and lovely Lord, laboured for me for more than thirty years. Ah, my sweet and lovely Lord, with what love you laboured for me and bore me through your whole life. But when the time approached for you to be delivered, your labour pains were so great that your holy sweat was like great drops of blood that came out from your body and fell on the earth ... Ah! Sweet Lord Jesus Christ, who ever saw a mother suffer such a birth! For when the hour of your delivery came you were placed on the hard bed of the cross ... and your nerves and all your veins were broken. And truly it is no surprise that your veins burst when in one day you gave birth to the whole world.[54]

Julian, however, does not dwell so much on the labour and pain, at this point, as on the healing and comfort which Jesus' mothering can give. Her ideas here lend themselves to a Jungian interpretation. In Christ our Mother, those whose earthly mothering was all that it should have been can find the archetype of that most beautiful relationship; and those whose earthly mothering left deep wounds through lack of love and care, and who thereby feel diminished in their personhood, can find healing and comfort and fulfilment by finding in Christ the Mother they have always longed for.

From our own perspective in the twentieth century, we may want to ask whether this is projection. It might be argued that it is a classic case of taking the unattainable ideals of an earthly relationship and pushing them up 'into the sky', creating God in our own idealized image. If this is what is going on, it is inauthentic and unhealthy, a way to avoid coming to terms with real relationships, inadequate though they may be, in favour of a fantasy whose indulgence distorts actual relationships even further.

This is a question that must be faced; but it must be faced in the whole context of Julian's theology. Her teaching on the motherhood of Christ does not stand on its own, but is bound up with her whole integrated theology of profound reflection on her own experience and the teaching of the Church. We have already noted how it is linked with the doctrines of creation, the Trinity, the incarnation, the Eucharist, and our salvation. The real question, therefore, is whether Christian theology has any implications for psychology; whether salvation remains purely theoretical, at best offering fulfilment in a future life only, or whether there can be genuine spiritual healing and fulfilment in our relationship with Christ in this life. Julian's whole approach is to emphasize the fact of healing; her repeated theme is that through the passion of Christ our wounds, like his, are turned into honours, the badges of glory. How this takes place we will explore more fully in the final chapter. But that it takes place is what makes the gospel good news, and makes Julian's message of healing an important one for the wounded and broken people of our time.

Notes to Chapter Seven

1. Whether her debt to Augustine was conscious, or whether it was the debt common to the centuries of Augustinian theology, is a matter of scholarly disagreement. (cf. Colledge and Walsh, who argue that she had an intricate theological background, vs. Pelphrey, who accepts that she might have been illiterate.)
2. LT 4.
3. ST 24.
4. ibid.; cf. LT 73.

5. LT 4.
6. cf. LT 57.
7. 2 Cor. 10.5.
8. *The Cloud of Unknowing*, Ch. 7.
9. ibid., Ch. 12.
10. ibid., Ch. 6.
11. ST 10–11; cf. LT 19.
12. Jaroslav Pelikan, *The Emergence of the Catholic Tradition*, pp. 344–9; and *The Spirit of Eastern Christendom*, pp. 65–8 and *passim* on the divine economy and the divine essence; James Walsh, Introduction to *The Cloud of Unknowing*.
13. The difference is one of emphasis; this ought not to be taken to imply that either the Pseudo-Dionysius or the author of *The Cloud* minimized the importance of the incarnation.
14. LT 58.
15. ibid.
16. ibid.
17. Augustine, *De Trinitate* XV.17, etc.; cf. John Burnaby, *Amor Dei: A Study of the Religion of St Augustine* (Hodder & Stoughton 1938), p. 175.
18. Hugh of St Victor, *De Sacramentum* I.2.6 (PL 176, col. 208).
19. Thomas Aquinas, *Summa Theologiae* I.1 Q9 a8.
20. Richard Rolle, *The Fire of Love*, Chaps. 6 and 7.
21. cf. A. Hyman and J. Walsh, ed., *Philosophy in the Middle Ages* (Hackett, Indianapolis, 1973), p. 164.
22. Thomas Aquinas, *Summa Theologiae* I.1 Q30 a2.
23. Augustine, *De Trinitate* XV and *passim*.
24. Anselm, *Monologium* XLIX and LIII, tr. S. N. Deane, *St Anselm Basic Writings*, 2nd edn (Open Court, La Salle, Illinois, 1962), pp. 113–15.
25. LT 36.
26. cf. LT 46. See below, pp. 173–80.
27. LT 36. In the context, this particular passage does not have specific reference to the Trinity, but to a 'great deed' which the Lord will perform: see below, p. 177. But it would have more general application as well.
28. LT 59.
29. cf. Caroline Walker Bynum, *Jesus as Mother: Studies in the Spirituality of the High Middle Ages* (UCLA Press, Los Angeles and London, 1982), Chapter 4.
30. Isaiah 49.15.
31. Galatians 4.26, 31.
32. Bynum, p. 126.
33. Irenaeus, *Against Heresies* I.11.1; cf. Elaine Pagels, *The Gnostic Gospels* (Pelican 1982), pp. 73f.
34. cf. Louis Jacobs, *Jewish Mystical Testimonies* (Schocken, New York, 1976); Gershom G. Scholem, *Major Trends in Jewish Mysticism*, 3rd edn (Schocken, New York, 1961), pp. 205–43.
35. *Regula Magistri*, Ch. 2. In what follows I have been helped by an unpublished dissertation by Margaret Bendelow Collier, 'Verily God is Our Mother': *A Study of the Doctrine of Julian of Norwich* (Pontifical Institute 'Regina Mundi', Rome, 1963).
36. cf. André Cabassut OSB, 'Une Dévotion Médiévale peu connue, la Dévo-

Julian's Theology of Integration

tion à Jésus notre Mère', in *Revue d'Ascétique et de Mystique* 99–100 (April-December 1949), pp. 234–45.

37. Bernard of Clairvaux, *On Consideration* prologue (Cistercian Fathers Series 37, Cistercian Publications, Kalamazoo, Michigan, 1976); cf. his letter to John, Abbot of Buzay, in Bruno Scott James, *The Letters of Saint Bernard of Clairvaux* (London, Burns Oates, 1953) No. 312; *Sermons on the Song of Songs* Nos. 9, 10, 23, 41, etc. See also William of St Thierry, *Exposition on the Song of Songs* (Cistercian Fathers Series 6, 1970) No. 30; Aelred of Rievaulx, *De Institutione*, in *Treatises and Pastoral Prayer* (Cistercian Fathers Series 2, 1971).
38. Anselm, 'Prayer to St Paul', in Sr Benedicta Ward SLG, *The Prayers and Meditations of St Anselm* (Penguin 1973), pp. 153–6.
39. Colledge and Walsh suggest many other possible sources, including in particular William of St Thierry's *Epistola ad fratres de Monte Dieu*, popularly known as *The Golden Letter*, as well as his other writings, where the same theme occurs. (C & W, pp. 151–62); cf. also Bynum, Ch. 4.
40. LT 46.
41. cf. C & W, pp. 153–5, and p. 607 n57.
42. LT 61, emphasis mine.
43. LT 58.
44. ibid.
45. The idea of Julian as a fourteenth-century feminist is of course anachronistic.
46. LT 57.
47. LT 58.
48. LT 22.
49. LT 58.
50. Aelred, *De Institutione* 31.
51. Bynum, pp. 132–3.
52. LT 60.
53. ibid.
54. Marguerite of Oingt, *Pagina*, Chaps. 30–9, quoted in Bynum, p. 153.

126

8 Creation and Asceticism: Expressions of Love

Julian's theological method, which allows for reciprocity between doctrine and experience, as well as for its practical consequences for the development of holiness and wholeness, is well illustrated by her understanding of the doctrine of creation and her own response to the created order. The doctrine itself emerges in her experience. At an early stage in the revelations, Julian is given a striking object lesson:

> And in this he showed me something small, no bigger than a hazel-nut, lying in the palm of my hand, and I perceived that it was round as any ball. I looked at it and thought: What can this be? And I was given this general answer: It is everything which is made. I was amazed that it could last, for I thought that it was so little that it could suddenly fall into nothing. And I was answered in my understanding: It lasts and always will, because God loves it; and thus everything has being through the love of God.[1]

As Julian contemplates this tiny ball which seems to her so delicate and fragile, she is taught that it is the whole universe, everything that exists. Because of the love God has for it, it is preserved in being, though without God it would be nothing. He is for it 'the Creator and the protector and the lover'.[2]

We might have expected that at this point Julian would do one of two things. She might have launched into praise of God for the beauty and wonder of all created things and for his care of them, becoming a fourteenth-century Psalmist. Or, perhaps more characteristically, she might have developed a theology of creation. She does neither. Later in the Revelations Julian does indeed consider more fully what the relationship is between God and the universe – what it means to say that he is its Creator. But when she is first shown the tiny ball lying in the palm of her hand, her thoughts do not immediately turn to doctrine but to the practical consequences of this experience for her relationship to God.

> This little thing which is created seemed to me as if it could have fallen into nothing because of its littleness. We need to have knowledge of this, so that we may delight in despising as nothing everything created, so as to love and have uncreated God. For this is the reason why our hearts and souls are not in perfect ease, because here we seek rest in this thing which is so little, in which there is no rest, and we do not know our God who is almighty, all wise and all good, for he is true rest.[3]

The thought which Julian is expressing here is her own experientially mediated version of the words of Augustine in the opening lines of his *Confessions*: 'You have made us for yourself, and our heart is restless until it rests in you.'[4] There is nothing odd about her use of the idea; Julian is deeply Augustinian, as we have seen already, and these words of Augustine's are among his most frequently quoted. What is striking, however, is the context in which she expresses this thought. Even allowing for the fact that Julian moves at once to the practical consequences of her hazel-nut experience, one would hardly have expected this apparent world rejection to be its consequence. The emphasis in that showing seemed to be on the tender love of God for this fragile world he created and preserves. Why should Julian interpret it to imply that we should despise as nothing that upon which God himself places so much value? It might seem that in this instance, far from integrating experience and doctrine, Julian is allowing a preconceived medieval world-renouncing asceticism to override her own experience which, had she but taken it seriously, would have undermined this negative attitude to the world.

This, I suggest, is to misunderstand Julian. As already indicated, the Long Text of the Revelations is a finely honed theological book; and it cannot be properly understood either by a strictly linear reading or by taking individual passages on their own. In this case in particular, there is a whole theology of creation and of human nature implicit between the world-affirming hazel-nut passage and the apparently world-renouncing implications which follow it. What that theology is can only be understood from a study of the rest of her book; and we are not in a position to evaluate her asceticism until we have explored it. I propose therefore in this chapter first to investigate her teaching on creation in general, and then her account of human nature as a particular aspect of it. With this as a basis, we will return to consider her asceticism to see whether it is consistent with her own thought and experience, and what its validity might be.

Creation

We in our culture tend to be somewhat embarrassed by the doctrine of creation. We are steeped in post-Enlightenment thought patterns, and have witnessed the unedifying spectacle of debates between creationists and evolutionists, and would not wish to choose between the strident dogmatism of the former and the reductionism of the latter. Yet the creativity of God is the first of his attributes to which Scripture calls attention, and we affirm it every time we repeat the Creed. Indeed, it is in one sense the foundation of all Christian belief. This, however, is not because it supplies a quasi-scientific answer to a question about the origin of all things, but because it points to the creativity of a God who can make all things new. God as Creator brings cosmos out of chaos and Easter out of Calvary; as such his creativity is the ground for hope that the tangled knots of individual and social existence may yet be woven into a pattern of dignity and beauty. If there were no doctrine of creation there could be no doctrine of salvation. Julian's theology, as we shall see, is emphatic in the claim that the creative attributes of God which brought the world and ourselves into existence are the very same creative attributes which bring about our fulfilment.[5] The converse is also true: it is our experience of the creative activity of God in our lives which qualifies our understanding of the creation of the universe.

As we have already seen, Julian believed that all the showings were in a sense one, unified as a single revelation of the love of God and displayed in the passion of Christ. Thus it comes as no surprise that she should root her understanding of the doctrine of creation firmly in that love. When she later reflects on the hazel-nut experience, which in turn had occurred within the vision of the bleeding head of Jesus, she recounts as some of its lessons, first,

> that he who created it [i.e. all things] created everything for love, and by the same love it is preserved ...

and furthermore,

> that God is everything which is good, as I see, and the goodness which everything has is God.[6]

This is very strongly stated. Julian does not say merely that God is the *cause* of everything that is good, or that the goodness it has is *from* God: she makes a much stronger identification. God *is* everything good; its goodness *is* God. She repeats that assertion in the next chapter:

> For God is everything that is good, as I see; and God has made everything that is made, and God loves everything that he has made ... For God is in man and in God is all.[7]

To understand more clearly what Julian intends by this passage, it is helpful to consider its two aspects separately, though ultimately they are connected: God's immanence, and God's goodness.

Beginning then with God's immanence, we find that it is in this that Julian's theology of creation and its consequences for spirituality are grounded. In one sense we make a correct distinction between the divine nature which is uncreated and the multiplicity of created natures in all the rich variety that we find in the world. Yet this variety of created natures is not utterly different from God as though the relationship of creation were a purely extrinsic one. Julian prefers the metaphor of parenthood. Children are indeed different from their

129

parents, and are individuals in their own right; yet they are also very like their parents, and indeed share their nature, in ways that artefacts made by their parents could never do. In some sense their parents' nature has flowed into them; and as we watch them grow we can see likenesses of various sorts to their mother or father. The distinction between producing children who share in the parents' nature and producing artefacts which do not, helps us to an initial understanding of a rather obscure but very important passage:

> God is essence in his very nature; that is to say, that goodness which is natural is God. He is the ground, his is the substance, he is the very essence or nature, and he is the true Father and the true Mother of natures. And all natures which he has made to flow out of him to work his will, they will be restored and brought back into him by the salvation of man through the operation of grace.[8]

Just how it is that the salvation of man is to bring about the revelation of all things will be seen better after we consider human nature, though it is at once plain that Julian is here echoing the thoughts of St Paul in the Epistle to the Romans:

> For the creation waits with eager longing for the revealing of the sons of God ... because the creation itself will be set free from its bondage to decay and obtain the glorious liberty of the children of God.[9]

The point is that although there is a vast variety of created natures, they are all related. It is a mistake to suppose that we and all other inhabitants of the planet are unconnected with each other. The universe is not like a department store where one can find things as unconnected as lawn-mowers and handkerchiefs. It is much more like a vastly extended family where everyone is related to everyone else, though it may take some effort to work out just how.

Julian's thought here, as elsewhere, is closely related to that of Thomas Aquinas, who in his discussion of the relationship between the will and goodness of God argued that any good being diffuses its goodness to all that it creates, thereby making it as much like itself as possible. God, therefore, as the supreme good, communicates his own nature of goodness to all created things, and they are all related to him and flow out from him.

> Thus, then, he wills both himself to be, and other things to be; but himself as the end, and other things as ordained to that end, inasmuch as it befits the divine goodness that other things should be partakers therein.[10]

Aquinas, like Julian after him, sees both the relatedness of all things in God flowing from his goodness, and also the difference between being a partaker in goodness, as all created things are, and being that goodness itself from which all created goodness flows.

Creation and Asceticism

Today we are less accustomed to this sort of talk from theologians than from ecologists who emphasize the fragility of the biological balance and the dangers of pollution. But what is now emphasized and confirmed by scientific research was for Julian an implication of her understanding of creation. All natures (again, the Middle English word is 'kyndes') are related, because they all flow out of God, who is 'the true Father and the true Mother of natures'. We ourselves, and the plants and animals and other natural things of this world, are all siblings. Julian is here giving the theological basis for the song of Francis of Assisi which she may have known:

Praised be You, my Lord, with all your creatures,
especially Sir Brother Sun ...
Praised be You, my Lord, through Sister Moon and the stars ...
Praised be You, my Lord, through Brother Wind ...
Praised be You, my Lord, through Sister Water ...
Praised be You, my Lord, through Brother Fire ...
Praised be You, my Lord, through our Sister Mother Earth,
who sustains and governs us,
and who produces varied fruits with coloured flowers and
herbs ...[11]

Not only are all created natures thus closely related to one another; they are also much more closely related to God than is often supposed. Indeed, it is this which is the basis for their relationship to one another. As Gerald Vann puts it, in words echoing Julian's thoughts,

All the things that God has made are made ultimately of the same stuff, so that there is a bond between them like the blood-tie that binds the members of a family; all the things that God has made have ultimately the same end, to worship and praise him in their different ways; most important of all, God himself is present in all the things that he has made, and his presence is discernible in them to the eyes of faith and love and worship – and we best assist the song of creation, and recognize our oneness with all things most truly and most fully, when we learn to see them in God and God in them; and then it is to him that they can lead us.[12]

This idea is not altogether acceptable to modern-day theologians. There are various historical reasons for the current theological idea that God and the world are only extrinsically related. They range from the Deist understanding of God as totally removed from his creation, so that, once made, it can go on without him, to the long-standing suspicion of matter as utterly alien to God and the double suspicion of our physical bodies as somehow dragging us away from him, to the account of God as Wholly Other than anything created.[13] Whatever the reasons, and whether they are orthodox or not, the idea is that God created the world and its inhabitants by *fiat*, his command bringing into existence things utterly unlike himself, to which he could then relate or not, as he chose.

131

Julian's conception is different from this. She takes it as basic that God 'is the ground, his is the substance' of all things, which 'flow out of him to work his will'. The differences between creatures are real, but they are not pointers to an ultimate difference, because at the most fundamental level they all participate in the divine substance, formed by God in a rich variety of ways. Similarly the difference between creatures and God is not a difference between substances but a difference between substance as divinely creative and its created manifestations.[14] Thus the various created natures are in a very strong sense divine self-expression. God is immanent in all things, preserving them in existence not just by command but by his being. 'In God is all.'

Julian's terminology, however, may bring to modern consciousness a lurking suspicion: is this not pantheism? Must we not maintain a stronger division than this between God and creatures – a division which would be indicated by the traditional terminology of creation *ex nihilo*? Julian would not have used the term 'pantheism', of course, but to say as Julian does that God 'is being' and that all natures 'flow out of him' might seem to reduce God to nothing but the sum total of all created things, so that it becomes impossible to speak of him as God over against creation, a personal being with attributes of his own. And if once we give up the personal nature of God, we have given up all that is significant for Julian's theology and spirituality.

I suggest, however, that this moves much too quickly, and that Julian's theology does not fail at this point. To see why, it is helpful to bring in the idea of divine goodness, which crucially qualifies the idea of immanence in her theology, and which, manifested in the crucified Christ, contains within itself all the revelations. As we saw, Julian believes that

> God is everything which is good ... and the goodness which everything has is God.[15]

But what is it for God to be good? In other words, how is that goodness expressed, particularly with reference to the creative activity of God? Julian uses a concept that is now not much used with reference to God: the idea of God's courtesy; and though for her the courtesy of God has ramifications far beyond the doctrine of creation, this is a good place to begin in understanding it. Her reflection begins from an example shown to her of a majestic lord and a poor servant: a theme she will later take up in her understanding of sin and salvation. If this lord, great as he is, desires the familiar friendship of the servant and shows him the courtesy of treating him as a valued human being, rather than as a chattel to be ordered around, this will be a greater honour and delight to the servant than the greatest of material gifts. Courtesy like this is not mere formality; it is rather the lord voluntarily forgoing his right to command the servant and to treat him as property, in order that the servant has being or status in his own right and therefore can enter into a relationship as of equals with the lord. The lord is not required to behave like this: in medieval times, especially the times surrounding the Peasants' Revolt, there were plenty of examples of lords treating their servants as utterly beneath contempt, as mere tools to serve the lord's purpose. In England in the late Middle Ages there would have been plenty of examples ready to hand; one which might have sprung to Julian's mind was the disastrous poll tax of 1380, that was levied without any regard for the welfare of those who had to pay, and thus helped precipitate the Peasants' Revolt. In a society such as that, it is all the greater an honour to a servant if his king or lord declines to exercise his rightful power over him and instead extends friendship to the servant.

Now, it is just such generous courtesy, forgoing his rights to domination, which Julian finds in the relationship between God and his creatures, including ourselves. She explicitly draws the parallel to the lord and the servant.

> So it is with our Lord Jesus and us, for truly it is the greatest possible joy, as I see it, that he who is highest and mightiest, noblest and most honourable, is lowest and humblest, most familiar and courteous . . . For the greatest abundance of joy which we shall have, as I see it, is this wonderful courtesy and familiarity of our Father, who is our Creator, in our Lord Jesus Christ, who is our brother and our saviour.[16]

There is no requirement laid upon God to treat us so generously; indeed it is the humility of God which places self-imposed restraints on the exercise of his power so that he can be, in Julian's words, 'familiar' with us, just as the lord would have to impose restraints on his own right to command if he were to treat his servant as a friend.

We are now in a position to see how this overcomes the difficulty we might feel with Julian's idea that God is a personal being over against creation even though all created natures flow out of him.[17] In one sense it is true that God is Being Itself; there can be no being utterly other than God, not deriving its being from him, both in its original creation and its preservation. If God were somehow to withdraw himself, all creatures, ourselves included, would instantly collapse into nothing. He is absolutely infinite, omnipotent, omniscient, omnipresent. This means that for God to bring creatures into existence, so that they are genuinely differentiated beings in their own right, he must impose restraints upon himself, so as to allow them to have being of their own. Although he is their substance, and they could have no existence at all without his will, he gives them existence in their own right, natures (kyndes) of their own, by the courteous self-limitation of his absolute right of command.

Thus the universe operates by what we might call 'natural law', the regular causal order of gravitation, motion, and the like, producing on earth such patterns as the seasons and the tides. As one moves through the sequence from inanimate entities to organisms, plants, the whole variety of animals, and human nature, we see that there is increasingly what we might call 'a nature of one's own'. For example, one fire is very like another given the same circumstances of fuel and oxygen; but one dog will wag its tail at an intruder while another will go into paroxysms of barking. Thus creatures, to be creatures in their own right at all, are increasingly dependent on God's self-limitation which allows them the freedom to act according to their nature, even while their substance and the very possibility of their acting at all is rooted in the being of God.

The most obvious case is of course that of human personhood, where the generous courtesy of God restrains his omnipotence and allows us freedom. God who is Being Itself, in his great humility 'lets be the beings'[18] – and in this self-imposed restriction on his interference in their natures which flow from him he allows them to be beings in their own right. But the effect of this is that insofar as he allows us and all creatures a created independence of being, he, by relating to us in this way, humbles himself to be a being among beings. Like the lord in Julian's example, he restricts his right of dominion and allows us to be individuals, treating us with love and courtesy. He is thus in one sense a personal being over against created beings, though in a prior sense he is Being Itself, the ground and substance of all things.

Should we call Julian a pantheist? Yes, if by this we mean that ultimately God is the source and substance of all reality. But no, if we mean that this is undifferentiated reality with divinity somehow diffused through it allowing for no individuality of creatures and no personal being in God. The label 'pantheism' has been used of a variety of positions, not all of them heretical; it is more profitable to consider the theology in question than to dismiss it with a label.

We can also see how closely Julian's understanding of the relationship between God and the world is to her vision of the crucified Christ. It is in the passion that we see most fully the self-giving love of God, Christ emptying himself of all power and self-assertiveness and giving himself up to the freedom of the very human beings he had himself created. Although without him they would not have had the life or the strength to do the deed, the Lord of life allowed himself to be put to death at their hands. This is the extreme case of divine humility. But it is not the sole case: the whole of the created order displays the same self-limitation of God as brought the world into being. We easily think of creation as the manifestation of God's supreme power, calling the beings into existence. There is truth in this; but it is truth which must be qualified by the cross. If the cross is the ultimate reference point, the supreme power is not domination; supreme power is the power to restrict one's own force and foster the being of the other. Love, in the end, is the strongest power of all; and God is love. By meditating on the bleeding head of Christ as given to her in the revelations, Julian is enabled to come to an understanding of creation as the self-giving love of God. It brings about an awe or fear of God, reflecting on the extent of his graciousness, which can be considered either by thinking of him directly, or of his presence in the least created thing:

> But this kind of trembling and fear will have no kind of pain, but it is proper to God's honourable majesty so to be contemplated by his creatures, trembling and quaking in fear, because of their much greater joy endlessly marvelling at the greatness of God, the Creator, and at the smallest part of all that is created.[19]

An immediate result of this understanding of the immanence of God in all things is that it makes it possible to appreciate that all created things are good. If their natures flow out from God, and God is the essence of goodness, then they also must be good. Julian is emphatic in her affirmation of the beauty and goodness of all created things. The passage about the hazel-nut illustrates the way in which she perceives God's high regard for his delicate creation which he preserves in being. As Julian reflects on this, she becomes more aware of the goodness of God in everything:

> And these words of the goodness of God are very dear to the soul, and very close to touching our Lord's will, for his goodness fills all his creatures and all his blessed works full, and endlessly overflows in them.[20]

Although Julian in her vocation as an anchoress had renounced much of the created order, in particular the enjoyment of people and places outside her own enclosure, she never for a moment rationalized her radical renunciation by seeing creation in negative terms.

Characteristic of her view of the physical world as good and noble is her account of the darkness and earthquakes and other physical phenomena with which the gospel writers surround their accounts of Jesus' passion. She says,

> Here I saw a great unity between Christ and us, as I understand it; for when he was in pain we were in pain, and all creatures able to suffer pain suffered with him. That is to say, all creatures which God has created for our service, the firmament and the earth, failed in their natural functions because of sorrow at the time of Christ's death, for it is their natural characteristic to recognize him as their Lord, in whom all their powers exist. And when he failed, their nature constrained them to fail with him, insofar as they could, because of the sorrow of his sufferings.[21]

The physical world is in sympathetic unity with its Maker, in such solidarity with Christ that Julian tells us that even those who, like Pilate, did not recognize Christ, were compelled to suffer with him, because creation withdrew the ordinary comforts of light and stability during his crucifixion. Whatever we make of this account of the phenomena surrounding the passion, it is an illustration of Julian's central point that all things were created and are preserved by the love of God immanent in them, and their natural state is to reciprocate that love as best they can.

This strong doctrine of divine immanence, however, raises for Julian the same sorts of problems which it would bring to our minds. To the extent that God is ultimately the substance of all things, to that extent he must be responsible for everything that happens. And if that is so, since God is all goodness, must it not follow that everything that happens is good? Julian pursues the logic of this:

> Therefore I was compelled to admit that everything which is done is well done, for our Lord God does everything. For at this time the work of creatures was not revealed, but the work of God in creatures; for he is the centre of everything, and he does everything.[22]

If in the final analysis everything that happens is done by the activity of God and therefore by his good will, nothing can happen by chance, and everything must flow from his goodness.

Now, this would be very nice if it were true, but it is all too obvious to us, as it was to Julian, that things do not fit easily into this description. What about the Black Death? And what about all the evil and injury which human beings inflict upon themselves and upon each other, all too often in the name of religion? Surely we cannot attribute these things to the activity of God – let alone to his goodness? Julian, as we have seen, is not the sort of woman to bask in the consolation of a vision, oblivious to the pain and evil of the world, and she never disengages her intellect in her experience of God. She is therefore immediately puzzled about how this understanding of God's goodness immanent in all things can be squared with sin and evil. Though she later receives further enlightenment, at this stage she is forced to admit the discrepancy between human judgement and the eternal perspective of God.

> For a man regards some deeds as well done and some as evil, and our Lord does not regard them so, for everything which exists in nature is of God's creation, so that everything which is done has the property of being God's doing.[23]

This turns into something of a crisis of conscience for Julian. It is quite impossible for her to deny her experience of sin and evil; yet it seems incompatible with the love and goodness of God which she is experiencing in an undeniable way. Which is she to trust? Her response is to wait, continuing in contemplation to see whether the Lord would reveal an answer to her perplexity. But he does not immediately do so; he shows her instead that since all things are done by God, God himself is pleased with it, and whether it looks like it or not, all is well.

> God revealed all this most blessedly, as though to say; See, I am God. See, I am in all things. See, I do all things. See, I never remove my hands from my works, nor ever shall without end. See, I guide all things to the end that I ordain them for, before time began, with the same power and wisdom and love with which I made them: how should anything be amiss?[24]

We might have thought that Julian was asking a question of God, examining the revelation she had been given, and so, in a sense, she was. But the vision of God's goodness in creation has turned the examination around: as well as being an examination of God, Julian finds that she herself is being examined: would she trust God's love? She concludes the chapter tellingly:

> So was the soul examined, powerfully, wisely and lovingly, in this vision. Then I saw truly that I must agree, with great reverence and joy in God.[25]

This is not the end of her questioning, nor a licence for credulity: she will continue to probe the apparent inconsistency between the immanent goodness of God and the sin and evil in the world, and we will follow her probing in the next chapter. Nevertheless, this affirmation of the goodness of God gives her the basic framework within which the questioning can go forward. We will have to wait to see how she progresses until we have considered some further dimensions of her integrated theology and experience, beginning with her understanding of human personhood.

Human Personhood

Nowhere else in creation is the theme of the interlocking goodness and immanence of God so fully realized as in the human being; and yet it is in the human that the problem of evil stands most acutely in tension with it. Julian emphasizes that our creation was the eternal intention of God; it was not a sudden whim.

> God the blessed Trinity, who is everlasting being, just as he is eternal from without beginning, just so was it his eternal purpose to create human nature ...[26]

Indeed, the human soul is the peak of creation; it is, in Julian's terms, where God did his very best.

> For I saw in the same revelation that if the blessed Trinity could have
> created man's soul any better, any fairer, any nobler than it was created, the
> Trinity would not have been fully pleased with the creation of man's soul.
> But because it made man's soul as beautiful, as good, as precious a creature
> as it could make, therefore the blessed Trinity is fully pleased without end
> in the creation of man's soul.[27]

Whatever the subsequent difficulties in understanding human sin and
wickedness, Julian begins from the premise that we are of value and
worth in the sight of God.

This positive conception of ourselves is grounded, as is the rest of
her theology, in her experience of the love of God manifested in the
passion of Christ. The love that he has for us, so that Christ would
gladly and joyfully suffer for us, shows that in his esteem we are worth
the very life of God. To say that we are nasty and worthless, therefore,
would be to say that he was misguided in his acceptance of the cross.
Our self-esteem is grounded in the boundless esteem God himself has
for us. It is true that this must be balanced by the recognition of our sin,
for it was this which made the suffering of Christ necessary; and we
will presently examine this further. Yet our basic worth remains.

When we fall into depression and despair, and deny our basic worth,
it is as though we think of ourselves as creatures of mud, on whom,
perhaps, a clean face can be painted, but who remain mud for all that. If
that were the case, no amount of washing would help; because for every
layer that was removed, more mud would remain. But we are not creatures of mud; we are God's dear children, sharing in his nature. To be
sure, we can get ourselves very muddy indeed, besmirched with all
manner of wickedness; but we can be cleansed by the blood of Christ
and reveal again the glory of his countenance. We are not fundamentally evil creatures who can sometimes be made better. We are fundamentally good creatures in spite of the fact that we sometimes do
wrong. Julian sees a striking image of this in one of her visions.

> And in this time I saw a body lying on the earth, which appeared oppressive
> and fearsome and without shape and form, as it were a devouring pit of
> stinking mud; and suddenly out of this body there sprang a most beautiful
> creature, a little child, fully shaped and formed, swift and lively and whiter
> than the lily, which quickly glided up to heaven.[28]

Julian identifies the pit with the wretchedness which we experience
while we are on earth, and the beautiful child with the cleanness and
purity of our souls. At first sight it might appear that she is making a
distinction here between our bodies, which are nasty, and our souls,
which are pure; but as we shall see later, that would be a misunder-
standing. The distinction is rather between our real self, our essence,
which is good and lovely, and the distortion and corruption of it by sin
and wretchedness, inflicted upon us by others as well as by our own

hand. Without in the least minimizing this wretchedness, Julian begins from the premise that the self which is created and loved and redeemed by God is of great beauty and worth in his sight.

Julian considers this positive self-conception to be of great import-ance in the development of our spirituality. She is very different from those in her time and our own who suppose that we must think of ourselves as worthless and despicable creatures, hardly worthy of con-tempt. Julian could never be accused of taking sin lightly, for in a sense the Long Text is the result of her continuous pondering and praying about it; yet sinfulness is not the first or the most important fact about us. That place is reserved for our goodness and beauty and nobility, created by God as the triumph of his whole creation.

This theme is of central importance to many spiritual writers. To cite only one example, Teresa of Avila in the sixteenth century uses strik-ingly similar language at the beginning of her account of human per-sonhood. She likens us to a beautiful castle of very clear crystal, in which are many mansions, and in the centre of which God himself dwells; and says, in typically forthright fashion.

> As he himself says, he created us in his image and likeness. Now if this is so – and it is – there is no point in our fatiguing ourselves by attempting to comprehend the beauty of this castle; for, though it is his creature, and there is therefore as much difference between it and God as between creature and Creator, the very fact that His Majesty says it is made in his image means that we can hardly form any conception of the soul's great dignity and beauty.[29]

Julian had also spoken of the soul as the citadel of God, his chosen dwelling place; indeed one might almost suppose that Teresa's *Interior Castle* grew out of a meditation on this chapter in Julian, though there is no external evidence to support this speculation. Julian says,

> I saw the soul as wide as if it were an endless citadel, and also as if it were a blessed kingdom, and from the state in which I saw it, I understood that it is a fine city. In the midst of that city sits our Lord Jesus, true God and true man, a handsome person and tall, highest bishop, most austere king, most honourable lord. And I saw him splendidly clad in honours.[30]

Both Teresa and Julian go on to develop the theme of God at the centre of the soul, drawing from it the consequence of the nobility of the soul. A king chooses the fairest part of his kingdom as the place for his dwelling, and then makes it even more honourable by making it his home, ruling the rest of his dominions from that centre. Just so, God rules heaven and earth from his dwelling place in the soul, where he has chosen to make his abode. This shows the wonder and beauty of the soul in the sight of God, for whom it is the greatest delight; and also the nobility conferred on it by being the home of God himself. It is there-fore a source of great joy as we begin to recognize our true worth.

139

This metaphor of the soul as a citadel in which God dwells is balanced in Julian by another metaphor which is in a sense its converse: not only does God make his home in the soul, but the soul also makes its home in God. This may at first seem like a contradiction; it is, on the contrary, Julian's rendition of the paradox of mutual indwelling that is found in the Fourth Gospel: 'Abide in me and I in you';[31] and occupies so important a place in Pauline writings with their emphasis on 'Christ in you' but also 'You in Christ'.[32] Julian juxtaposes the two ideas as she delights in the relationship with God:

> Greatly ought we to rejoice that God dwells in our soul; and more greatly ought we to rejoice that our soul dwells in God. Our soul is created to be God's dwelling place, and the dwelling of our soul is God, who is uncreated. It is a great understanding to see and know inwardly that God, who is our Creator, dwells in our soul, and it is a far greater understanding to see and know inwardly that our soul, which is created, dwells in God in substance, of which substance, through God, we are what we are.[33]

We have already seen that in all of creation God is in one sense the Being or substance of all things, for all created natures flow from him. This is pre-eminently true of the human soul: we are what we are through the substance of God.

Julian is here affirming the same position as that held by many another mystic, a position which has caused the spilling of much theological ink: the identity of the soul and God. Furthermore, Julian affirms this identity because of her understanding of the ontological basis of creation and human personhood. It is not an identity achieved only in intense mystical experience of union or merging with the divine, but is a fact of our personhood at all times. This is therefore not reducible to a psychological unity subjectively experienced. Indeed, quite the opposite is the case: this identity is a fact of our creation, the fact of our nature, like all created natures, flowing forth from God and thus being of his substance whether we experience this to be so or not. For Julian, this is a simple fact of our being; to recognize it is very helpful to us, because it brings home to us how worthwhile we are, but it is true whether we recognize it or not.

Like other mystics, she immediately qualifies this to retain the Creator–creature distinction.

> And I saw no difference between God and our substance, but, as it were, all God; and still my understanding accepted that our substance is in God, that is to say that God is God, and our substance is a creature in God.[34]

The idea is parallel to that of Eckhart, with his elaborate metaphor of a mirror reflecting the sun so brightly that in one sense the mirror *is* the sun, yet without losing its ontological distinction;[35] or John of the Cross who speaks of a glowing log as a picture of a soul so aflame with the love of God that, although in one sense the log and the fire are two different things, they cannot be divided.[36] There are those, like Eckhart's judges, who would turn this into a Western form of absorption mysticism; but this would be to misunderstand the metaphors and to fly in the face of their explicit statements to the contrary.[37]

Furthermore, at least in the case of Julian, this insistence on the fact that in one sense there is no difference between the soul and God, while in another sense retaining the Creator–creature distinction, need not be taken as the stammerings of intense experience on the border of inarticulateness. Indeed, Julian writes of this in the same careful but unself-conscious way that she uses for the rest of her book, and does not complain of any inadequacy of language. There is therefore no warrant for seeing her discussion as an example of the alleged ineffability of mystical experience.[38]

The considerations of the previous chapter have in fact provided the framework within which this apparent paradox can be understood. We saw there that in one sense God is All, he is Being Itself, and nothing could exist without his continuous preservation of it. Yet in order for beings to exist in their own right, God restricts himself, 'letting be the beings'. This is taken farthest in the creation of humankind. Although in the ultimate sense we are not of some substance alien to God, 'but, as it were, all God', in order for us to be individuals God imposes self-restraints on his omnipotence so that we are allowed independence and freedom. This independence is of course not absolute: we have no choice at all about a great many fundamental features of ourselves. We did not choose to be born, and had no say in what sort of creatures human beings should be. Nevertheless we have, within boundaries, freedom of thought and behaviour; and in creating this to be so God made us individuals in our own right, creatures whose substance is in God and yet who, in their created nature, are to that extent distinct from God.

Within this framework we can now make sense of the quotation with which this discussion began. There is 'no difference between God and our substance, but, as it were, all God'; and yet God in creating us gave us, though we are of his substance, freedom of intellect and will and the ability to express that freedom. In that sense, therefore, 'God is God, and our substance is a creature in God.'

Because of this, it should come as no surprise when Julian says that human persons have the same attributes as God himself; after all, we participate in the divine substance by which we are what we are.

> For God is endless supreme truth, endless supreme wisdom, endless supreme love uncreated; and a man's soul is a creature in God which has the

same properties created. And always it does what it was created for; it sees God and it contemplates God and it loves God.[39]

Now, however, it seems that Julian's 'kyndly reson' has led her down a path of its own. Surely it is far from obvious, whatever Julian's logic may say, that we have the attributes of God: which of us would lay claim to endless truth, wisdom, and love?

We might just have managed to swallow this if Julian had said that in human nature this is potential, and gradually realized by the grace of God, perhaps to reach fulness of fruition in heaven. It is after all true that we never come to the end of knowing and loving, as though we could imagine that we might reach a point after which we will have attained the limit of our capacity to know or to love. That *capacity* is indeed endless. Yet even if we grant this, it is entirely contrary to our experience to suppose that, even given this understanding of the purpose of our creation, we always fulfil that purpose. Time after time we are precisely *not* doing that for which we were created; we are constantly failing in our love for God and for one another, failing in our prayer and contemplation, falling short in every way of the glory of God. And Julian, of all people, is well aware of this. What, then, could she possibly mean?

A first step in interpreting her meaning is to consider the distinction she draws between substance and sensuality. She says,

> We are double by God's creating, that is to say substantial and sensual. Our substance is the higher part, which we have in our Father, God almighty; and the second person of the Trinity is our Mother in nature in our substantial creation, in whom we are founded and rooted, and he is our Mother of mercy in taking our sensuality.[40]

Another way of putting this is that our substance is our created nature that flows out from God and is constitutive of the essence of our humanity as rooted in God; whereas our sensuality is that which constitutes our God-given independence. Sensuality as Julian is using the term is not quite what we might at first think. It does not mean 'sensuous', and does not refer exclusively to the physical senses, let alone to sexuality, though all of that would be included. It includes, rather, all of our psychology and physicality as individual human beings: our capacities for perception in sight, hearing, touch, and so on, our whole sensory consciousness, and our capacity for action. In other words, sensuality refers to our existence as psychosomatic beings in a physical world. In terms of the discussion of the previous section, our substance is the substance of Being Itself; our sensuality individuates us, making each of us one among many beings.

This distinction between substance and sensuality must not be confused with a dualism between soul and body, as though substance is soul and sensuality body. To the extent that Julian does retain a body-soul dichotomy in her understanding of personhood, both substance and sensuality belong to the soul; though without embodiment there could be no sensuality. We are made sensual, she says, 'when our soul is breathed into our body';[41] but the sensuality consists of the union of the two, not of either soul or body on its own.[42] Julian was more accustomed than we are to thinking of our sensory abilities as involving both soul and body. For example, when we think of vision, we are preoccupied with the physical apparatus of the eye and the way in which it responds to the varied stimuli of light and colour. But without minimizing the marvellous intricacy of the physical organism, we must recognize that this is not the whole story. In order for vision to occur, there must be not only a functioning eye and physical light; there must also be consciousness. We can perhaps imagine a highly skilled medical team constructing an exact working replica of human visual apparatus, so exact that it could be used for eye transplants to eliminate blindness. Yet until such an artificial eye is actually connected to human consciousness – until the transplant occurs – this visual apparatus can see nothing at all. We can only speak of vision taking place when there is someone – some conscious being – actually seeing, and being aware. This illustrates the twofold nature of our sensuality. The functioning physical apparatus is indispensable: a person whose eyes have been gouged out is blind. Yet by itself this physical visual equipment does not produce vision, even if it is in perfect working order: an unconscious person sees nothing, even though he or she may have perfectly good eyes and have them wide open.

The same, of course, applies to all our senses. In order for sensory perception to occur, it is necessary that the appropriate parts of our body are functioning, but it is also necessary for us to be conscious. It is this union of consciousness with embodiment that Julian calls sensuality. A human body without consciousness would not be sensual, no matter how perfect the body might be. On the other hand, neither would a disembodied spirit be sensual. This is why Julian says that all three persons of the Trinity share our substance, but only the Son, who became incarnate, shares our sensuality:

> And our substance is in our Father, God almighty, and our substance is in our Mother, God all wisdom, and our substance is in the Lord God, the Holy Spirit, all goodness, for our substance is whole in each person of the Trinity, who is one God. And our sensuality is only in the second person, Christ Jesus, in whom is the Father and the Holy Spirit ...[43]

A consequence of the fact that sensuality requires both consciousness and the physical organism is that our bodies are not accidental to us, as though our real self is a soul which has somehow been attached to a physical body from which we will escape at death. Our real self, according to Julian, is precisely the *combination* of consciousness and the physical in sensuality, integrated with our substance, the ground of our being which is Being Itself. Julian meditates on the biblical account of the creation of human beings:

> And so I understood that man's soul is made of nothing, that is to say that it is made of nothing that is made, in this way: When God was to make man's body, he took the slime of the earth, which is matter mixed and gathered from all bodily things, and of that he made man's body. But to the making of man's soul he would accept nothing at all, but made it. And so is created nature rightfully united to the maker, who is substantial uncreated nature, that is God.[44]

The matter of which our physical bodies are composed is itself created by God, and flows from his immanent goodness; but it is, as it were, at one further remove than our soul, which God makes 'of nothing that is made'. In other words, he makes it from his own uncreated substance, and in the union of this with our physical bodies, makes us sensual.

This in turn means, however, that the body cannot be looked upon as evil or blamed for sin and wickedness. The body, like all things created by God, flows from his goodness. Julian firmly rejects the idea derived from a one-sided reading of Plato that the body is independent recalcitrant matter, always tending to evil, while the soul is the divine principle tending toward good. The body itself is good; and whatever the answer to the problem of evil and sin, it does not, for Julian, lie in body-soul dualism. Julian illustrates her positive evaluation of the body in rather unusual ways, contemplating, for instance, how the love and care which God has for us extends to the humblest of our physical functions:

> A man walks upright, and the food in his body is shut in as if in a well-made purse. When the time of his necessity comes, the purse is opened and then shut again, in most seemly fashion ... For he [God] does not despise what he has made, nor does he disdain to serve us in the simplest natural functions of our body, for love of the soul which he created in his own likeness. For as the body is clad in the cloth, and the flesh in the skin, and the bones in the flesh, and the heart in the trunk, so are we, *soul and body*, clad and enclosed in the goodness of God.[45]

We are hardly accustomed to finding this sort of illustration in theological treatises; but for Julian, this straightforward reflection on our physicality is all of a piece with her meditation on the showings of Christ who took our flesh upon himself in its lowliness as well as its dignity. When once the doctrine of the incarnation is taken fully seriously, the physicality of our nature can no longer be despised.

For him [Christ] was this fair nature prepared for the honour and nobility of man's creation, and for the joy and bliss of his salvation, just as he saw, knew, and recognized from without beginning.[46]

Julian saw more clearly than many a theologian influenced by the anti-physical strand of Neoplatonic thought that if Christ took our physical nature upon himself, he thereby proclaimed it to be of dignity and worth. This in turn has a profound effect on her understanding of asceticism and spiritual development, as we shall see below.

This brings us back, however, to the passage already quoted about the wretched body lying in the pit of stinking mud, out of which the beautiful lily-white child escapes to heaven. Julian explicitly identifies the foul pit with the body, and the beautiful child with the soul, when she says,

The pit which was the body signifies the great wretchedness of our mortal flesh; and the smallness of the child signifies the cleanness and purity of our soul. And I thought: In this body there remains none of the child's beauty, and in this child there remains none of the body's foulness.[47]

At first sight, this quotation seems to undermine the positive evaluation of the body which Julian otherwise maintains: it seems that we have here after all a dualism of body and soul, in which the soul is good and the body loathsome.

The context, however, makes clear that this is not so. The passage occurs in an account of how Julian in her illness longs to die and thereby be released from all her pain. She is assured by the Lord that this will happen in his own good time, and that when it does, the pain will be altogether a thing of the past, and she will be filled with joy and bliss. Given this context, and the wider context of the book as a whole and the society in which it was written, it is not necessary to suppose that Julian here thought of the body in itself as evil 'stinking mud'; she is rather thinking specifically of the body – her own, in the first instance – when it is wracked with dreadful pain and illness and becomes loathsome to all around, and even to the sufferer. It is noteworthy that it is not the flesh as such which is signified by the stinking pit, but the *wretchedness* of the flesh. The foulness and wretchedness of which she speaks is not a moral description but a physical one, the miserable state to which we can be reduced by certain forms of disease. And when death occurs, and all that remains is the corpse, it is very soon a putrid, unclean thing.

In modern times we are largely insulated from this unpleasantness. People suffering putrefying illnesses are hospitalized, and medical methods and modern sanitation do much to neutralize or at least camouflage the worst odours and protect us from the most distressing sights. But in days before antiseptics, and with poor sanitary arrangements, there must have been many instances of wounds which became infected and putrid, the sight and stench of which we can hardly imagine. And whereas today death is so sanitized and cosmeticized that we are scarcely aware of the decomposition of the corpse, in those times there was, at least for the common people, no escaping the fact of the foulness of a corpse. Julian had lived through the successive waves of the Black Death, and could therefore have been no stranger to the most odious aspects of disease and the disposal of its victims. And she herself at the time of the vision was ill to the point of death. Indeed it has been suggested that it was her own disease which produced the 'foul stink' which accompanied her nightmare of the devil and which persisted even after the nightmare was gone.[48]

However that may be, it is certain that Julian, like almost anyone in her society, would have had more first-hand knowledge of the un-pleasant physical aspects of disease and death than most of us need ever encounter. It is no wonder that she sees a disease-ridden human body as a loathsome thing; nor that in her own severe pain she longs for release. But it would be a mistake to conclude from this that she considered the body itself, in its normal healthy condition, to be a vile or evil thing. Physicality is not in itself foul, let alone morally evil, for it is the creation of God and flows from his essential good-ness. It is diseased and decomposing flesh, not flesh in itself, that becomes offensive. Of course this raises yet again, in a slightly different form, the problem of evil: how can a good God permit his good creation to endure such suffering that it turns into a rotting, stinking thing? This must be considered in the next chapter.

Many of Julian's themes regarding personhood are directly related to her understanding of the incarnation. By reference to Christ, she shows more clearly what she means by the importance of the body and its creation, the necessity of the body for sensuality, the sub-stance-sensuality distinction, and the difference between this and a soul-body distinction. Regarding substance and sensuality, she says,

> And these two parts were in Christ, the higher and the lower, which are only one soul. The higher part was always at peace with God in full joy and bliss. The lower part, which is sensuality, suffered for the salvation of mankind.[49]

Now, it would clearly be a mistake to suppose that in the case of Christ, the substance or 'higher part' which was united with God was the soul and did not suffer when his body suffered: Christ in his passion suffered mental and spiritual torment as well as physical. Julian in fact explicitly says that the 'two parts', substance and sensuality, are 'only one *soul*' – neither of them are the body.

146

She makes her meaning clearer by referring back to the eighth revelation in which it was suggested to her that she raise her eyes from the suffering of Christ on the cross and look up instead to heaven. She refused this, as we noted. Looking back to this, she says that the reason for her refusal, and for her insistence on Jesus as heaven, was that she saw, hidden in the agony of the crucified one, 'a perception and a secret inward vision of the higher part', that is, the substance. This was then revealed to her in a

> mighty contemplative vision of the inward life, which inward life is that high substance, that precious soul which is endlessly rejoicing in the divinity.[50]

Since this was the case, there was nothing to be gained by looking away from Jesus; there is no way of coming to the divinity of Christ except through his suffering humanity. To yield to the temptation to look up to heaven to the Father would not in fact reach to union with God. Instead, by attempting to bypass the condition of humanness, both the humanity and the divinity would be lost.

The substance or inward life of Christ which she perceives is therefore not Jesus' soul as contrasted with his suffering body, but rather the divinity of Christ which she perceives hidden in his humanity. Though Christ suffered in the fulness of his humanity, body and soul, his divinity or 'higher part' was never alienated from God: indeed, according to Christian tradition, it *was* God, in continual union with the Father and the Holy Spirit. This is not to say that Jesus was conscious of it: to insist that he was would be to slip back into reducing Jesus' substance to his subjective psychology. Yet the dimension of his essential selfhood, the deepest ground of the soul, is the divine substance, continually united with God even while also being united with his human sensuality, the two parts together being 'only one soul'.

Now this, according to Julian, is also true of ourselves, with the important qualification that for Jesus it was true because he was the *begotten* Son, whereas for us it is true because we are *created* in the image of God. Since we are created in his image, the substance-sensuality distinction which is true of Christ is also true of us. Our essential selfhood, our substance, is eternally united with God from whom it flows forth, though we are certainly not always aware of it, and can never be fully aware of it in this life. Our sensuality, our ordinary physical and psychological life, is something else, and is very far from being always united with God. In each of us, as in Christ, there is what Julian has here called the higher, inner self and the lower self. As in Christ, this is not a distinction between soul and body, let alone a distinction between good and evil, but the distinction between substance, always united with God, and sensuality, which can have a

147

different focus. When our sensuality is not focused on God as the centre of our lives, then we are broken, fragmented because our higher self and our lower self are out of tune with one another. As Julian presents it, the task of spirituality, made possible by the incarnation in which Christ fully united sensuality and substance, is to follow him and find in him the reunification of our own sensuality with our substance and become whole again in God.

The idea that our essential self is always united to God, no matter how we feel or what we are conscious of or even how sinfully we are behaving is not an easy one to grasp. Yet Julian's ideas here have a long history in Christian theology and spirituality in their connection to the concept of the image of God. The idea of being created in God's image occurs from the first chapter of the Bible onwards, and became an important theme in Christian thought regarding the nature of personhood. It signifies an essential relatedness to God, which is central to our humanity. Although this relatedness can be distorted, clouded over by sin, it can never, so long as we are human, be eradicated utterly, for it is ultimately constitutive of humanness. Putting it in 'image' language, the image of God in ourselves may be bent and twisted and nearly unrecognizable, but it can never be destroyed without simultaneously annihilating ourselves as selves. This is what Julian means by substance: it is that essential ground of our being which constitutes our selfhood, flowing from Being Itself, and, no matter what we do, it is always still what it is.

Augustine, in that famous quotation with which we began this chapter, says the same thing when he recognizes that God has made us for himself, and as long as we are human, we will be restless and divided against ourselves unless we find integration and rest in God. This gives rise to the same paradox for Augustine as it does for Julian, when he recognizes his alienation from God and his need to call upon him, and yet at the same time the central truth of his existence in God.

> How shall I call upon my God, my God and my Lord, since in truth, when I call upon him, I call him into myself? ... O Lord my God, is there anything in me that can contain you? In truth, can heaven and earth, which you have made and in which you have made me, contain you? Or because without you whatever is would not be, does it hold that whatever exists contains you? ... I would not be, I would in no wise be, unless you were in me. Or rather, I would not be unless I were in you, 'from whom, by whom, and in whom are all things' ... To what place do I call you, since I am in you?[51]

We are made with an orientation to God in our inmost self, and are at odds with ourselves until this orientation is the focus of our whole life, integrating our sensuality with our substance, which is always united with God.

This, of course, is not to deny our sinfulness; indeed it is to emphasize it. In our consciousness and behaviour we are very far from union with God: the image of God, though not destroyed, is marred and layered over with so many patterns of thought and action that we may lose touch with it altogether. The traditional language for this uses terms like 'original sin' and 'fall': our sensuality is focused away from God and fragmented from our substance, and we are divided against ourselves. Yet while Julian fully recognizes this, she is emphatic that this does not destroy the union of our essential substance with God: the image of God is the inalienable essence of what it is to be human. Thus we have to say very different things about our substance and our sensuality in terms of our relationship to God:

> As regards our substance, he made us noble and so rich that always we achieve his will and his glory ... For truly I saw that we are that which he loves, and that we do what is pleasing to him, constantly, without any stinting ... And so in our substance we are full and in our sensuality we are lacking ...[52]

Just as Julian sees the true Church as pure and spotless in the sight of God, though she was well aware that the empirical Church of her time was corrupt and impure, so also she sees that our substance is hidden with Christ in God, while our sensuality is in need of healing and purifying. The question is what to do about it. We will explore this question, first in relation to Julian's teaching of asceticism, then in terms of the problems of evil and suffering, and finally in considering her teaching on the development of wholeness. This will enable us to understand her anthropology more fully, and also to see how profoundly it stands in reciprocity to her spirituality.

Asceticism

The interlocking nature of Julian's theology, in which the understanding of each doctrine presupposes and completes the others and all are focused in the passion of the incarnate Christ, becomes more and more involved, as also does the reciprocity between Julian's experience and her reflection within this theological framework. This makes for difficulty in exposition; it is impossible to do justice to Julian's thought by treating it as a linear sequence, yet that is how a book must be written. In particular, Julian's account of the incarnation as the response to the problem of evil, which she develops in the parable of the lord and the servant is, I believe, the crux of the whole book and the key to understanding it; yet it cannot itself be understood without a grasp of the surrounding doctrines of the Trinity, creation, and human nature. Nowhere is the incarnation more fully presupposed than in Julian's teaching on asceticism, because her asceticism is based on her teaching about the reunion of substance and sensuality. Therefore as we explore this in this chapter, it is well to keep in mind that its foundation in the parable of the lord and the servant will be more fully explored in the final section of Chapter Nine.

Very few in Western society in our time would deny that we are individually and collectively fragmented. That is obvious enough from the mess and muddle of our own lives and of the society around us. Julian would say that the root of all this is that we are quite literally heart-broken. Our heart, our being, is split in two by the division between our substance and our sensuality. Human wholeness can never be achieved until this brokenness is healed. Our substance is always united to God; but our sensuality all too easily focuses on other things, most obviously on ourselves. We may call this sin, or brokenness, or soul-sickness, or alienation; but whatever term we use, there is this fracture at the centre of our personhood, the deep wound which divides us from ourselves and makes us hurting and hurtful people, spreading pain like an infectious disease in which everyone contaminates everyone else.

Not everyone will find Julian's diagnosis easy to accept. That we are alienated from ourselves and from one another is obvious enough; but it is less easy to recognize that the root of this is alienation from God. Yet as we have seen, for Julian these two are one. It is important to notice that our brokenness is not a punishment which *God* inflicts on us because of our sin. Rather, turning from God *is* turning from our deepest self. Because our substance is essentially united with God whether we know it or not, and because that is constitutive of our being human at all, the denial of God in our lives actually is the denial of our deepest reality. Julian goes so far as to say that a person who persists in this denial ultimately annihilates himself or herself:

> Sin is neither death nor delight, but when a soul deliberately chooses sin, which is pain, to be his god, in the end he is nothing at all.[53]

Julian uses the concept of the godly will in connection with her teaching that our substance is united to God:

> In this revelation I saw and understood very surely that in each soul which will be saved there is a godly will which never assented to sin nor ever will, which will is so good that it can never will evil, but always constantly it wills good and it does good in the sight of God.[54]

Now it is quite clear from the rest of her book that Julian is not denying that we do wrong on purpose, with the deliberate consent of the will. She is far too realistic to suppose otherwise. Nor, of course, is she thinking of the two wills as two parts or pieces of us, the way we have two eyes or two hands.

The account of the godly will is rather a consequence of the distinction between our substance and our sensuality. Our substantial self, united with God, is godly; but our sensuality, as long as it is focused away from God, cannot get anything right.

> Just as there is an animal will in the lower part which cannot will any good, so there is a godly will in the higher part, which will is so good that it cannot ever will any evil, but always good.[55]

The reference to the animal will here needs to be clarified and distinguished from various ideas with which it might be confused. In the first place, as is clear from the previous discussion, it must not be confused with physicality as such. The body itself is not what makes us go wrong. The body goes wrong when the mind and will are focused on it, rather than on God. Self-centred preoccupation, whether physical or psychological, is what is being referred to here as animal will, because this focus is inadequate for us as human beings made in the image of God. There is nothing wrong with animal will as such. It would be entirely appropriate for Julian's cat to be concerned only with its food and warmth and comfort and the mice and rats which it might catch. A cat is not immoral because it takes thought only for itself: that is its nature. But if human beings take thought only for ourselves, that is not our nature, and by concentrating on the animal will, we thereby sell ourselves short and divide ourselves against our higher nature.

This also makes it clear that the animal will is not to be equated with sensuality. The substance, because it is the outflowing of the immanent goodness of God, must have a godly will; it would not be itself if it did not. But the converse is not the case. Sensuality can have an animal will, but it need not. It can be wholly preoccupied with itself, and thereby be at odds with the substance, or it can, by repentance, training, and the grace of God, come to focus on God and thereby be reintegrated with the substance and bring new wholeness to the person.

This notion of a godly will at the centre of our being is neither so paradoxical nor so far from our experience as it might at first seem to a modern reader. There is in each of us at some level a desire to be good. No matter how badly we behave, and how miserable a mess we get ourselves into, and although we recognize, often, that it is at least in part by our own hand that we are in this wretched state, we never intended things to be like this. I do not mean just that we are content to have behaved badly and only wish that we had been able to get away with it, though of course we do sometimes feel that way too. But at a more fundamental level, we do not mean to be bad. We do bad things, and we do them on purpose, but part of us wishes we didn't. We want to be good, and we wish we could say that we were good.[56]

This is well illustrated by the immediate impulse to self-justification when we are (rightly or wrongly) accused of something. We are not content to say, 'Yes, I did wrong, and I don't mind that I did.' There is always some reason or excuse for what we did, so that we persuade others and ourselves that we were not wrong after all: the action was somehow justifiable. If, on the other hand, we do admit that we did wrong, we do not feel satisfied but sorry. We mind about being bad; we want to be good. Human beings, for all our capacity for deliberate wickedness, are fundamentally good and want to be good: to use again the illustration of the previous section, we are not mud figures on which clean faces can be painted, but beautiful creatures who get ourselves into a mess, but are able to be cleansed. Once we recognize this, we have come a fair way to understanding what Julian means by the godly will, and the way that our selfish will is at variance with this fundamental goodness of our being.

The implication of this is that there is hope for people. If we were fundamentally bad, if that were the central fact about us, then no remedy would be possible, because the more unified and integrated we became, the worse we would get. Julian's view is just the opposite. The more we truly know ourselves and become whole, the better we will be. Because we are good and of worth, there is hope; if we were evil, we would have to be destroyed in order to make the world good. Since, however, we are good, a good world comes about not by destroying us but by bringing us to our true and integrated selfhood. This is why Julian says,

> We ought to have three kinds of knowledge. The first is that we know our Lord God. The second is that we know ourselves, what we are through him in nature and in grace. The third is that we know humbly that our self is opposed to our sin and our wickedness.[57]

The opposition of our true self to our sin and wickedness is the basis for refocusing our sensuality from its inadequate orientation to be integrated with our substance in union with God.

This is the purpose of asceticism. Asceticism is not a hatred or indifference for created things; this would be quite incompatible with Julian's teaching that all things flow from God's goodness and are grounded in him. But because of the relative independence which we have in order to be individuals at all, and because of the loss of focus of our sensuality upon God, it is possible for us to be totally oriented to things – things in nature, artefacts, other people, or even ourselves – without reference to God. To be focused on them in that way is to misunderstand them too, of course, for just as it divides us from our own roots, so it ignores their roots in God. Thus alienation multiplies itself.

> And I saw very certainly that we must necessarily be in longing and in penance until the time when we are led so deeply into God that we verily and truly know our own soul ...[58]

We long for God in our innermost being, even when our lives are so fragmented and mis-focused that we do not recognize the longing for what it is. Penance is literally repentance, which means 'turning around': penance is the continuous practice of turning back to God as the central orientation of our lives.

It is this, rather than any devaluation of the world, which lies behind Julian's teaching on asceticism. Only God himself can satisfy human longing; anything else, even the most valuable, cannot take his place.

> For the natural desire of our soul is so great and so immeasurable that if all the nobility which God ever created in heaven and on earth were given to us for our joy and comfort, if we did not see his own fair blessed face, still we should never cease to mourn and weep in spirit, because, that is, of our painful longing, until we might see our Creator's fair blessed face.[59]

Julian is not talking here only about herself and a few other specially devout Christians who want union with God more than anything else; still less is she talking about a desire for special ecstasies or visions. Her claim is that this deep longing for God is true, if unrecognized, in all of us, and that the reason for our mad quest for more and more things, activities, and power, and our dissatisfaction when we get them, is that we are made so that we literally cannot be satisfied with anything less than God. She would have agreed with Traherne's observation that human discontent is not the problem; the real problem is that we persuade ourselves that we will be contented much too easily, with the wrong things, and consequently do not own up to the restlessness which is our common inheritance until we find our rest in God.

This explains how it is that Julian moves directly from the hazel-nut passage, in which she recognizes the goodness and beauty of creation, to what seems to be world-renunciation.

> I know well that heaven and earth and all creation are great, generous and beautiful and good. But the reason why it seemed to my eyes so little was because I saw it in the presence of him who is the Creator. To any soul who sees the Creator of all things, all that is created seems very little.[60]

Creation could be compared to a letter from a friend: it is special and valued, and brings the friend to mind. Yet it is not itself the friend, and in a way makes the friend's absence more poignant than before. Now, should the friend arrive while we are still treasuring the letter, it would be ridiculous to have nothing to do with him or her because we are absorbed in the letter. Similarly, created things, beautiful and good as they are, are 'very little' compared with their Creator, so that it is perverse to cling to any of them as a substitute for God. No matter how worthwhile or good the thing may be, it can never give us the spiritual fulfilment and rest which can be found only in God. The comparison with the letter must be modified, for as we have seen, in Julian's view God is immanent in creation far beyond the way that a person is immanent in what he or she writes; creation is not detachable from God. But this only makes it all the more mistaken to prefer some created thing to God, valuing it for its own sake rather than for the sake of God's purpose in and through it.[61]

This is as true of spiritual consolations as it is of physical ones. It is relatively easy to see that focusing our attention on acquiring money or prestige is a distortion of our true nature and will have a fragmenting effect; it is more difficult to recognize that a quest for pleasant spiritual experiences can be just as harmful. Julian reminds us that anything, even the comforts of prayer and religious experience, can become a trap if they are preferred to God himself as he is revealed in the cross of Christ. We recall again the instance where Julian is offered release from her pain by looking away from the dying Christ, and steadfastly refuses to do so, thus being taught 'to choose Jesus for my heaven'.[62] Spiritual things like consolation and delight, good as they are, are still created things, and even they are not to be preferred to their Creator, who is definitively revealed in the passion of Christ.

It is instructive to compare Julian's attitude to created things with that of her contemporary, the author of *The Cloud of Unknowing*. While both of them agree on the centrality of God himself, and on the necessity of being focused on him rather than fixated on created things, the *Cloud* author has a rather different stress on the negative effects of attention to created things for the purpose of contemplative prayer. All things, he says, are to be trampled down under a 'cloud of forgetting' and are not to be allowed to take up room in the mind of the solitary at prayer.

> Try to destroy all understanding and awareness of anything under God and tread everything down deep under the cloud of forgetting. Understand that in this exercise you are to forget all other creatures besides yourself, or their deeds or yours; and in this exercise, you must also forget yourself and your own activities, as well as all creatures and their activities, because of God.[63]

The author of *The Cloud* finds it necessary to insist in detail on the dangers of all created things, as we saw when we considered the contrast of his views with those of Julian on the use of intermediaries in prayer. These things are the source of endless distractions in contemplative prayer. This applies even to 'our Lady or the saints or angels in heaven',[64] which, though good in themselves, must likewise be trodden underfoot in this cloud of forgetting so that the soul may reach out to God alone. The author of *The Cloud* does recognize that God is the Creator of all these things, and as such they cannot in themselves be evil, but he considers them injurious in their distracting influence on the person at prayer.

In some ways Julian agrees. As we have seen, she too insists that in comparison with the Creator, all that he has created is very little indeed, and can provide no resting-place for human longings. She also agrees that in our prayer, the use of many intermediaries may be because of our ignorance of God's courteous willingness for us to approach him directly. God is not an aloof medieval lord whose favour we can hope to gain only if we seek it through the mediation of his friends.

> Then I saw truly that it is more honour to God and more true delight if we faithfully pray to him for his goodness, and adhere to this by grace, with true understanding and steadfast belief, than if we employed all the intermediaries of which a heart may think.[65]

Yet her difference in emphasis from the author of *The Cloud* is not superficial. Her whole perspective finds its focus in the generous love of God, by which he is immanent in all things. It is in the light of that immanent love that all things are to be appreciated. Because of this, it is possible for Julian to be much less suspicious of created things, and to feel less need to emphasize their dangers and distractions. It is only when they are split off, in our attitude, from their rootedness in God that they turn our attention away from him; and that is not their fault but our own. Their natural function is to point toward God, not away from him.

The balance Julian strikes here is the balance found by Augustine, who also emphasized the immanence of God while yet recognizing that God is not reducible to all created things, but that they point toward him. He says,

> I had already searched for him by means of the body, searching from earth to sky, as far as I could direct the beams of my eyes as messengers ... [My soul] sat in judgment weighing the replies of heaven and earth and all things within them when they said: 'We are not God', and when they said: 'He made us' ... I asked the whole mass of the world about my God, and it answered me: 'I am not he, but he made me.'[66]

Thus also Julian says that intermediaries, the angels and saints, the holy cross, our Lady, and all others are given to us to help us, not to hinder or distract us; and it is the goodness of God which comes to us through them. Of course it would be wrong for us to suppose that it was their own goodness rather than God's which helps us, or that he is wrathful and they placate him on our behalf; nevertheless Julian never talks about trampling them underfoot even for purposes of contemplative prayer.

> For the intermediaries which the goodness of God has ordained to help us are very lovely and many ... Therefore it pleases him that we seek him and honour him through intermediaries, understanding and knowing that he is the goodness of everything.[67]

Although the author of *The Cloud* does not deny this, his stress is more pessimistic, warning against the dangers of things and intermediaries more than delighting, as Julian does, in their goodness and beauty from the generous hand of God.

Nevertheless, Julian, like the author of *The Cloud* and the whole tradition of Christian spirituality, recognized our propensity to be disorientated from God, and therefore saw the need to take whatever measures necessary to heal the fracture within us, bringing our external self, our sensuality, into line with our true self or substance in union with God. She was, after all, an anchoress, and had chosen a life of solitude and silence, and, we may assume, the regular monastic vows of poverty, chastity and obedience. Yet here also, both in what she says and in what she does not say, her positive evaluation of created things and especially of human nature is in evidence. Christ became incarnate, took upon himself our sensuality, not to destroy it or to rid us of it but to reintegrate our sensuality with our substance. This, therefore, is the aim of the anchoritic life, as it is of any Christian life: not to suppress our personhood, but to bring it to its full potential in wholeness of being.

> For until the time that it is in its full powers, we cannot be all holy; and that is when our sensuality by the power of Christ's Passion can be brought up into the substance, with all the profits of our tribulation which our Lord will make us obtain through mercy and grace.[68]

The whole emphasis is on developing calmly and joyfully, finding the inner liberty that allows one to be wholly attentive to God and to others, rather than on a cramping of talent or of happiness. It would be hard to find anyone who took more delight in God's world or who developed her talents more fully than Julian did, in spite of – or perhaps because of – the fact that she was an anchoress. Because she had given herself wholly to God, she was able to take wholesome delight in the works of God and give whole-hearted attention to those who came to her.

This is not to minimize her renunciation; it is rather to see the point of it. Poverty is not, for Julian, an end in itself, but is rather a means of freeing herself from false attachments to created things so that she is free to love them properly in the liberating love of God. For she would have agreed with Walter Hilton in his book written for an anchoress when he reminds her that physical enclosure does not produce holiness all by itself, as though one could be fully turned to God 'as easily as you can have your body enclosed in a religious house'.[69] Physical enclosure is only a means of coming to be completely attentive and available to God. And although this singleness of heart is the aim of all Christians, the means by which it should be pursued will vary: not everyone should take up the anchoritic life. It is noteworthy that Julian, though her avowed aim in writing her book is to foster the deepening of love for God in her fellow-Christians, never mentions poverty let alone the anchoritic life. For herself these were clearly important means to that end, but she does not so much as hint that others should follow her in them.

Even more striking is the fact that Julian never mentions chastity. At least by the time she became an anchoress, if not before, she had herself doubtless taken the vow; and it may well be that she took it for granted as a necessary condition for her own life of prayer. Yet in her repeated affirmations that she is writing for all her fellow-Christians she does not once suggest that chastity is an important element in the development of deepening moral and spiritual integrity in response to God. It is simply not discussed. When this is taken together with her deep appreciation of God's creative love in our other physical functions, and in the context of a society which would be inclined to link celibacy with godliness, her silence is eloquent.

Julian's balanced and wholesome view of the physical body is very different from that of her younger contemporary, Margery Kempe, whose attitude reflects a prevalent medieval view of the 'stains of marriage' as preventing whole-hearted love for God.[70] Margery expended much emotional energy bewailing her lost virginity and pestering her husband into an unwilling vow of sexual abstinence; and seems to imply that as a token of his special love for her the Lord restored her to her virginal state, though she had borne thirteen children.[71] It is true that Margery Kempe was a psychologically tumultuous woman and would not be altogether representative of ordinary Christian piety of her time. However, though she was an extreme case, she did reflect the wide-spread feeling that sexual enjoyment even within marriage was not fully compatible with holiness of life.[72] Julian, by contrast, concentrates all her energy into turning toward Christ. Whenever one turns toward something, one necessarily simultaneously turns away from something else; but what this is will differ for different people, depending on what it is that has been the distraction from total love for God. For Julian, the life in which she could best develop in love for God presumably meant the renunciation of sexual activity, but she does not waste time discussing it. All her attention is taken up in the delight in the one to whom she has turned, Christ himself.

Julian's attitude toward sexuality is also apparent in the light of her appreciative discussion of the motherhood of God. In seeing Jesus as Mother as well as Father, she reveals that for her, reflection on human sexuality and parental relations has become a meditation on the nature of God and provides a natural way to think of him. Furthermore, Julian herself had become a highly unconventional woman, even by modern standards, not to mention fourteenth-century ones, in her acquisition of the solid theological background and acute literary skills which enabled her to communicate the love of God which she experienced. Julian is in no sense a feminist for its own sake; all her efforts towards liberation for herself and others were in terms of response to the liberating love of God and her own efforts to communicate it. Yet the fact that she was a woman was not allowed to prevent her from studying and writing, and her writing does not concern itself with any such sexual preoccupations as beset poor Margery Kempe.[73]

Julian's view of the created nature of human personhood is, as we saw, not restricted to physicality; the soul, too, is created by divine love. Indeed the soul has been created with such great nobility and dignity that God simply could not have done it any better.[74] Julian was by no means the first to speak of the nobility of the soul and of the delight which God takes in it. The theme had been a prominent one throughout the centuries in relation to the notion of the image of God.[75] Of special interest is the parallel between Julian's thinking and that of Bernard of Clairvaux on the one hand, and Meister Eckhart on the other. Bernard, in his enormously influential book, *On the Love of God*, had centred an argument for loving God in the *dignitas* of the human being.

> When man fashioned in honour does not perceive the honour that is his, he is, by reason of such ignorance justly likened to the beasts of the field that share his present corruption and mortality. It happens, therefore, that a creature distinguished by the gift of reason, through not knowing itself begins to be herded with the droves of unthinking beasts ... and becomes one with the rest of visible creatures because he thinks that he has received nothing beyond the rest of them. And so we must be especially on our guard against this ignorance by which, perchance, we think of ourselves as being less than we really are.[76]

The equal and opposite error, of course, is to suppose that this *dignitas* is of our own making, rather than a gift of God and a reflection of his glory: Julian, like Bernard, emphasizes the importance of recognizing that all created goodness flows from God's substantial goodness, and cannot be understood or properly appreciated except in this relationship.

Eckhart, also, speaks of the soul as 'nobler than all created things',[77] and uses language similar to that of Julian's in speaking of the joy that God takes in human personhood.

> So like himself has God made man's soul that nothing else in heaven or on earth, of all the splendid creatures that God has so joyously created, resembles God so much as the human soul.[78]

Characteristic of all three of these great spiritual writers, different as they are from one another in other respects, is the way that they move immediately from this account of the soul's worth to the implications for spirituality, stressing the need for detachment from all things, material or spiritual, good or bad, in order to be devoted completely to God. As Julian puts it, since God himself takes such a delight in us, seeing us of value and worth, it follows that he

> wants our hearts to be powerfully lifted above the depths of earth and all empty sorrows, and to rejoice in it [the Trinity].[79]

For all of them, asceticism does not spring from any hatred or devaluation of the self, which must somehow be stripped away before God can take pleasure in the soul. It springs instead from an altogether positive evaluation of self-worth; so positive, indeed, that nothing but the best is good enough for the self, and that best is God himself. Because this is so, all that is of lesser worth, or anything which in a particular case would interfere with the total response to God (even if the thing is good in itself and would not be an interference to someone else's response) can be gladly given up.

> God, of your goodness give me yourself, for you are enough for me, and I can ask for nothing which is less which can pay you full worship. And if I ask for anything which is less, always I am in want; but only in you do I have everything.[80]

Julian is thus by no means the only mystic who has a deep appreciation of God's creation and especially of ourselves as of dignity and worth, who finds this the basis of true asceticism. Whether there was actual historical influence from Bernard and Eckhart cannot be established, though it is certainly possible, given the spread of Cistercian monasteries in England, on the one hand, and the flourishing trade between East Anglia and the Rhineland on the other. This, however, is less important than the fact that for all three of them, beginning from a profound grasp of the love of God for his creatures leads them to recognize that only the love of God can fully satisfy us, made, as we are, for himself.[81]

In contrast to this, we find a passage typical of the author of *The Cloud of Unknowing* in which he is discussing obstacles to perfect communion with God:

> You should loathe and hate to reflect on yourself, since you must always experience sin as some sort of foul fetid lump between yourself and your God. This lump is nothing else than yourself; it shall seem to you that it is one with it, congealed with the substance of your being, as though there were no division between them.[82]

The contrast here should not be overdrawn; the author of *The Cloud* would affirm with the other three mystics that the 'substance of our being' as created by God is good and noble, and that the 'foul fetid lump' is the accretion of sin which must be removed by the grace of God; it is not our original or true self. And Julian, for her part, takes the doctrine and experience of sin very seriously indeed, as we shall see more fully in the next chapter. Yet once again because the starting point for Julian's understanding of creation is the *love* of God, and because this permeates her reflection, her emphasis is on the nobility of the soul and the delight God takes in it, rather than upon the sin which in the view of the author of *The Cloud* makes it into a stinking mess. For Julian the primary fact is that we are loved by God and are the honourable place of his dwelling.[83] The author of *The Cloud* would not disagree, but his accent falls differently.

This in turn leads to a marked difference between Julian and the author of *The Cloud* in their respective teaching about how we may know God. For whereas the author of *The Cloud*, having emphasized our sinfulness, says that to know God

> you must destroy all knowing and feeling of every kind of creature, but most especially of yourself,[84]

Julian says,

> we can never come to the full knowledge of God until we first clearly know our own soul.[85]

This knowledge, to be sure, is reciprocal: we know ourselves only in relation to God. We shall explore this reciprocity more fully in the final chapter. But the difference of emphasis from *The Cloud* is not trivial: Julian could never be used to support the attitude that love for God undermines our concept of self-worth.

In summary, Julian's meditation on the loving creativity of God

Creation and Asceticism

helps her to resolve a tension which had a long history in theology and spirituality before her time, and which is still with us. On the one hand, she took no part in disparaging or devaluing the created world, including our bodies and their functions; she does not share the suspicions of those strands of Christianized Platonic thought mediated by Augustine who saw his most important conversion as a conversion to chastity.[86] Julian, for sound theological reasons mediated by her experience of the love of God made visible to her in the dying Christ, affirms instead the other strand of Augustinian thinking which rejoiced in the goodness and nobility of creation. Yet she does so without losing her grip on the littleness of creation in comparison with its Creator. The need for detachment from created things arises not out of dislike of them, but because in themselves they cannot fulfil our longing, which is for God himself.

> Therefore God rejoices in the creature and the creature in God, endlessly marvelling, in which marvelling he sees his God, his Lord, his Maker, so exalted, so great and so good in comparison with him who is made that the creature scarcely seems anything to itself. But the brightness and clearness of truth and wisdom makes him see and know that he is made for love ...[87]

There is the balance.

Notes to Chapter Eight

1. LT 5.
2. ibid.
3. ibid.
4. Augustine, Confessions I.1.
5. LT 58.
6. LT 8.
7. LT 9.
8. LT 62.
9. Romans 8.19–21.
10. Thomas Aquinas, Summa Theologiae Ia, 19.2 (Anton C. Pegis, Basic Writings of Saint Thomas Aquinas, vol. 1 (Random House, New York, 1945).
11. Francis of Assisi, 'The Canticle of Brother Sun', in Francis and Clare: The Complete Works, tr. Regis J. Armstrong OFM, and Ignatius C. Brady OFM, Classics of Western Spirituality (SPCK, London, and Paulist Press, New York, 1982), pp. 38–9. Franciscan spirituality was widely disseminated in England by the fourteenth century.
12. Gerald Vann, The Divine Pity (Fontana, London, 1956), pp. 24–5.
13. I have explored these notions more fully in God's World God's Body (Darton, Longman & Todd, London, 1984).
14. The distinction is expressed technically in the terminology of natura naturata and natura naturans, and finds its most prominent medieval source in John Scotus Eriugena's De Divisione Naturae (PL 122.

125–1244). The frequent accusations of pantheism which were levelled at him can, I think, be answered in the same way as they can be answered for Julian, as I outline in the following paragraphs.

15. LT 8.
16. LT 7.
17. What follows is treated more fully in *God's World God's Body*.
18. The phrase, and much of the train of thought, is from John Macquarrie's *Principles of Christian Theology*, rev. edn (SCM, London, 1977).
19. LT 75.
20. LT 5.
21. LT 18.
22. LT 11.
23. ibid.
24. ibid.
25. ibid.
26. LT 58.
27. LT 68.
28. LT 64.
29. Teresa of Avila, *Interior Castle* I.1, tr. E. Allison Peers, *The Complete Works of Saint Teresa of Jesus*, vol. 2 (Sheed & Ward, London, 1946), p. 201.
30. LT 68.
31. John 15.4.
32. Rom. 8.9; 2 Cor. 5.17; Col. 1.27; etc.
33. LT 54.
34. ibid.
35. Meister Eckhart, *Sermons and Treatises*, vol. II tr. M. O'C. Walshe (Watkins, London, 1979), p. 81 (Quint Sermon No. 26).
36. John of the Cross, *Spiritual Canticle* XXXVIII.2, tr. E. Allison Peers, *The Complete Works of John of the Cross*, vol. ii (Burns, Oates & Washbourne, London, 1953), pp. 172–3; cf. *Living Flame of Love* I.4 (Peers, vol. III, p. 18). It must be said that for John, as for Eckhart, this is not spoken of as the continuous ontological truth about the soul, but as the summit of spiritual union.
37. See my 'Luther and the Mystics', in *King's Theological Review*, vol. VIII No. 2 (Autumn 1985).
38. As in Walter Terence Stace, *Mysticism and Philosophy* (Macmillan, London, 1961), Ch. 6.
39. LT 44.
40. LT 58.
41. LT 55.
42. This closely parallels Thomas Aquinas' account of personhood and his insistence that the body is essential to it. *Summa Theologiae* I.i. Q75–6.
43. LT 58.
44. LT 53.
45. LT 6, emphasis mine.
46. LT 62.
47. LT 64.
48. LT 67, cf. James T. McIlwain, 'The "Bodelye syeknes" of Julian of Norwich', in *Journal of Medieval History*, vol. X No. 3 (Sept. 1984), p. 171. McIlwain suggests that Julian's inflamed mucous membranes made a

stench to her which in this case was not perceived by the others who were present.
49. LT 55.
50. ibid.
51. Augustine, *Confessions* I.2, tr. John K. Ryan (Image Books, Doubleday, New York, 1960).
52. LT 57.
53. ST 18.
54. LT 53.
55. LT 37.
56. The terms 'good' and 'bad' beg many questions; for this exposition all that is necessary is to recognize that we mean to do what we (rightly or wrongly) consider is good, etc.
57. LT 72.
58. LT 56.
59. LT 72.
60. LT 8.
61. cf. Augustine, *Confessions* X.6.
62. LT 19.
63. *The Cloud of Unknowing*, Ch. 43.
64. ibid., Ch. 5.
65. LT 6.
66. Augustine, *Confessions* X.6, tr. Clark.
67. LT 6.
68. LT 56.
69. Walter Hilton, *Scale of Perfection*, I.1.
70. cf. Peter Damian in Jaroslav Pelikan, *The Growth of Medieval Theology*, p. 112.
71. *The Book of Margery Kempe*, Ch. 22, on the dance in heaven in which Margery is taken by our Lord to join with our lady and 'other holy virgins'.
72. cf. Maureen Fried, 'Margery Kempe', in Paul Szarmach, ed., *An Introduction to the Medieval Mystics of Europe*.
73. It must be granted, however, that sexuality may have been connected with authority, and that Margery Kempe was also unusual – a woman and a writer – and perhaps had to lay the stress she did in order to show to her society that her views were legitimate in spite of the fact that she had been sexually active.
74. LT 68.
75. cf. William of St Thierry, *Cantica Canticorum* I (PL 494); Thomas Aquinas *Summa Theologiae* I.i Q29 a3.
76. Bernard of Clairvaux, *On the Love of God* II.4, tr. Terence L. Connolly sj (Burns, Oates & Washbourne, London, 1937); cf. Etienne Gilson, *The Mystical Theology of St Bernard* (Sheed & Ward, London, 1940).
77. Meister Eckhart, Sermon 23.
78. ibid., Sermon 6.
79. LT 68.
80. LT 5.
81. There is of course established historical linkage between Bernard and Eckhart, who cites *On the Love of God* at least five times. See Bernard McGinn, 'St Bernard and Meister Eckhart', in *Cîteaux Com. Cist.*, vol. I (1980).

82. *The Cloud of Unknowing,* 43; cf. 40.
83. LT 68.
84. *The Cloud of Unknowing,* 43.
85. LT 56.
86. It is true that Augustine himself came to a much more positive attitude toward physicality later in life, but as regards sexuality, it was his early rather troubled view which profoundly influenced medieval thinking; cf. Margaret R. Miles, *Augustine on the Body,* AAR Dissertation Series 31 (Scholar's Press, Missoula, Montana, 1979).
87. LT 44.

PART FOUR

Wounds into Honours

9 Sin and Suffering

The task of spirituality is to become a whole person, to reunite our sensuality with our substance in union with God. But how did this fracture at the centre of ourselves ever occur, and why did God permit it? This question has been emerging in various ways as we have considered Julian's teaching, and in one sense it could be called the central question of the book.[1] It raises its head at every turn: if the Church is holy and blameless in the sight of God, how are we to account for its corrupt bishops and the schisms in the papacy? If God is all goodness and is immanent in all things and events, then, as we saw, logic compels the admission that all things must be well – in flat contradiction to human experience. How, for instance, can such an assertion be squared with the Black Death? If our substance, our essential self, is continually united with God and there is in each of us a godly will, how is it that we so regularly and by our own hand get ourselves, individually and collectively, into such disastrous situations?

Julian's teaching is, as we have seen, anchored at every point in the passion of the incarnate Christ. Yet even this passion itself, considered in terms of the human behaviour it displayed, was a paradigm of hideous wickedness, a manifestation of malice, deceit, cruelty, and religious and political hypocrisy. In spite of this, the teaching of the Church and Julian's experience are unanimous in holding that although the crucifixion displayed human wickedness at its worst, it occurred as a remedy for that very wickedness. But why should it have been necessary at all?

It is this cluster of questions which keeps Julian's mind alert throughout the showings themselves, not allowing her simply to bask in the glow of God's love but continuing to require explanations. Her prayer had been for increasing compassion for Jesus in his sufferings, and solidarity with him; and as this is increasingly granted to her through the visions, her compassion for him raises in most acute form the question of why all his suffering should have been necessary. It is this question which she ponders for twenty years between the experiences themselves and the writing of the Long Text. We might plausibly see the primary theme of the Long Text as the fruit of her meditation on the problem of evil and its remedy.

The problems raised by evil and suffering are often presented nowadays as though they were an objection brought against Christianity by unbelievers. There is no doubt that suffering can be a barrier to Christian belief; but it must be recognized that the problems arise at least as forcefully within Christian commitment itself. If Christian belief takes its point of departure from the cross of Christ, as Julian emphasizes, then it is theology which must be done 'within earshot of the dying cry of Jesus'.[2] But if the death of Jesus is normative for theological considerations then it follows that the problems of evil and suffering must be a central item on the agenda of practical and doctrinal Christianity. It raises the obvious question about the sort of God who wills or even permits such suffering. It also, however, makes a practical response imperative. Jesus went to the cross because of his solidarity and compassion for suffering and sinful humankind: he would rather die than give up his claims on their behalf. Any theology and spirituality which ignores this fact has betrayed the death of the one whom it calls its Lord.

It follows from this that sensitivity to the problems of evil and suffering become an important criterion upon which claims to religious experience and spirituality can be assessed; and on this assessment, Julian must be rated very highly indeed. The inward quest, the desire for deepened spirituality, has often been criticized as a self-indulgent exercise, catering for the improvement of the individual soul while the rest of the world can go to hell.[3] To the extent that this is the case, however, it is a travesty of the spirituality whose paradigm is the crucified Christ. Jesus did not go to the cross for the improvement of his soul; he went there because of his refusal to compromise his claims of God's love and compassion for suffering human beings.[4] The development of Julian's spirituality of contrition, compassion, and longing with her will for God led her to her own Calvary, but it did not do so for the sake of an introverted spirituality that cared little about her fellow human beings: her whole book is written expressly to communicate her insights to her 'even Christians' for whom she has come to share the divine delight and compassion.

Julian's central message is her echo of Jesus' manifestation on his path to the cross that the most important thing we can say about God is that he loves. It was because of his love and compassion which Jesus had offered to outcasts and sinners and sufferers in the name of this God whom he called 'Abba' that they found him compelling, and that they found in him a manifestation of a God worthy of respect and love. Jesus never minimized the problems of evil and suffering, or offered explanations which trivialized real human anguish. Instead, he offered renewed human dignity by taking human suffering seriously and attempting to do something about it, even at ultimate cost to himself.

This, therefore, becomes a standard against which theology and spirituality must be measured, not merely because of the demands of an indignant world, but because of its own internal logic. If Jesus' experience of God is normative, then those who most truly experience God are those who are most sensitive to human hurt and can respond to it most helpfully, mediating God's own compassion. Julian's desire for compassion and her willingness to experience the sufferings of Christ show how deeply she had pondered this already before her experiences; and though we know little about it, her ministry as an anchoress to those who came to pour out their troubles to her would have been a taxing outpouring of her own compassion. And in the experiences themselves, even while they lasted, and in her subsequent meditations on them, the suffering of humankind is laid before the suffering Christ.

The theology and spirituality which Julian develops in the Long Text ought not to be detached from the context of intense suffering in which the revelations occurred. Julian herself had been in acute pain and believed herself to be dying; and Jesus in her visions was likewise *in extremis*. Although Julian's physical suffering ceased during the time of the vision, her identification with Christ produced in her even more intense suffering than before.

> This revelation of Christ's pains filled me full of pains ... And in all this time that Christ was present to me, I felt no pain except for Christ's pains; and then it came to me that I had little known what pain it was that I had asked, and like a wretch I regretted it, thinking that if I had known what it had been, I should have been reluctant to ask for it. For it seemed that my pains exceeded any mortal death.[5]

Pondering the tension between the experience of the love and compassion of God on the one hand, and the suffering, both physical and spiritual, in the world as it was shared by Jesus on the cross, on the other, was thus no abstract issue for Julian. It arose directly out of the context of the revelations.

Julian experiences to the full the tension between her intense awareness of the overwhelming love of God in Christ and her first-hand knowledge of pain and evil. Indeed, the more intense is the former, the more acute is the latter, in reciprocal relationship: the more one is aware of the suffering of humanity, the more one needs the insight and compassion of Christ to alleviate and remedy evil; but the more one is aware of the compassion of Christ, the more horrendous evil and suffering appears.

> So I saw how Christ has compassion on us because of sin; and just as I was before filled full of pain and compassion on account of Christ's Passion, so I was now in part filled with compassion for all my fellow Christians, because he loves very dearly the people who will be saved, that is God's servants.[6]

And in that compassion which she feels for her suffering fellow-Christians she finds it inadequate just to accept that all the harm and suffering will be well, as Christ has promised her.

> But in this I stood, contemplating it generally, darkly and mournfully, saying in intention to our Lord with very great fear: Ah, good Lord, how could all things be well, because of the great harm which has come through sin to your creatures? And here I wished, so far as I dared, for some plainer explanation through which I might be at ease about this matter.[7]

We see in this quotation Julian's urgent desire for an explanation of how all things could be well when it seems so obvious that things are not at all well. We also see how she moves from the problems of pain and suffering to that of sin as the cause of suffering. Several strands come together to provide this focus. Most immediate is the suffering of Christ himself. Julian takes this to be the most severe suffering imaginable, and takes it also to be the divine response to sin: sin, therefore, is the cause of the most intense suffering that the world could ever see.

> And so I saw our Lord Jesus languishing for long, because the union in him of the divinity gave strength to his humanity to suffer more than all men could. I mean not only more pain than any other one man could suffer, but also that he suffered more pain than all men who are to be saved, from the first beginning to the last day, may tell or fully think ... And he suffered for the sins of every man who will be saved; and he saw and he sorrowed for every man's sorrow, desolation and anguish, in his compassion and love.[8]

The sin which is the cause of Jesus' suffering is also the basic cause of all human suffering.

> In this naked word 'sin', our Lord brought generally to my mind all which is not good, and the shameful contempt and the direst tribulation which he endured for us in this life, and his death and all his pains, and the passions, spiritual and bodily, of all his creatures ... Sin is the cause of all this pain.[9]

Sin is the cause of the fracture within the human being, the breakage which splits the substance from the sensuality. This fracture has the immediate effect of self-alienation and thus of the mental and spiritual anguish of the inevitably restless heart; it is the woundedness at the centre of the personality. Now because of the unity of the sensuality with the physical organism which we explored in the previous chapter, the dis-integration of the sensuality from the substance cannot but have physical effects of pain and illness. Julian is very much aware that we are a psychosomatic unity: the wound of the personality caused by sin is therefore bound to have psychosomatic consequences. It is not clear what Julian would say about diseases caused by biological organisms: the fourteenth century did not know about viruses and germs. What is clear is that she would have been whole-heartedly

170

behind the growing recognition of modern medicine of the psycho-somatic dimension of a huge amount of human illness.

This does not, of course, mean that Julian supposed that it was possible to make straightforward inferences from the state of an individual's body to the state of his or her soul, as though holiness was a guarantee of health. Such naiveté would be impossible for a woman who had witnessed the indiscriminate swathes of suffering cut by the Black Death, and the particularly high casualty rate among priests willing to minister to the dying. The fourteenth century may not have known about viruses, but it surely knew about contagion, marking with a huge red cross the doors of houses containing the plague as a warning to others to keep away.

Reflection on this shows that the human race is a solidarity; it is impossible for one person to sin and others to remain unaffected. There is not only a psychosomatic unity within each individual, but a unity of human beings, and, even more widely, a unity with all of creation. The fracture at the heart of humankind is a fracture that is contributed to by everyone and that has consequences for everyone. The suffering of a particular individual is therefore no indication of that individual's sinfulness or otherwise; it is, however, an indication of the sinfulness and suffering of the whole of humankind of which that individual is a member. Putting it another way, when our sensuality will be fully reintegrated into our substance – when we are entirely made whole in union with God – and when this is true for all human beings, then there will be no more illness or physical pain. In heaven there will be neither viruses nor hypochondria!

It is in this sense that sin is the cause of all suffering, spiritual, psychological and physical; and thus sin is revealed to Julian to be the central focus of the multi-faceted problem of evil and suffering. She asks, as we saw, for further explanation.

> And to this our blessed Lord answered, very meekly and with a most loving manner, and he showed that Adam's sin was the greatest harm ever done or ever to be done until the end of the world.[10]

We hear in Julian's words an echo of St Paul: 'in Adam all die ...' Julian, like St Paul, presumably believed in an historical Adam and a temporally first sin, but her argument does not depend on this any more than his does. What is crucial is that we are all sinful, and our sinfulness is both individual and corporate. In other words, our sin is both by our own choice and because of the damage done to us by others. The context of our lives and thus of our choices is a damaged and sinful context, and we both reflect and augment that sinfulness, 'through negligence, through weakness, through our own deliberate fault'. The damage we suffer at the hands of others we perpetuate by our own hand.

The modern reader may feel a considerable reluctance to think about sin. This is partly a matter of vocabulary. For historical reasons, sin and sex have become closely associated in popular thinking, so that talk about sin may seem either like prudery or like intellectual voyeurism. There are, however, plenty of linguistic alternatives which indicate some of the dimensions of sin. People today who would feel unable to respond to the term 'sin' nor consider themselves particularly sinful (in that their primary problems and misdeeds are not sexual ones), would often recognize their own brokenness and hurt, and admit that it is in part inflicted upon them, and in part their own fault, and that they have passed on to others their wounded and wounding attitudes and behaviour.

The vocabulary of woundedness was an important one when medieval writers considered sin. As usual, a major source for this was Augustine. His *Confessions* are full of references to himself as wounded and damaged by sin, in intellect, will, and feeling, to Christ as the Great Physician, and to the medicine which he made available in his crucifixion.[11] While not ignoring the dimension of blameworthiness for sin, the vocabulary of woundedness leads Augustine and those who took up his language to look upon themselves also with compassion, and to appreciate something of the compassion of Christ and the way in which he looks at us with mercy, not only with judgement. Many writers took up the theme,[12] among them, once again, Thomas Aquinas who pondered the woundedness of nature consequent upon the fall.[13] Julian takes the theme of woundedness to great lengths, in the fine counterpoint between the wounds of sin, the wounds of Christ, and her own prayer for the three wounds of contrition, compassion, and longing with the will for God. In this chapter we are mainly concerned with her understanding of the wounds of sin.

To look seriously at sin, means to inquire into its causes and extent; and this Julian finds difficult to do because it means self-scrutiny at a most painful level.

> Sin is the sharpest scourge with which any chosen soul can be struck, which scourge belabours man or woman, and breaks a man, and purges [or 'makes despicable'] a man in his own sight so much that at times he thinks himself that he is not fit for anything but as it were to sink into hell ...[14]

Probing sin and pain is both theologically and psychologically threatening because it strikes at the root of thinking about God and ourselves as good. Yet if we shy away from it in fear or distaste (perhaps disguised as optimism preferring to think of more cheerful things) nothing can really be resolved, because we have refused the knowledge of ourselves and God which alone can reunite our sensuality and our substance and thus bring healing. Julian, characteristically, faces these issues relentlessly, at both the theological and the psychological levels.

The theological question of sin first arises acutely for Julian in the context of her vision of God as present in all things. If all things and events flow forth from his goodness and are inseparable from him, then how can there be sin – which seems to be by definition contrary to the goodness of God?

> I marvelled at that vision with a gentle fear, and I thought: What is sin? For I saw truly that God does everything, however small it may be, and that nothing is done by chance, but all by God's prescient wisdom.[15]

Now, if it is true that nothing happens by chance, and that God has made us for integration with ourselves in union with him, and sin is a fragmentation of ourselves and of that union, then it seems unthinkable that God should have allowed sin.

> I saw that nothing hindered me but sin, and I saw that this is true of all of us in general, and it seemed to me that if there had been no sin, we should all have been pure and as like our Lord as he created us. And so in my folly before this time I often wondered why, through the great prescient wisdom of God, the beginning of sin was not prevented. For then it seemed to me that all would have been well.[16]

Julian is assured that all will be well in spite of sin, and that sin was necessary, but this does not really answer her question. Before she finds any understanding of why it was that God permitted sin, however, it was necessary for her to recognize several other things about it.

The Great Mystery and the Great Deed

As Julian gazed upon the vision of love in the passion of Christ, it was simply not clear to her how 'all will be well', or how the sin and misery of this world could be turned to good account with none of it wasted or unnecessary. As Julian pondered this, 'darkly and mournfully', the Lord added another dimension to her experience.

> I saw hidden in God an exalted and wonderful mystery, which he will make plain and we shall know in heaven. In this knowledge we shall truly see the cause why he allowed sin to come, and in this sight we shall rejoice forever.[17]

Although we cannot now see the purpose of all the world's suffering, Julian is assured that this will not always be the case.

Julian discusses the knowledge that we have of God and the knowledge that we do not have in terms of 'two portions' which are in God's gift. The first of these 'portions' is freely open to us to explore and

ponder in ever-increasing depth; it consists of the truths of our salvation in Christ. The more we absorb these truths and make them our own
so that we live in them and by them, the more we advance in grace and
are transformed into the joyful wholeness which our Lord desires for
us. This, however, is only half the matter.

> The other portion is hidden from us and closed, that is to say all which is
> additional to our salvation; for this is our Lord's privy counsel, and it is
> fitting to God's royal dominion to keep his privy counsel in peace, and it is
> fitting to his servants out of obedience and respect not to wish to know his
> counsel.[18]

It is to this 'portion' that full understanding of the purpose of evil and
suffering belongs. Julian seems here to be suggesting that we ought not
to insist upon understanding it in this life, but that we should rather
occupy ourselves with those things which God does now lay open to
our exploration.

When Julian discusses this in the Short Text, she indicates that the
Lord's assurance that he will make all things well and that there will be
no purposeless sin or pain is part of the portion that is open to us, but
the specific way in which he will do this is not. This we simply do not
know; though we shall know it hereafter. Julian comments,

> I understand this in two ways: One is that I am well content that I do not
> know it; and the other is that I am glad and joyful because I shall know it. It is
> God's will that we should know in general that all will be well, but it is not
> God's will that we should know it now except as it applies to us for the
> present, and that is the teaching of Holy Church.[19]

With this, therefore, she exhorts her readers, and herself, to be satisfied.

It is amusing to see how unsuccessful the exhortation was, at least on
one level. Julian had a much too inquisitive mind and compassionate
heart simply to leave matters there. To say that evil and suffering represent a mystery which will be resolved in due time is in itself not very
helpful in dealing with it now; and Julian is sufficiently assured of the
love and goodness of God to be certain that this is not the end of the
matter. So she continues to probe it, not in a belligerent or merely
curious way, but seeking aid and comfort for herself and for her fellow-
Christians.

Why, then, does she speak of a mystery which is God's privy counsel
and which we are not to probe? Is she being inconsistent, or
disobedient to her own experience and the instruction it contained?
She had after all said that even the saints in heaven do not try to probe
into things that are none of their business but are content with that
which God intends them to know, and that it would please God and be
to our profit if we resembled them in this. Now, however, she seems to
fly in the face of her own counsel.

Such flagrant disobedience would be contrary to the whole tenor of the book, and it is necessary to look more closely. Clearly Julian cannot have understood God to tell her that she must not ask further questions about the problem of evil, and then have spent the next twenty years doing exactly what she was forbidden to do. The differences between the Short Text and the Long Text show that in the intervening time Julian became much more intellectually confident, willing to ask difficult questions and explore uncomfortable issues:[20] it must therefore be the case that her experiences acted to liberate rather than fetter her mind for such exploration. Indeed, in the very next sentences, in both the Short Text and the Long, Julian continues to ponder what Jesus meant when he told her from the cross that all shall be well; and in the Long Text she discusses this in terms of further dialogue with him, in which

> Our good Lord answered to all the questions and doubts which I could raise, saying most comfortingly: I may make all things well, and I can make all things well, and I shall make all things well, and I will make all things well; and you will see for yourself that every kind of thing will be well.[21]

This becomes the basis for sustained further reflection, culminating in the parable of the Lord and the servant which will be discussed below. It is clear, therefore, that Julian did not take our Lord to be discouraging her from further pondering of the matter. What, then, does she mean by the mystery, the 'closed portion' that we are not to pry into?

I suggest that the distinction between the general and the specific is significant. The prohibition is not on further investigation of the 'great mystery' in general, but on specific applications of it. The term 'mystery' itself is, as we have seen, not treated as a 'No Trespassing' sign over a closed door, as we might have feared. Rather, as in the case of the mystery of the Trinity, a mystery is seen by Julian in the traditional theological sense as a deep well from which, no matter how much one draws, there is always more and more, springing up to eternal life'. A theological mystery is an inexhaustible source of truth and wonder; it is anything but a prohibition of reflection.

When Julian says that she saw 'hidden in God an exalted and wonderful mystery' which, when fully revealed, will make plain the cause of suffering and sin, she is suggesting two things. First, negatively, until God does make it plain, there is a great deal of suffering for which we can see no explanation and which does just appear pointless. Julian is far from offering facile 'solutions' to that before which we can only keep silence. In situations of intense suffering, the appropriate response must often be respect for the reality of the situation, standing with the sufferer so far as possible, but not offering cheap answers. Of this, Julian is well aware. The most that we can hope for is that the point of that which is now so opaque and bitter to us will one day become clear. It is insensitive and wicked to pretend that we have clarity already.

But secondly, while it is true that for many – probably most – instances of suffering we cannot see their purpose or offer any justification, the more general question of why any sin was allowed in the first place is a mystery in the positive sense. The more Julian ponders it, the more theological and spiritual insight she receives. It is because of this that her book has so much depth. It brings together the urgent anguish of the world and the loving compassion of God in the person of the suffering and dying Jesus, and from this juxtaposition finds insight, both about ourselves and about God. It is not too much to say that Julian's whole anthropology, theology, and spirituality are rooted in this conjunction. Modern theologians have sometimes suggested that any theology must begin from the empirical facts of this world's suffering.[22] Julian would agree, but would say that this is only one half of the story; the other half is the personally experienced overwhelming love of God in Christ. When these two are brought together, it is indeed a great mystery, but the mystery is the source of insight as she ponders it more and more fully.

In subsequent sections of this chapter we will explore some of these insights. It is well, however, first to consider more fully the negative aspect of the mystery, the 'closed portion' that is not for our present understanding. Julian says that when she had become aware of the goodness of God in her vision of Christ's suffering, she wanted to inquire about a particular friend of hers whom she hoped had begun to live a good life. Julian was concerned to know whether her friend would continue in this. But this concern, she tells us, blocked her own understanding, and was inappropriate. Rather than receiving an answer to her inquiry, she was told,

> Accept it generally, and contemplate the courtesy of your Lord God as he revealed it to you, for it is more honour to God to contemplate him in all things than in any one special thing. I agreed, and with that I learned that it is more honour to God to know everything in general than it is to take delight in any special thing. And if I were to act wisely, in accordance with this teaching, I should not be glad because of any special thing or be greatly distressed by anything at all, for all will be well; for the fulness of joy is to contemplate God in everything.[23]

When she says that we are to understand it generally rather than specifically, she does not mean that God required her to content herself with vague generalities that have no actual application. Her insights which derive from this are anything but vague, as we shall see. However, they are not about particular individuals or instances of pain.

For these, all too often we have no answers. The path of compassion in such cases is not to pretend that we do, but to stand with the sufferer – and it might be ourselves – in faithful silence. Julian does not trivialize misery by pretending that an explanation for it somehow takes it away. It is indeed a great mystery. But we are helped to bear it by the mystery of the suffering Lord who fully shares it with us; and with the knowledge that in his good time we will understand completely and specifically as we now understand in general and in part.

> And for the great love which he has for us he reveals to us everything which is at the time to his glory and our profit. And those things which he now wants to keep secret he still in his great goodness reveals, but not openly. In this revelation he wants us to believe and understand that we shall truly see it in his endless bliss. Then we ought to rejoice in him for everything which he reveals and for everything which he conceals; and if we do so, willingly and meekly, we shall find great comfort in it, and we shall have endless thanks from him for it.[24]

Because we cannot see the point of a great deal of the suffering around us, and cannot conceive of how all this could be well, we can only trust in God's power and goodness and take his word for it that it will be so. In Julian's pondering of our Lord's promise that he will make all things well, her understanding moves toward the future and she looks forward to that which God will yet do. She says that there will be a great and wonderful deed which we cannot now know, but which God has planned and treasured in his breast since before the creation of the world, by which he will make all things well.

> There is a deed which the blessed Trinity will perform on the last day, as I see it, and what the deed will be and how it will be performed is unknown to every creature who is inferior to Christ, and it will be until the deed is done.[25]

She is not told what this deed is, except that it will put right everything that is wrong, and heal all sorrow and pain and grief, and the fracturing of sin, so that none of it will be wasted. How this could come about she does not understand, nor is she told; but she accepts both the revelation and the concealment as given by the love of God for our betterment.

> The goodness and the love of our Lord God want us to know that this will be, and his power and his wisdom, through the same love, want to conceal it and hide it from us, what it will be and how it will be done. And the cause why he wants us to know it like this is because he wants us to be at ease in our souls and at peace in love, disregarding every disturbance which could hinder our true rejoicing in him.[26]

Here, as always, Julian's primary concern is for undisturbed joyful growth in wholeness. The sin and pain in our world and in ourselves is the great disturber of our souls. Unless we were assured by God himself

that this would be made well, we could not find peace in our disturb-
ance. Yet it is for our good, Julian is assured, that we cannot now see the
means by which God will accomplish this. By resting in our knowledge
of those great deeds which he has already done, and in particular by
focusing on his suffering and death for us, we can be assured that all
the rest of what he will do will also be done with power and great
tenderness.

> It is God's will that we pay great heed to all the deeds which he has per-
> formed, for he wishes us to know from them and to trust and believe all
> which he will do. But always we must avoid pondering what the deed will
> be, and wish to be like our brothers, who are the saints in heaven, who want
> nothing else than God's will. Then shall we rejoice only in God, and be well
> satisfied both with what he conceals and what he reveals.[27]

In this way our peace and growth in spiritual wholeness will be steady,
as we draw deeply from the mysteries which are open to us, and leave
in God's hands those that are his 'privy counsel' until such time as he
chooses to make them plain.

Julian is not one to give up easily in her search for understanding;
and her theological method requires her, as we have seen, to bring
together the teaching of the Church with her own spiritual experience.
On this particular point the two seem to clash. Whatever exactly the
'great deed' is that God promises to do, he has assured her that by this
deed he will make all things well. Yet the teaching of the Church has
been that many would be damned: angels who had fallen through
pride, pagans, and even those who, although baptized, live unchristian
lives.[28] But if this is so, how could God possibly make all things well?
Surely all cannot be well so long as even one of his creatures suffers
damnation? Julian seeks for further enlightenment on this, because it
seems to her impossible to reconcile the Church's teaching about hell
and purgatory with her experience of the love and mercy of God. Her
request, however, is not granted.

> To this I had no other answer as a revelation from our Lord except this: what
> is impossible to you is not impossible to me. I shall preserve my word in
> everything, and I shall make everything well.[29]

How this will come about is not shown to her: it is part of the concealed
great deed which the Lord will do, and he asks her to trust him to keep
his word.

Because of Julian's faithfulness both to her experience of God's love
and to the teaching of the Church, she is unable to resolve this tension.
There have been those who have wondered aloud whether Julian is a
universalist, that is, one who believes that everyone will ultimately be
saved.[30] Yet her affirmation of her belief in the teaching of the Church
on this point is clear. She, like any Christian who believes in the

goodness of God and who has compassion for human frailty, would *like* to be a universalist. Nevertheless, the freedom that God has given in our creation is such that we have a choice to turn away from him; and this turning away can persist to such an extent that literal self-annihilation takes place. Sin is the opposite of God, and God is substance; therefore there is a sense in which sin is nothing – we will explore this more fully in the next section. If someone chooses so to identify himself or herself with this nothingness of sin, then he or she ultimately comes to be nothing: one cannot deliberately and consistently choose evil and still remain human, for to be human means, as we have seen, to have a core which longs for God. There is a terrible alternative to the unification of substance and sensuality in the love of God, and that is to turn away from God so utterly and deliberately that all true selfhood is eroded and only the hell of nothingness remains. Perhaps this is what Julian means when she says,

> By this sight I understand that every creature who is of the devil's condition in this life and dies is no more mentioned before God and all his saints than is the devil, notwithstanding that they belong to the human race ...[31]

The deliberate choice of the absence of God is therefore the deliberate choice of hell. This must not, however, be understood as in any sense God's punishment; it is rather his gracious self-emptying to such an extent that although he fills all things, he has made it possible for people to choose to be absent from him. There is no question of God disowning us or being angry with us so long as there is the faintest flicker of desire for him left in us. Hell, whether in this life or the next, is not a place to which God sends us for punishment, but a condition in which he respects our willing of his absence. This is why it is impossible for Julian to be a universalist: it would trivialize the freedom which God has given us, and the courtesy and humility by which he allows us not to be in his presence – though we thereby create our own hell. Julian may hope, as indeed all Christians may hope, that the compassionate love of God which reaches even into hell to woo all men and women will eventually triumph, so that all will finally turn to him. But this hope cannot be translated into a doctrine. So long as there is human freedom, the choice of the absence of God, hell, must remain a possibility; though we may hope that the possibility will not be actualized for anyone.

Julian insists that there is no wrath in God: the wrath is in us, when we choose to separate ourselves from him. God does not blame us for our sins; he sees the frailty of our nature and our fractured contrariness, and recognizes that sin is both a consequence and an augmentation of our brokenness. He longs to help us and heal us; he is not angry with us nor does he wish to punish us. She puts this in very strong terms: she says that there is a sense in which it is inaccurate to speak of God forgiving us for our sins, because to forgive presupposes that there must be something needing to be forgiven, and God does not look upon us in that way. Rather, he sees us as perfect in Christ, our substance entirely united with him, and longs to unify our sensuality with our substance so that those things which we rightly consider to be sinful will plague and destroy us no longer.

> I saw truly that our Lord was never angry, and never will be. Because he is God, he is good, he is truth, he is love, he is peace; and his power, his wisdom, his charity and his unity do not allow him to be angry. For I saw truly that it is against the property of his power to be angry, and against the property of his wisdom and against the property of his goodness. God is that goodness which can never be angry, for God is nothing but goodness. Our soul is united with him in unchangeable goodness. And between God and our soul there is neither wrath nor forgiveness in his sight. For our soul is so wholly united to God, through his own goodness, that between God and our soul nothing can interpose.[32]

Indeed, if God really *were* to be angry, even for a moment, his wrath would utterly obliterate us: 'we should have neither life nor place nor being',[33] because all these come from the generous and loving preservation of God.

Though it is against *God's* nature to be angry, however, it is all too possible for *us* to be angry and frustrated. Julian sees this as a division against ourselves, a lack of integration with our substance which is rooted in God.

> For I saw no wrath except on man's side, and he forgives that in us, for wrath is nothing else but a perversity and an opposition to peace and to love. And it comes from a lack of power or a lack of wisdom or a lack of goodness, and this lack is not in God, but it is on our side. For we through sin and wretchedness have in us a wrath and a constant opposition to peace and to love ... But yet in all this the sweet eye of pity is never turned away from us, and the operation of mercy does not cease.[34]

What the great deed is that the Lord will do to make all things well, Julian is not told. But she is assured that there will be such a deed; and she can accept the assurance because of her deep conviction of the love of God who looks on us, in all our sinfulness, with pity, not with blame.

Sin has no Substance

In the vision of God which Julian has, in which she sees God 'in an instant of time', she sees that he is present in all things, and therefore that all things have their being in him, all finite substances flowing from his substance, and all events occurring through his goodness and wisdom.

And here I was certain that sin is no deed [or 'is nothing'], for in all this sin was not shown to me.[35]

Julian sees God, and sees all things in God, in a mystical vision; and though she sees all things she does not see sin. This leads her to conclude that sin is nothing.

At first sight this seems facile: surely one cannot dismiss sin by declaring it non-existent? Nor should we suppose that someone of Julian's integrity would do so: her visions, after all, are visions of the suffering Saviour whose crucifixion and death were precisely because sin had to be taken seriously. Furthermore, Julian does not say that there is no sin; she says that sin is nothing. To us this might seem like the same thing, but for Julian this represents a distinction. She has explained that all things – all substances – flow from the divine substance. Sin, however, does not come from God, for sin is evil and God is all goodness. This means that whatever sin is, and in whatever way it is to be understood, it cannot be a substance. This is both the conclusion of logic and the fruit of her experience in which she sees all things in God but does not see sin. Later, she makes this more explicit:

But I did not see sin, for I believe that it has no kind of substance, no share in being, nor can it be recognized except by the pain caused by it.[36]

This cannot be a casual dismissal of sin; that would run counter to the whole tenor of Julian's book and the experience of the passion of Christ upon which her writings are based. It is, rather, a statement about the ontological status of sin: it is a denial of sin as an ultimate and irremediable fact about the world, a rejection of the notion that sin can never be overcome.

In one way we have already seen this in the discussion of the godly will in the previous chapter. Our true substance is founded in God, according to Julian, and this is unalterably the case if we are human at all, in spite of the fact that our sensuality turns away from our substance and we are fractured beings. Putting it another way, we are made in the divine image, and although that image is distorted, it is never erased. Now, the distortion of an image has no new ontological status, no separate being. We are still the children of God; no matter how muddy and messy we become, we do not thereby become creatures of mud. We may be badly distorted, and no longer beautiful, but we are still the same beings, created in God's image; we have not suddenly become altogether different entities. Sin, according to Julian, is the marring and twisting of the image of God; but it is not the replacement of the image of God with a different image – say, the image of evil. As long as we are human we bear the image of God, even if in a scarcely recognizable way. To say that sin is no substance is to say that sin is not an alternate image which could exist in its own right, but is rather the warping of the image which is there.[37]

Another way of saying this is to say that evil is parasitic upon good. As a parasite feeds on its host and could not exist without it, so evil feeds on good and is dependent on it. The host could exist without the parasite, but if the host should die, all its parasites would die too. Similarly, there can be good without evil; but there could not be evil without good, because evil is good gone wrong. Evil has no independent existent; it is no substance.

Here as elsewhere, Julian stands firmly in the Augustinian tradition. Like Julian's Long Text, Augustine's *Confessions* can be read as the history of his personal pondering of the problem of sin and evil and its origin. He also had come to the conclusion that evil cannot be a substance, because all substances flow from God. In his words,

> If things are deprived of all goodness, they will have no being at all . . . If they were deprived of all goodness, they would be altogether nothing. Therefore, as long as they are, they are good. Therefore, all things which exist are good, and that evil the origin of which I sought is not a substance because, if it were a substance, it would be good.[38]

This does not of course mean that evil does not matter at all; but it does mean that evil does not matter ultimately. While Julian gazes upon Jesus, he shows her that by his death the fiend, the embodiment of evil, is overcome; and because he has been overcome, he can be scorned. Julian bursts into delighted laughter, making those around her laugh too, because she sees that Jesus has overcome evil.

> And after this I became serious again, and said: I see three things: sport and scorn and seriousness. I see sport, that the devil is overcome; and I see scorn, that God scorns him and he will be scorned; and I see seriousness, that he is overcome by the blessed Passion and death of our Lord Jesus Christ, which was accomplished in great earnest and with heavy labour.[39]

Indeed, the insight that evil has no substance is the ground of great optimism, because it means that sin can be utterly abolished without destroying anything that is good. If the image of God were not merely warped but were actually removed and replaced by an evil image, so that we had become essentially evil rather than good, then no remedy would be possible, because the more 'ourselves' we became, the worse we would be. To destroy evil it would be necessary that we ourselves should be destroyed. The assertion that we are fundamentally good and want to be good (that we have a godly will) is the assertion that there is hope: the more we become at one, integrated, the better we will be. It is because of this denial of ontological status to sin that Julian can see the force of the divine promise:

It is true that sin is the cause of all this pain, but all will be well, and every kind of thing will be well.[40]

This does not yet answer the question of why sin should have been permitted in the first place, or of *how* it will be remedied, nor does Julian take it as such. But it is the necessary condition for optimism that evil can be utterly eradicated without destruction of our fundamental selfhood. In the Short Text, therefore, Julian summarizes this aspect of sin in a series of observations written as a direct address:

O wretched sin, what are you? You are nothing. For I saw that God is in everything; I did not see you. And when I saw that God has made everything, I did not see you. And when I saw that God is in everything, I did not see you. And when I saw that God does everything that is done, the less and the greater, I did not see you ... And so I am certain that you are nothing ...[41]

'Suddenly You Will be Taken'

Because sin has no substance, it is not an essential aspect of personhood. It is consequently possible to look forward to a day of complete wholeness and fulfilment when all sin and its consequences of pain and sorrow will be taken away. If sin is not the first thing that must be said about human beings, but is rather parasitic upon our substance made in the image of God, neither is it the last thing which must be said about us. Julian receives the Lord's assurance that sin and its afflictions are temporary and will come to an end.

Suddenly you will be taken out of all your pain, all your sickness, all your unrest and all your woe. And you will come up above, and you will have me for your reward, and you will be filled full of joy and bliss, and you will never again have any kind of pain, any kind of sickness, any kind of displeasure, no lack of will, but always joy and bliss without end.[42]

This assurance that sin and suffering will come to an abrupt end and be replaced with endless consolation is intended to give us patience and fortitude to endure the suffering while we must. In comparison with the everlasting bliss which we shall enjoy, this life and longing is as merely an instant of time, and when we are released from it, 'then pain will be nothing'. Although now while we are in it suffering may seem to be interminable, reflection on the relative brevity of life restores a sense of proportion and gives us patience.

Julian has been given an example of this in her vision of the suffering of Christ, and more than one parallel in her own experience. During her observation of Jesus on the cross, she watched as he came progressively nearer to death. After the intense bleeding from the crown of thorns, his body was without moisture, bloodless and dry in the tormenting wind, so that he sagged down and shrivelled as he hung on the cross.[43] As she watched, in sorrow and compassion, she fully expected to see him die. But just when she thought that he must expire at any moment, suddenly his countenance changed to one of triumph and joy, and he spoke to her cheerfully, asking whether she still had any pain or grief. Though in the first instance the reference is to the pain and grief she suffered because of his agony, she soon takes the point that it has a much wider reference, encompassing all pain and suffering. As suddenly as his appearance changed to joy, leaving no trace of the agony behind, so we also shall suddenly be delivered from all sadness.

> And I was very joyful; I understood that in our Lord's intention we are now on his cross with him in our pains, and in our sufferings we are dying, and with his help and his grace we willingly endure on that same cross until the last moment of life. Suddenly he will change his appearance for us, and we shall be with him in heaven. Between the one and the other all will be a single era; and then all will be brought into joy.[44]

The phrase which Colledge and Walsh here translate, 'between the one and the other all will be a single era', is in Middle English, 'shalle alle be one tyme', or, in a variant, 'no tyme'. The text itself is uncertain, but in view of Julian's emphasis on the suddenness of the transformation, it is plausible to suppose that she had in mind St Paul's comment that we shall all be changed 'in a moment, in the twinkling of an eye'.[45]

The sudden change from *extremis* to delight which Julian observed in Christ on the cross had a physical as well as a psychological parallel in her own experience. The physical parallel was her own abrupt passage from severe pain and suffering, the shortness of breath which she and those around her took to be the immediate harbinger of death, to a sense of soundness and wholeness. Though she still thought she would die, she received this complete cessation of pain as God's secret doing, giving her strength and consolation to meet her end.[46]

The psychological parallel came in a series of abrupt emotional swings from intense delight and consolation to extreme depression and mental pain, and then back again, 'I suppose about twenty times'. The suddenness of the changes makes it clear to her that this is not a matter of reward or punishment, but is rather part of the whole revelation of God's love. She experiences the desolation of one who is allowed to feel abandoned by God, and the great comfort and consolation of his loving presence, and sees that God intends both to increase our trust in him.

> For it is God's will that we do all in our power to preserve our consolation, for bliss lasts forevermore, and pain is passing, and will be reduced to nothing for those who will be saved. Therefore it is not God's will that when we feel pain we should pursue it in sorrow and mourning for it, but that

suddenly we should pass it over, and preserve ourselves in the endless delight which is God.[47]

Characteristically, Julian moves from her vision of the dying Christ and her own physical parallel to his suffering, to the spiritual implication. Just as he changed suddenly from pain to delight, and she from illness to comfort, so also we should 'suddenly pass over' our mental pain, and foster in ourselves the 'delight which is God', while looking forward to our sudden transformation from the sorrows of this life to everlasting happiness. She is much too realistic to suppose that we can ever in this life completely escape depression and anguish, but she is also aware that we are often perverse enough actually to *want* to be depressed, to *pursue* sorrow and mourning, and cling to it. Although it would be futile to deny these negative feelings and unhealthy to repress them, Julian gently points out that we ought not to feed and nourish them, but rather foster in ourselves as much as we are able the positive feelings and attitudes. These are not wishful thinking or subjective fantasy; they are based on the reality of the love of God and the endless bliss which this love holds for us. It is the pain, not the joy, which is ultimately unreal. Therefore as quickly as we are able we are to put down the things that give us pain; 'suddenly we should pass it over'. Rather than nourishing these feelings, we should nourish ourselves in the delights of God.

It would of course be naive for Julian or for ourselves to suppose that all psychological pain is of this variety and that it is possible always to 'pass it over': many of life's griefs require far more than a positive attitude to resolve them. For someone who is really ill with depression it is impossible just to 'snap out of it', to 'suddenly pass it over'. Furthermore many of the things which cause us mental anguish are not of this variety, and are beyond our control: bereavement, loss, heartache for the brokenness of those we love. Thus while it is quite true that we should not perversely foster mental pain within ourselves, this cannot possibly be the whole solution. Rather, it is because all sorrow will one day be healed in the endless bliss of the love of God that it is ever possible to 'pass over' pain. Julian looks forward to this time of ultimate restoration and whole-making with very much joy.

In this joy she is again taking her cue from her vision of Jesus on the cross. With great gentleness he puts to her the question: 'Are you well-satisfied that I suffered for you?'[48] When she replies emphatically in the affirmative, he rejoices: if she is satisfied, then so is he, and more than satisfied. He tells her that if he could suffer more he would suffer more, because our redemption is so joyful and pleasing to him that he would count all his sufferings on our behalf as nothing by comparison. Great as was his suffering

The love which made him suffer it surpasses all his sufferings, as much as
heaven is above the earth.

In just the same way as his love surpasses all his sufferings, so will our
eternal bliss and reward far surpass our own.

For I saw most truly that always, as our contrariness makes for us on earth
pain, shame and sorrow, just so in contrary manner grace makes for us in
heaven solace, honour and bliss, so superabundant that when we come up
and receive that sweet reward which grace has made for us, there we shall
thank and bless our Lord, endlessly rejoicing that we ever suffered woe...[49]

Although at the present it seems impossible to conceive of ever giving
thanks for all the suffering we are forced to undergo, and it seems
wicked even to contemplate giving thanks for such tragic events as the
Black Death and all the suffering this caused, Julian is clear that the
rewards will be so great that we will actually be glad that we suffered.
Just as Jesus rejoiced in his suffering, because it resulted in that which
he greatly desired, so also will we: as, indeed, Julian herself rejoiced in
the deeper experience of God which came through her own illness and
suffering in answer to her prayer.

As it stands, this clearly cannot be a solution to the problem of why
God allows suffering in the first place. It would be a perverse parent
who tortured his child or allowed it to undergo excruciating physical
and mental pain, justifying himself with the promise that he will
subsequently reward the child. Even if the parent *did* subsequently
reward the child, and even if the pleasure of the reward far outweighed
the pain of the suffering, this still would not make it all right for the
parent to have allowed the child to be tortured if he could have prevented it. The only way in which subsequent reward could compensate for suffering would be if the reward were intrinsic to the suffering,
and impossible without it. Otherwise we would expect God to behave
as a loving parent, giving good gifts to his children and taking away
pain from their lives. All the joys of heaven cannot justify previous
pain and suffering unless those joys are in some way a direct result of
the suffering, not just as compensating rewards, but as intrinsically
impossible without the pain.

Julian would not disagree. Although it is important to her that suffering will be rewarded, this is not an external relationship, as though a
certain number of units of pain merited a certain number of units of
reward. Again, the fixed point is the suffering of Jesus. The joy and
delight which for him made his suffering worthwhile is in the fact that
it results in Julian's salvation – and ours. For this, no price is too high.
The redemption brought about by his passion

is so great a joy to Jesus that he counts as nothing his labour and his sufferings and his cruel and shameful death ... This deed and this work for our

186

salvation were as well devised as God could devise it. It was done as honourably as Christ could do it, and here I saw complete joy in Christ, for his joy would not have been complete if the deed could have been done any better than it was.[50]

The example which Julian follows in her thinking, therefore, is one in which the reward of the suffering could not have come about unless Jesus had suffered: the two are intrinsically related. Consequently one would expect that this would also be her view about the relationship between our suffering and the bliss of heaven; and this, indeed, is the case. The pain which we bear, she says, is directly related to the reward, because it is through the pain that we develop the 'wounds' of contrition, compassion, and the longing for God without which we could never be receptive to the delights of his love.

Julian, as we have seen, considers sin to be the most grievous of all the pains we have to bear, because it fractures our personality and sets our sensuality against our godly will which is united to God. Therefore if the heavenly reward is to compensate for suffering, it must above all compensate for sin and all its pain. This must be so not merely in an extrinsic sense, but as a direct consequence of the sin, so that the sin is a necessary condition of the reward which would be impossible without it. We are not accustomed to thinking along these lines: we might perhaps think that God will remove sorrow and pain from us in heaven, but we are more inclined to think that God's rewards will be for good deeds done in this life than for bad ones. Yet Julian boldly says that sin itself will be rewarded.

And God showed that sin will be no shame, but honour to man, for just as there is indeed a corresponding pain for every sin, just so love gives to the same soul a bliss for every sin. Just as various sins are punished with various pains, the more grievous are the sins, so will they be rewarded with various joys in heaven to reward the victories over them, to the degree in which the sin may have been painful and sorrowful to the soul on earth.[51]

At the heart of her thinking here is her notion of the godly will at the root of our personality. At bottom, because of this godly will, there is a level within us at which we do not consent to sin. However, because it is also true that at another level our sin is indeed voluntary, the consequence is that sin divides us against ourselves and sets up a conflict within us. This conflict is between that in us which does not want to be wicked and the godly will which never gives its consent as long as we are human beings bearing the image of God.[52] This internal fracture and the suffering it causes Julian considers to be the worst of all suffering and in some sense the cause of all the rest. Therefore if suffering is to be rewarded, it is sin above all which must find compensation, and this must be somehow intrinsic to the sin itself, so that the sin is necessary for it.

This, indeed, Julian takes to be so. It is because of the brokenness brought about by sin that the three wounds of contrition, compassion, and longing for God are developed.

> Sin is the sharpest scourge with which any chosen soul can be struck, which scourge belabours man or woman, and breaks a man, and purges him in his own sight so much that at times he thinks himself that he is not fit for anything but as it were to sink into hell, until contrition seizes him by the inspiration of the Holy Spirit and turns bitterness into hope of God's mercy. And then the wounds begin to heal and the soul to revive, restored to the life of the Church.[53]

The confession to which the Holy Spirit leads the contrite individual, and the humility and willing submission to penance, heal the fragmentation of our sinful state and gives us in place of this ignoble wounding the honourable wounds. But these, far from being marks of shame, are turned into marks of honour, just as the wounds of the crucified Jesus are turned into the badges of his glory.

> For every sinful soul must be healed by these medicines. Though he be healed, his wounds are not seen by God as wounds but as honours. And as we are punished here with sorrow and penance, in contrary fashion we shall be rewarded in heaven by the courteous love of our almighty God, who does not want anyone who comes there to lose his labours in any degree. For he regards sin as sorrow and pains for his lovers, to whom for love he assigns no blame. The reward which we shall receive will not be small, but it will be great, glorious and honourable. And so all shame will be turned into honour and joy.[54]

Just how this process takes place we will consider in more detail in later sections, for Julian meditates on it at length until it becomes both her understanding of the problem of evil and the basis for her teaching on the development of spiritual wholeness. We should note, however, that she never supposes that it is always obvious that sin and its fragmentation are having this positive effect: we will in many cases have to wait until heaven before it becomes apparent. Nevertheless Julian is bolstered in her thinking by some of the heroes of the Church who are known to have been miserable sinners and who became great saints, with a greatness not unrelated to their previous condition. In the case of David, Mary Magdalene, Peter and Paul, their spiritual greatness is partly a result of their sin, grievous though it was. Especially dear to Julian's heart is the account of John of Beverley, a monk of Whitby and a bishop of York in the early part of the eighth century. During his bishopric, he founded a monastery at Beverley, which was at that time in a heavily forested area, where he retired to pray. Julian tells us that in spite of his sanctity, 'God allowed him to fall': she seems to expect her readers to know about this and goes into no detail, and no record or even legend is now extant. Although our curiosity remains unsatisfied, however, the point of her comments is in any case not his fall but its aftermath:

> Afterwards God raised him to many times more grace, and for the contrition and meekness that he had as he lived, God has given him in heaven manifold joys, exceeding what he would have had if he had not sinned or fallen.[55]

From this example Julian took comfort, accepting that although it is only in a few instances like this that we can actually see how the fragmentation of sin is turned into honour, they do illustrate that it is more generally true. When we have the longer view of heaven as well as earth, we will be able to say that none of our pain and suffering was wasted; all was taken up in the mercy of God to bring about a result impossible without them and out of comparison greater than any suffering that was a part of it.

This is not a complete response to the problem of sin and pain, and Julian never pretends that it is. It is very difficult indeed to see how the illness and pain and grief and distress caused by the Black Death, or the corruption and pomposity of the Church which generated the abortive Norwich crusade under Bishop Despenser are in any way intrinsically connected to the whole-making and ultimate honour which she envisages. We can perhaps see in the cases of her examples how a fall into sin resulted in a more complete sanctity; yet it is not difficult to think of examples where the opposite takes place. In far too many cases instead of suffering resulting in greater wholeness, it brings about bitter, twisted personalities, broken in themselves, and inflicting further harm and brokenness on others.

Julian is aware of this, and speaks, as we have seen, of the great mystery which we cannot penetrate. Yet her assurance that all sin and pain will be rewarded and will bring about a good out of comparison to the pain itself is of great significance. Just as the idea that sin has no substance is not by itself any solution to the sin and pain of this world, so neither is the idea that it will all receive full compensation. Yet if the idea lying behind the former is that sin is not the first thing to be said about the human condition, but is rather a warping and fracturing of something intrinsically good and beautiful, so also the idea lying behind the teaching that all will be rewarded is that sin is not the last thing to be said about human nature. In the end it will be abolished. And its abolition will not be just as something that had no point or use, but as a necessary, but temporary, state of affairs which we will 'suddenly pass over'. No matter how widespread and powerful they now are, sin and suffering will not triumph. The greatest suffering there ever was, that of Jesus on the cross, ended in the joy of Easter. Though we cannot see how all pain and sin can be taken up into a greater wholeness, Julian is assured by the living Lord that we too can anticipate resurrection in delight and joy, where nothing will have been wasted. God longs, she says,

> to bring us up into bliss, as souls are when they are taken out of pain into heaven ... and that will be fulfilled on the last day, to last forever. For I saw what is known in our faith, that pain and sorrow will be ended then for those who will be saved.[56]

The Lord and the Servant

Although Julian has been assured that sin and its attendant suffering will not be wasted in the good purposes of God, and has been given examples of how the grievous wounds of sin have been turned into honours, she is still not fully satisfied. It does not seem possible to her to reconcile the teaching that there is no wrath in God with the teaching of the Church that those who rebel against him will be condemned to hell; and it is on this point that she focuses all her perplexity about the problem of sin and suffering. The only thing for her to do is to pursue the question further with God himself; and so she says,

> Good Lord, I see in you that you are very truth, and I know truly that we sin grievously all day and are very blameworthy; and I can neither reject my knowledge of this truth, nor see that any kind of blame is shown to us. How can this be?[57]

Julian's continued bewilderment here, in the context of her direct experience of the powerful love of God, is instructive. We have already noted how fully this speaks for her integrity and sturdy common sense: not even the most overwhelming experience could shake her from seeking answers to hard questions or make her content to bask in emotional glow. However, it also shows that even direct experience of God such as she had is not any guarantee that all questions will be answered and all bewilderment resolved. For Julian, quite the contrary is the case: the bewilderment about the problem of sin and suffering in the world is increased in intensity, rather than resolved, by her experience of God's love in the passion of Christ, and we have seen why this should be so.

Furthermore, this bewilderment is not dissipated by the fact that she has already been given partial answers. Although she accepts that in the sense described sin is 'nothing', and although she recognizes that in some ways it must remain an irresolvable surd, a mystery which only God can explain and which we will not fully understand until he makes all things clear to us, she nevertheless does not leave it alone. She has been given the assurance *that* all wounds will be turned into honours, but she feels a need to be clearer about *how* this might come to pass. Because she does not as yet understand the means by which such a triumphant conclusion could be reached, the moral and spiritual and intellectual difficulties raised by sin and suffering are for Julian a great affliction, even in the context of an unmistakable experience of the love of God. Nor is there the slightest hint in her writing that she considered this affliction inappropriate. It is simply not the case that the experience of God's love is a panacea for mental and spiritual anguish.

> And between these two oppositions my reason was greatly afflicted by my blindness, and I could have no rest for fear that his blessed presence would pass from my sight, and I should be left in ignorance of how he may look on us in our sin ... My longing endured as I constantly beheld him; and yet I could have no patience because of great fear and perplexity ...[58]

Julian, therefore, takes courage to ask for yet further enlightenment, and considers that it is appropriate for her to do so. Her reasons are interesting: first, she thinks that it is a very little thing that she is asking God to do in asking him to grant her further enlightenment. Had she been requesting a great matter, she says, she would have been afraid; but because it is such a small thing her fear can be transcended. We might take a slightly wry view of this: if a resolution to the problem of evil is small, what would be big? For Julian, however, her understanding of the loving power of God is such that she sees her request for enlightenment as a very small thing for him to grant. He, after all, has already assured her that

> I may make all things well, and I can make all things well, and I shall make all things well, and I will make all things well; and you will see for yourself that every kind of thing will be well.[59]

In the light of this assurance, the request for understanding *how* this could be true seems to her to be a very small one.

Secondly, she is prepared to make the request because it is general rather than specific. As we noted, she had earlier been warned against asking for information about specific people and events, and encouraged to understand the will of God in more general terms, applicable to all her fellow-Christians rather than only to some specific ones. She seems to be referring back to this instruction when she says that because she is now asking for general enlightenment about how God looks upon sin, rather than asking how some particular sin or hurt will be turned into honour in her own case or the case of another person, she need not be afraid.

Finally, it is a practical request. It seems to Julian that if she is to go on living after her illness, and is to be able to discern good from evil, then it is necessary for her to know how God looks upon sin and its attendant suffering, and also how to square this with the teaching of Holy Church whose precepts she is bound to obey. If Julian could not reconcile what she experienced to be true of God with what she had been taught by the Church, that would put her in a highly untenable position. Therefore it was necessary to her to have further enlightenment, so that she might take such practical steps as were necessary, and might know how to go on with her vocation, discriminating between good and evil.

In the light of these reasons, therefore, Julian appeals to the Lord for help.

> I cried within me with all my might, beseeching God for help in this fashion: Ah, Lord Jesus, king of bliss, how shall I be comforted, who will tell me and teach me what I need to know, if I cannot at this time see it in you?[60]

From what we have already seen of the depth and effectiveness of Julian's prayer, we can be sure that this is no trivial request, and that there is a high probability that it will be granted. And granted, indeed, it is; though not, perhaps, in the way that Julian expected. In answer to her request, she is by the courtesy of the Lord given further revelation in the form of a complex vision.

The vision is of a lord and a servant. It is shown both 'spiritually, in a bodily likeness', and also 'more spiritually, without bodily likeness': that is, both as a vision and as spiritual understanding which goes beyond and interprets the contents of the vision itself. In the vision, the lord sits in state, while the servant stands before him, eager to do his bidding. When the lord sends him off on a task, the servant 'dashes off, and runs at great speed, loving to do his lord's will'.[61] Almost at once, however, he comes to grief.

> He falls into a dell and is greatly injured; and then he groans and moans and tosses about and writhes, but he cannot rise or help himself in any way.[62]

Worst of all is the fact that he cannot be comforted. It was not, indeed, that the lord was angry with him. Quite the contrary: the lord was very close to him, and was full of compassion and consolation, but the servant was unable to turn his face to look at the lord, and instead of drawing hope and consolation from him in his afflictions, he concentrated on his misery and distress, the pain of his body and his mind which was so intense that not only could he not rise, but he hardly even remembered his love for the lord. Most astonishing of all to Julian was the fact that he was completely isolated in his misery: she says that

> I looked all around and searched, and far and near, high and low, I saw no help for him.[63]

In all this, Julian says that she looked very carefully to see whether the servant's fall into the ditch and his continued suffering there was in any way blameworthy, but she could find no reason to suppose so. His fall was a result of the alacrity with which he obeyed his lord, not of any wilfulness on his part. Having noted this, Julian repeats that she saw that the lord himself imputed no blame to his servant, and was not in the least cross with him, but rather was planning a reward for the servant after he would be rescued.

> Then this courteous lord said this: See my beloved servant, what harm and injuries he has had and accepted in my service for my love, yes, and for his good will. Is it not reasonable that I should reward him for his fright and his fear, his hurt and his injuries and all his woe? And furthermore, is it not proper for me to give him a gift, better for him and more honourable than his own health could have been? Otherwise, it seems to me that I should be ungracious.[64]

When she moves from the vision itself to the spiritual understanding of it, this aspect is deepened: she reports that it was revealed to her that the reward of the servant would be far beyond what it would have been had he never fallen into the ditch, and indeed that the wounds and distress he received from the fall would be 'turned into high, surpassing honour and endless bliss'.[65]

In itself, this is not new: it is the theme of wounds being turned into honours which we have already considered. It takes Julian no further in her perplexity of *how* this might come about, nor does it resolve her worry about the deliberate and (at least in the eyes of the Church) blameworthy nature of much of our sinfulness. How can this vision of the lord and the servant help her? The vision and its bearing on her dilemma is so hard to understand that at first she feels she is hardly anything further forward as a result of it. She does not even include it in the first account of her showings: she says that although she believed that it came as an answer to her prayers, she was so bewildered by it that she could not be comforted.[66] Nevertheless, she recognized that somehow it contained what she was looking for: 'The secrets of the revelation were deeply hidden in this mysterious example.' Some glimmerings of its meaning she had from the time that it was revealed; and gradually more became clear to her. Yet it was twenty years less three months later when she was still pondering it that she received what she calls an 'inward instruction':

> You ought to take heed to all the attributes, divine and human, which were revealed in the example, though this may seem to you mysterious and ambiguous.[67]

With this she gladly complies, and its result is its exposition in the Long Text, a discussion which might with justification be considered the key to her whole teaching.

She began by considering all the details of what she had seen, in case some of them had a significance which she had missed; and she says that in her prayerful contemplation of them, the Lord continued to instruct her as she used her own intellect and understanding to the greatest extent of her capability. She focused first of all on the outward details: the colour and style of the clothing worn by the lord and the servant, the posture and place of each of them, and their demeanour toward one another. It was from the first clear to her that the lord represented God, and that the servant represented Adam and his fall; and from the first also she understood Adam here to stand for all human beings and their falling, rather than simply a historical figure.[68]

One major result of the servant falling into the ditch, she perceives, was that his understanding was injured because he could no longer look upon his lord; and although his good will was intact, he himself was not able to recognize this because of the impairment of his understanding. Thus he did not even recognize that he still loved his lord and wanted to serve him; he felt completely alienated. His affliction here is double: he knows neither his lord nor himself. Because of this, there is no rest or peace possible to him.[69]

This is a return to a theme which we have already explored: the good will or image of God which remains within us despite our sinfulness. Julian sees that because of the blindness of our understanding, we are prevented from knowing the goodness of our own souls, and thus we despair. We feel guilty and alienated and utterly unworthy of love and unable to receive it. Until the love of God penetrates us so that we know ourselves as lovable we can find no peace. Julian believes that through his courtesy, his love is available to us so that we can come to know ourselves and be reintegrated with our substance in a gradual process which begins here and will be completed in heaven: the more fully this is received, the more we are able to enter into peace and rest.

The blindness, however, is all too real; and it effectively prevents us from recognizing that at bottom we really do want to be good and to know the love of God. Julian assures us that God understands even this. He is not vexed with us because of our blindness; he recognizes that this is an injury from a fall which was sustained in the very eagerness to do his will.

> And the loving regard which he kept constantly on his servant, and especially when he fell, it seemed to me that it could melt our hearts for love and break them in two for joy . . . The compassion and pity of the Father were for Adam, who is his most beloved creature . . . The merciful regard of his lovely countenance filled all the earth, and went down with Adam into hell, and by this continuing pity Adam was kept from endless death. And this mercy and pity abides with mankind until the time that we come up to heaven. But man is blinded in this life, and therefore we cannot see our Father, God, as he is.[70]

The obvious question in all this is why the blindness was permitted to occur. Even if it be true that there is a sense in which our wills are good and we retain the image of God, so that in that sense no sin is deliberate (no matter how wilful it is in the more conventional sense), it still remains the case that we are badly fragmented creatures. If the fragmentation is in our understanding, so that often we do not even recognize our longing for God and his goodness, this explains how it is that we can have a godly will without knowing it. What it does not explain is why God permitted the fall and its resultant blindness in the first place.

By attending to the details of the vision, Julian makes a little more progress. She sees that the servant, having great love for his lord, wished to do the thing that would most honour him. And that thing, it turns out, is to serve him with some special delicious food. The food, however, is not yet prepared; indeed, it is not even grown. The servant

> was to be a gardener, digging and ditching and sweating and turning the soil over and over, and to dig deep down, and to water the plants at the proper time. And he was to persevere in his work, and make sweet streams to run, and fine and plenteous fruit to grow, which he was to bring before the lord and serve him with to his liking.[71]

The idea of the servant as a gardener, 'digging and ditching and sweating', has overtones of the parable of the vineyard in Isaiah 5, and of Jesus' elaboration of it in the Gospels,[72] where he identifies himself with the gardener trying to bring fruit to his lord.

At first it might seem as if it was very selfish of the lord to require his servant to go and work so hard for him, especially given the dangers involved; but Julian does not intend such an implication. In her vision, the servant longs to do something special for the lord, as we might long to do something special for a dearly loved friend for a birthday. Rather than rejecting such a self-offering of love and saying that he had everything he wanted already, the lord in his courtesy made it possible for the servant to do something to honour him, and was willing to receive the servant's expression of love and devotion.

A parent who knows that their child wishes to give them a present as an expression of love may well have to supply the child both with the money and the idea for the gift. If the parent says that they don't want anything, or if the parent brushes aside the child's generous desire by saying that it is the intention that counts and refuses to make it possible for the child to express that intention, the effect is a rejection of the offered love. Part of what it is to receive the child's love is to give the child an opportunity to express it. The same is true, of course, of adults as well: to receive the love of others we cannot merely sit passively and wait for them to love us, but must be willing to make occasions and opportunities for them to express it. It takes as much imaginative effort to receive love with joy and delight as it does to give it.

The lord in Julian's example does not brush aside the servant's desire to express his love; in his courtesy he gives the servant the means of showing that devotion. But why the ditch? Couldn't the lord have foreseen that the servant would fall headlong into it? It seems to me that the answer must be that he could, if not with certainty, at least with probability. Why, then, did he allow it to happen?

We might reflect that a parent who gives a child opportunity to express love does not remove the possibility of any cost to the child; otherwise the child's efforts and generosity are demeaned. If the situation is made such that the child really contributes nothing, whether in money or in effort, then the whole thing has become a charade and the child is made to feel that his or her generosity counts for nothing after all. Thus also the lord, if he removed all danger and all possibility of fall from the servant, would hardly have been allowing the servant to express the generosity and love which was his intention.

Nevertheless, no parent who can foresee it allows a child to contribute so much that the child's whole life and happiness is at risk. There is a mean between allowing no contribution at all and requiring the life's blood! Surely it would have been enough if the lord had allowed and received with thanks the toil and sweat of the servant, without also allowing him to fall into the ditch?

Here Julian has some further insight. She had said at the beginning of the exposition of this vision that it had been shown 'doubly with respect to the lord, and ... doubly with respect to the servant'; and we now come upon the second aspect. Not only does the servant represent Adam, and with him all humankind; he also represents Christ, the true Adam.

> When Adam fell, God's Son fell; because of the true union which was made in heaven, God's Son could not be separated from Adam, for by Adam I understand all mankind. Adam fell from life into death, into the valley of this wretched world, and after that into hell. God's Son fell with Adam, into the valley of the womb of the maiden who was the fairest daughter of Adam, and that was to excuse Adam from blame in heaven and on earth; and powerfully he brought him out of hell ... For in all this our good Lord showed his own Son and Adam as only one man.[73]

The lord had indeed foreseen the fall into the ditch; but he had also foreseen the rescue.

It is the Augustinian theme of *felix culpa*, the happy fault which resulted in the coming of Christ, and thus of greater honour and delight both to ourselves and to the Father than there would have been had there never been a fall. Wounds turned into honours are far more glorious and more beautiful than unbruised and untried innocence. The Father has made provision in Christ for all wounds to be healed, and thus for a development of a mature love which far surpasses the possibilities of a naive state.

> We know that when man fell so deeply and so wretchedly through sin, there was no other help for restoring him, except through him who created man. And he who created man for love, by the same love wanted to restore man to the same blessedness *and even more*. And just as we were made like the Trinity in our first making, our Creator wished us to be like Jesus Christ our saviour in heaven forever, through the power of our making again.[74]

Many Fathers and doctors of the Church had pondered this theme, among them Thomas Aquinas, meditating on the writings of Gregory the Great. No one would want to say that innocence was a bad thing, nor would one deliberately corrupt such innocence in order to bring about maturity. Nevertheless, Aquinas says that in spite of innocence being good,

> Yet God is said to rejoice more over the penitent than over the innocent, because often penitents rise from sin more cautious, humble, and fervent. Hence Gregory commenting on these words says that, 'In battle, the general loves the soldier who after flight returns and bravely pursues the enemy, more than him who has never fled, but has never done a brave deed.'[75]

In the same way, Julian holds that there is even more blessedness for the person who has fallen into the ditch than there would be for one who had remained spotless. It is not that spotlessness is a bad thing; but that God has special tender care for one who has 'fallen into a ditch'.

Julian, seeing this in the context of her visions of the dying Christ, is also made aware of his rejoicing in the fact that he could offer her his suffering love: it is a parallel theme to the theme of the servant who longed to do something costly for his lord. Just as the servant ran gladly to take the opportunity to toil and labour and bring treasure to the lord, so also the Son of God went eagerly to give his love and restoration through his suffering: we recall his words in an earlier vision:

> If you are satisfied, I am satisfied. It is a joy, a bliss, an endless delight to me that ever I suffered my Passion for you; and if I could suffer more, I should suffer more.[76]

This is not a masochistic delight in suffering, but rather gladness at the opportunity of giving himself in love, as we on a much smaller scale are glad and delighted when we can do something to express what we feel for someone we dearly love.

This identification of Adam with Christ brings Julian to a resolution of part of her dilemma about the blame that seems to attach to sin. It had seemed to her that sin must be blameworthy; yet she saw no blame in the countenance of the lord – nor, indeed, any blame in the servant's fall into the ditch and his resultant blindness. Though there was great hurt to the servant in this, it was not through any evil intention. Yet the Church does and must assign blame to sin. How is it that the Church does so, when the Father does not? Julian now recognizes that the blame that attaches to our sin attaches only in consequence of our fragmentation. Because we are not inwardly integrated, and our sensuality is not united with our substance, we act blindly and wilfully; and in one sense this is indeed blameworthy. Yet in another sense all of this is a result of the blindness and fragmentation that is not our fault and that, did we but fully recognize it, we do not desire.

There is therefore a sense in which, in the sight of God, we are not blameworthy for our sins; and another sense in which the Church can best help us toward integration by holding us responsible and attaching blame. In terms of God's point of view,

> Our good Lord Jesus [has] taken upon him all our blame; and therefore our Father may not, does not wish to assign more blame to us than to his own beloved Son Jesus Christ. So he was the servant before he came on earth, standing ready in purpose before the Father until the time when he would send him to do the glorious deed by which mankind was brought back to heaven.[77]

Though there may be elements of a theology of penal substitution here, a theology mediated to the Middle Ages partly by Anselm's famous *Cur Deus Homo?*, Julian's theology is fundamentally different. According to the doctrine of penal substitution, God does initially assign blame to humankind for our sin; but because the Son takes the blame in our place, we can be saved. Julian's view, by contrast, is that God does not attach blame at all. There is no fault in the servant's fall into the ditch, and the lord never looks on him with anger but only with compassion and plans for a reward for his faithfulness. Even when the servant is blinded and divided against himself, no longer even realizing that his deepest will is still to love and serve his lord, the lord does not impute blame, but looks upon him with pity; because the blindness and the self-fragmentation is itself a result of a fall which was suffered in the course of great eagerness to do something especially loving for the lord. Therefore the blame which Julian is speaking of when she says that the Lord Jesus has 'taken upon him all our blame' is not the blame of God upon us. Just as God does not blame his Son, who is utterly beloved in his eyes, no more does he blame us, who are equally beloved, despite our wretchedness. The blame, rather, is part of our own confusion, our self-blame, the unproductive sense of guilt and worthlessness which make us feel that we are utterly unlovable even – or especially – in the sight of God, and that he could not possibly love and want us. It is this blame and self-loathing which Jesus has taken upon himself, coming to show us his endless love and the endless love of the Father to us, so that we can find dignity and worth and integration in that love of his.

This, however, is not to minimize sin or its guilt or blameworthiness at another level. Sin is both a symptom and an exacerbation of our fragmentation and wretchedness. Not only does it result from our blindness, it actually makes it worse, deepening the wounds of our personality and inflicting those wounds on others. Furthermore, in our dis-integrated state, some part of our personality does actually *want* to sin, even though another part of ourselves wants to be good. In that sense we are indeed blameworthy for our sins; though the fact of wanting to sin is itself a result of our fractured personality. Thus we sin 'through negligence, through weakness, through our own deliberate fault'; and we need to be delivered from all of this and made whole again.

It is just this that is the primary task of the Church: mediating the love of God to broken men and women so that they may find deliverance from their sinfulness and healing for their wounds. In this connection it is useful to return to Julian's earlier comments about sin and the devastating effect of guilt and self-loathing which it produces, so that a person 'thinks himself that he is not fit for anything but as it were to sink into hell'.[78] This bitterness of soul can be turned into an occasion for the mercy of God; and the Church has a primary role to play in this transformation.

> The Holy Spirit leads him to confession, willing to reveal his sins, nakedly and truthfully, with great sorrow and great shame that he has so befouled God's fair image. Then he accepts the penance for every sin imposed by his confessor, for this is established in Holy Church by the teaching of the Holy Spirit; and this is one meekness which greatly pleases God.[79]

The Church attaches blame to sin, not in the sense that it rejects the ultimacy of God's love, but in the sense that it recognizes sin's seriousness and the need to be healed from the bitterness of its wounds, and provides means for the cure of souls. The Church's reason for existence is to enable broken human beings to be made whole in the love of God.

For this healing, it is necessary that the Church provides the means of making renunciation of sin concrete, and enables real repentance and opportunity for newness of life. Confession and penance facilitate this. They can of course be wrongly used; the Reformation was a protest against their use as though they were a form of magic by which the seriousness of sin could be ignored. But used properly, they help an individual to make a concrete act of turning from the ways of brokenness and renew the longing for God which is met by his love.

> By contrition we are made clean, by compassion we are made ready, and by
> true longing for God we are made worthy. These are three means, as I under-
> stand, through which all souls come to heaven, those, that is to say, who
> have been sinners on earth and will be saved. For every sinful soul must be
> healed by these medicines. Though he be healed, his wounds are not seen by
> God as wounds but as honours ... For he regards sin as sorrow and pains for
> his lovers, to whom for love he assigns no blame.[80]

This is not, of course, to say that formal confession and penance as
practised by the Church in Julian's time is the only way in which sin
and the things exacerbating brokenness can be forsaken and one can be
enabled to turn to God to receive his love and goodness, nor did she
ever think it was. It is, however, *a* way. Whatever way the Church uses,
it will have to proceed by taking seriously and indeed assigning blame
for those things which display and deepen the fracturing of the personality; even though at a deeper level these are only symptoms of a
wound for which God does not assign blame.

Thus some of Julian's perplexity about the conflict she perceives
between God's continuous love and the absence of wrath in God, as
contrasted with the blame which the Church assigns to sin, can be
resolved. The Church must assign blame, in the sense that it must take
seriously our responsibility for the manifestations of the brokenness of
our deepest selves; yet that brokenness is itself not blameworthy in the
sight of God but is rather a wound suffered in his service.

This does not resolve all the problems, however. In particular, it does
not solve the question of why the wounding was permitted: why was
the particular blindness and fragmentation of the personality allowed
to be a result of trying to love and serve God? Julian does not know the
answer to this, except insofar as she trusts God that there will be far
greater honour to him and fulness of life for us because of this wounding than would ever have been possible without it: the wounds will be
turned into honours. At once we want to ask whether this will be so for
everyone: is it really true that, even in the light of eternity, everyone
will have greater fulness of life because of sin and its attendant suffering – not just as an external reward, but in a way that would not have
been possible without sin? Julian affirms that this is so, as we have
seen; but also affirms that it is a great mystery which God will reveal in
his own time. We might almost say that she looks forward to a seventeenth revelation, one which we will all share with her, of the loving
purposes of God. She has, indeed, a foretaste of it:

> Now the lord does not sit on the ground in the wilderness, but in his rich and
> noblest seat, which he made in heaven most to his liking. Now the Son does
> not stand before the Father as a servant before the lord, pitifully clothed,
> partly naked, but he stands immediately before the Father, richly clothed in
> joyful amplitude, with a rich and precious crown upon his head. For it was
> revealed that *we are his crown*, which crown is the Father's joy, the Son's

honour, the Holy Spirit's delight, and endless marvellous bliss to all who are in heaven.[81]

Notes to Chapter Nine

1. As, in a sense, it was for Augustine, whose ideas Julian also ponders (whether or not she knew them to be his); cf. G. R. Evans, *Augustine on Evil* (Cambridge University Press 1982).
2. The phrase is from Jürgen Moltmann, *The Crucified God* (E. tr. SCM, London, 1974).
3. See for example John Passmore, *The Perfectibility of Man* (Duckworth, London, 1970), Chaps. 6 and 14.
4. See my 'Ethics and Mysticism: Friends or Foes', in *Nederlands Theologisch Tijdschrift*, vol. 3 No. 4 (1985).
5. LT 17.
6. LT 28.
7. LT 29.
8. LT 20.
9. LT 27.
10. LT 29.
11. Augustine, *Confessions* VII.8; VIII.9; X.3; X.41–3, etc.; cf. *Homilies on the Gospel of John* XII.11; *De Lib. Arb.* III.18, etc.
12. Among them the English writers Bede, *In Luc.* III, super X, 30; and Anselm, *Prayer to St Mary* (1), etc.
13. *Summa Theologiae* I.2, Q85, a3.
14. LT 39.
15. LT 11.
16. LT 27.
17. LT 28.
18. LT 30.
19. ST 15.
20. cf. Simon Tugwell, *Ways of Imperfection*, Ch. 16.
21. LT 31.
22. cf. Stewart Sutherland, *God, Jesus and Belief* (SCM, London, 1985).
23. LT 35.
24. LT 36.
25. LT 32.
26. ibid.
27. LT 33.
28. LT 32.
29. ibid.
30. Robert Llewelyn, *With Pity not with Blame* (DLT, London, 1982), p.130.
31. LT 33.
32. LT 46; cf. Richard Harries, 'On the Brink of Universalism', in Robert Llewelyn, ed., *Julian, Woman of our Day* (DLT, London, 1985); Robert Llewelyn, *Love Bade me Welcome* (DLT, London, 1984).
33. LT 49.
34. LT 48.
35. LT 11.
36. LT 27.
37. In this she is consistent with the theme of the image of God in Bernard of

Clairvaux, which can be defaced but never removed; cf. *Sermons on the Song of Songs* 82.5; Étienne Gilson, *The Mystical Theology of St Bernard* (Sheed & Ward, London, 1940), p. 54 & *passim*.
38. Augustine, *Confessions* 7.12, tr. Clark.
39. LT 13.
40. LT 27.
41. ST 23.
42. LT 64.
43. LT 17.
44. LT 21.
45. 1 Cor. 15.52.
46. LT 3.
47. LT 15.
48. LT 22.
49. LT 48.
50. LT 22.
51. LT 38.
52. cf. Augustine, *Confessions* 8.9.
53. LT 39.
54. ibid.
55. LT 38.
56. LT 75.
57. LT 50.
58. ibid.
59. LT 31.
60. LT 50.
61. LT 51, p. 267.
62. ibid.
63. op. cit., p. 268.
64. op. cit., pp. 268–9.
65. ibid.
66. op. cit., p. 269.
67. op. cit., p. 270.
68. In this and what follows, of course, she is Pauline in her theology; cf. Romans 5.12–21; 1 Cor. 15.21–3, 45.
69. Note the parallels with Bernard of Clairvaux, *Sermons on the Song of Songs*, 82.5, yet also the compassion and absence of accusation in Julian by comparison.
70. LT 51, pp. 271–2.
71. op. cit., pp. 273–4.
72. Mark 12.1–12; Matt. 21.33–46; Luke 20.9–19.
73. LT 51, p. 274.
74. LT 10; italics mine.
75. Thomas Aquinas, *Summa Theologiae* Ia. 20.4. ad 4. The reference to Gregory is from his *In Evang.* II.34 (PL 76. 1248).
76. LT 22.
77. LT 51, p. 275.
78. LT 39.
79. ibid.
80. ibid.
81. LT 51, p. 278.

10 Spiritual Growth and Healing

In the previous chapter we considered Julian's insight into the problem of sin and suffering, and her assurance, derived partly from the parable of the lord and the servant, that nothing would be wasted. No matter how grievously wounded and damaged we are by sin and by the suffering which is the consequence of human selfishness, Julian has God's promise that all will be well; all will be turned to good account. She continues to ponder *how* this may come about, seeking to understand more of the means by which our wounds may be turned into honours as she has been promised; and she never pretends she understands it fully. This is the 'great mystery' reserved in God's private counsel until he is ready to reveal it. We might say that there is a seventeenth revelation still to come; one, however, which is not private to Julian, but will be experienced by all her 'even Christians'.

Nevertheless, although we do not have exhaustive knowledge, neither are we left in complete ignorance. We have, in the first place, the example of Christ himself, and the wounds in his hands and feet and side which have become the symbols of his glory. Furthermore, there are the examples of the spiritual heroes Julian admires, among them David, Mary Magdalene, and St John of Beverley. When Julian pondered their lives she saw that their spiritual maturity after – and in some sense because of – their sin far exceeded that of their unsullied naiveté. Julian therefore compares their sins to the wounds of Christ: they become the badges of glory.

This is a shocking comparison. Is it not verging on sacrilege to compare the wounds of Christ sustained in compassionate solidarity unto death with the human race, with the wounds inflicted on ourselves by selfishness, murder, and adultery? The wounds of Christ are indeed cause for pride and glory; but surely the wounds resulting from these sordid sins are cause only for shame and repentance.

It would be far from Julian's teaching to minimize the importance of repentance and contrition: indeed, it is only when one is brought to the point of contrition that the wounded personality can begin to heal. Sin causes the individual to despair of life itself

> until contrition seizes him by the inspiration of the Holy Spirit and turns bitterness into hope of God's mercy. And then the wounds begin to heal and

203

the soul to revive, restored to the life of Holy Church. The Holy Spirit leads him to confession, willing to reveal his sins, nakedly and truthfully, with great sorrow and great shame that he has so befouled God's fair image.[1]

Contrition, thus, is a means of healing, a medicine necessary for every sinful soul.

A fine counterpoint emerges in Julian's writings. We have noted that early in her life she prayed earnestly for 'three wounds': the wounds of contrition, compassion, and longing with the will for God. We find now that these wounds, though in some ways they are not without pain, are themselves the medicines which heal the deeper fracturing of the personality.

By contrition we are made clean, by compassion we are made ready, and by true longing for God we are made worthy ... for every sinful soul must be healed by these medicines.[2]

The same sort of counterpoint applies to the parallel she draws between our woundedness as a result of sin, and the wounds of Christ. In one sense our woundedness is indeed a source of shame and regret at spoiling the beauty of the image of God which we are. Yet it is precisely because of our sinfulness that Christ suffered his wounds, and 'with his stripes we are healed'. His wounds, like the three wounds for which Julian prayed, are wounds that heal, though in this case the wounding is his and the healing ours.

In the terms of the parable of the lord and the servant,

when Adam fell, God's Son fell. Adam fell from life to death, into the valley of this wretched world, and after that into hell. God's Son fell with Adam, into the valley of the womb of the maiden who was the fairest daughter of Adam, and that was to excuse Adam from blame in heaven and on earth; and powerfully he brought him up out of hell.[3]

Thus there is a double sense in which our sins, though a cause of shame and sorrow, are also a cause for rejoicing. In the first place, the fall of Adam resulted in the 'fall' of Christ, and therefore in the redemption that we have in him. It is as we have seen an ancient idea, reaching at least as far back as St Augustine, that because our sin had this magnificent result, we can in some ways rejoice that it happened: 'O felix culpa', happy fault, that resulted in such a stupendous restoration.

Secondly, however, as Julian sees it in her reflection upon her flawed heroes, this restoration is itself a better state than unblemished innocence could ever have been. The wounds not only provide the occasion for our salvation, they make that salvation into something which could never have been known without the brokenness which precipitated it. To a certain extent this is already available on earth: we can develop a maturity and balance because of our sins and our deliverance from them and their attendant suffering which is of value out of comparison to our innocent state. Julian, however, does not lose sight of the fact that a great deal more must wait for heaven: not all brokenness finds compensation on earth. Sometimes, indeed, it is so great that the person seems to be utterly destroyed by it, spiritually and mentally as well as physically; and even those who are much more fortunate would be rash indeed to say that they completely overcome all brokenness and find total integration in this life. Nevertheless, the fact that such growth is possible at all for anyone serves as a foretaste and promise of the day when all sin and suffering for all who will be saved shall turn into badges of glory. It is this which gives courage and hope, and delight in God who heals.

> The reward which we shall receive will not be small, but it will be great, glorious and honourable. And so all shame will be turned into honour and joy. For our courteous Lord does not want his servants to despair because they fall often and grievously; for our falling does not hinder him in loving us.[4]

The graciousness of our courteous Lord, the depth and safety of his love for us whatever happens, and the assurance that we are of incomparable worth in his sight, encourages and enables us to enter as fully as possible even now into the wholeness and healing which will one day be consummated. Because we do not have to be afraid that he will cease to love us if we fall, we are free to venture forward, taking risks if necessary, in the exploration of his healing love. Although Julian is clear that it is only in heaven that we will fully see our wounds turned into honours, she is equally clear that the assurance that this is so enables the process to take place already partly in this life, as indeed it did in the case of the heroes she cites. She offers considerable insight into how we may begin to move into the healing and delight of God, reversing the shattering effects of sin and developing an integrated and happy personality. In this final chapter, therefore, we return to her practical spirituality, drawing from her theological insights the basis for spiritual growth and healing. Julian herself, in her capacity as a counsellor to those who came to her in their need, must often have applied her teaching to them; and her book contains much solid wisdom, grounded in theology and experience, which must have stood the test of repeated application to concrete cases.

Knowing God and Knowing Ourselves

The sharpest scourge and the deepest wound we suffer according to Julian is sin, and it is of this that we must be healed. It is important, however, not to confuse 'sin' in Julian's sense with 'sins' or moral failures. Although these are not trivial, they are only symptoms of the deeper problem, the fracturing of our sensuality from our substance which is united to God. Because we have become dis-integrated from our substance, we act out our brokenness in ways that cause further injury to ourselves and others: these are sins. But sin is much deeper than sins, and is at the root of them.

In the parable of the lord and the servant we have some indication of the ways in which sin – the fracturing of the personality – leads to sins. Among the most striking of these to Julian's mind is the blindness which the servant suffers when he falls into the ditch. His whole perspective was distorted in a threefold way.

In the first place, he was blinded to his lord's loving compassion, and because of this he concentrated entirely on his own great distress rather than on any comfort or alleviation of distress which the lord might have been able to offer him.

> The greatest hurt which I saw in him was lack of consolation, for he could not turn his face to look on his loving lord, who was very close to him, in whom was all consolation; but like a man who was for the time extremely feeble and foolish, he paid heed to his feelings and his continuing distress.[5]

Like many of us when we are in trouble, his attention was riveted on his trouble and distress, and there was blindness to the compassion of God on this situation.

Secondly, he was blinded to his continued worth in his lord's sight. Because he had been unable to fulfil his intention, he felt that his lord was angry with him and no longer esteemed him:

> He neither sees clearly his loving lord, who is so meek and mild to him, nor does he truly see what he himself is in the sight of his loving lord.[6]

Because his attention was completely taken up with his distress – for which he was not blamed – he was unable to see that he was still of worth and value. He was still the bearer of the divine image, befouled though it might be by his fall into the mud. He needed radical cleansing, to be sure, but the beauty of the divine image was still there underneath the mud; it had not been destroyed.

Third, because he was blinded to himself and his own worth in the sight of his lord, he was also blinded to his own deepest nature and was unable to recognize that in spite of what had happened he still longed to serve his lord. Although 'his will was preserved in God's sight', he was so bewildered by what had happened to him that he did not even realize it,

> but he himself was blinded and hindered from knowing his will. And this is a great sorrow and a cruel suffering to him.[7]

Although he still had a 'godly will' and intended to serve his lord, his blindness about himself prevented him from recognizing this, and thus kept him at odds with himself.

This threefold blindness on the part of the servant is, according to

Julian, a parable of the threefold blindness from which we all suffer. Like the servant, we are blind to God's continuous love and care for us, looking on us with compassion, not with blame, when we wallow in a 'deep ditch' of misery.

> Our spiritual eye is so blind, and we are so burdened with the weight of our mortal flesh and the darkness of sin that we cannot see clearly the blessed face of our Lord God. No, and because of this darkness, we can scarcely believe or have faith in his great love and his faithfulness, with which he protects us.[8]

This, however, is not the whole story. Our situation is not totally that of the servant who has come to grief; it is also that of the servant who has been rescued by Christ. Although the full implications of the rescue and the reward for all our misery is in large part still future, it is nevertheless true that we can begin already to claim it and make it our own. Thus even while we are blinded creatures, we are also in increasing measure enlightened by the light of Christ. We are what Julian calls a 'marvellous mixture'.

> We have in us our risen Lord Jesus Christ, and we have in us the wretchedness and harm of Adam's falling ... And we are so afflicted in our feelings by Adam's falling in various ways, by sin and by different pains, and in this we are made dark and so blind that we can scarcely accept any comfort. But in our intention we wait for God, and trust faithfully to have mercy and grace; and this is his own working in us, and in his goodness he opens the eye of our understanding, by which we have sight, sometimes more and sometimes less, according to the ability God gives us to receive.[9]

It is important to notice what the blindness and the contrasting illumination come to. There is no implied accusation here. What Julian is saying is emphatically not that we are blind to our sinfulness and the miserable wickedness of our doings, and occasionally are enlightened to see God's dreadful displeasure. There have been sermons enough of this sort in the history of Christianity, but Julian is not one of their preachers. Her understanding rests securely in her experience of the deep love of God, who looks on us always with compassion. It is God's gentleness and comfort to which we are too often blinded, unable to receive the generosity of his acceptance and love.

Julian is much more concerned with impressing upon us the compassionate understanding of God than with making us own up to our sinfulness. In her view we are all too aware of the intolerable burden of guilt already. What we need is not to be reminded of it even more, but to be enabled to turn from absorption in our guilt and despair and its attendant depression and look instead at the comfort and mercy of God. Concentrating on our sin and guilt will never rid us of them; looking instead at the loving face of God will so deeply attract us to him that we will be drawn increasingly toward him and away from our wretchedness.

This, of course, is not to deny our sinfulness or repress our feelings of guilt and wretchedness. Only by acknowledging our actions and feelings, owning our wounds, can we be healed: this is the importance of confession and contrition. Yet this is not the same as concentrating on them. Julian strikes the balance when she says,

> So does our good Lord want us willingly to accuse ourselves, and to see truly and know our falling, and all the harms which come from it, seeing and knowing that we can never repair it; and also we willingly and truly see and know the everlasting love which he has for us, and his plentiful mercy.[10]

Rather than acquiescing in continuing guilt and despair, we are invited to turn 'willingly', that is, by a deliberate act, to the love and mercy of Christ, receiving it as he enables us.

The second form of blindness from which the servant suffered, namely blindness to his own selfhood and worth in the sight of God, is also, according to Julian, applicable to all of us, and is closely related to the first. As long as we are unable to see the love and esteem which God has for us, and instead are glued to our guilt and misery, we will be able to think of ourselves only as wicked and worthless, having lost all dignity and self-esteem. Whatever behaviour we assume for the benefit of others, at bottom we will feel ourselves to be beneath contempt, of no real value.

This is because, so long as we concentrate on our sinful condition rather than on God, we are identifying ourselves not with our true self or substance, which in Julian's teaching is continually united to God, but with our sensuality which has turned away from him. Yet it is our substance that is the image of God and the bearer of our true worth. If we concentrate on our wretchedness, it follows that we are looking away from our worth, and thus will not be able to perceive it.

As far as Julian is concerned, feelings of guilt and worthlessness are far more serious than the moral failures which are usually called sins. Partly this is because unresolved feelings of these sorts prevent us from living in the joy and freedom of God's loving presence. Partly also it is because they represent unhealed fracturing and pain at the core of the personality. The result of such pain will inevitably be pain-behaviour, actions arising out of the depths of our wounded psyche which only serve to deepen the hurts even further, and in the process hurt others as well. Indeed it is from this source that sins in the sense of moral failures usually arise. If the deep wounds are cured, the sins which are symptomatic and expressive of them need no longer occur.

The deep sense of worthlessness, like our blindness to the love of

God, can already be healed in part, though in part it still waits for consummation. The face of God is seen by Julian as the face of the compassionate Christ; and his face is our face. Looking on Jesus Julian sees the dignity and value of humankind demonstrated in his humanity. If once it is fully accepted that Jesus was truly man, then it is no longer possible to despise human nature, because Jesus is the manifestation of what that nature truly is.

> That honourable city in which our Lord Jesus sits is our sensuality, in which he is enclosed; and our natural substance is enclosed in Jesus, with the blessed soul of Christ sitting at rest in the divinity. And I saw very certainly that we must necessarily be in longing and in penance until the time when we are led so deeply into God that we verily and truly know our own soul; and I saw certainly that our good Lord himself leads us into the high depth, in the same love with which he created us and in the same love with which he redeemed us, by mercy and grace, through the power of his blessed Passion.[11]

Contemplation of Christ enlightens us so that we are able to see the worth of our own selves in the love and delight which God has for us.

Thus it emerges that the blindness we have of ourselves is linked to the blindness we have of God; and in just the same way knowledge of ourselves and knowledge of God are also interlinked. We might have supposed that knowledge of ourselves was much easier to attain than knowledge of God, because we are always available to ourselves for direct introspection, whereas God often seems far removed and inaccessible. Julian, however, takes the opposite view. We are too deeply wounded and blinded by feelings of guilt and worthlessness to be able to know ourselves rightly apart from the love and affirmation of God; and it is only in knowing him that we can know ourselves.

> And so I saw most surely that it is quicker for us and easier to come to the knowledge of God than it is to know our own soul. For our soul is so deeply grounded in God and so endlessly treasured that we cannot come to knowledge of it until we first have knowledge of God, who is the Creator to whom it is united. But nevertheless I saw that we have, naturally from our fulness, to desire wisely and truly to know our own soul, through which we are taught to seek it where it is, and that is in God.[12]

Because we are created in God's image and restored by his grace, the sense of worthlessness and of being out of touch with ourselves can be removed, not by endless investigation of ourselves, but by contemplation of God in Christ. Thus Julian continues,

> God is closer to us than our own soul, for he is the foundation on which our soul stands ... For our soul sits in God in true rest, and our soul stands in God in sure strength, and our soul is naturally rooted in God in endless love. And therefore if we want to have knowledge of our soul, and communion

and discourse with it, we must seek in our Lord God in whom it is enclosed.[13]

The same contemplation of God which brings about enlightenment from blindness regarding God's loving compassion and our worth in his sight is also the remedy for the third form of blindness with which we, like the servant in Julian's parable are afflicted. Because we do not perceive our worth in God's sight, and his deep abiding love for us, we do not perceive how very much we long for him and desire to live to his glory. As we saw when we explored Julian's understanding of the godly will, there is that in us which does desire to do right; but because of the brokenness of our personality it is often impossible for us to recognize this. Because of our weakness and foolishness, Julian says, we frequently get into situations in which we are at odds with ourselves, snarled up in internal struggles in which guilt, worthlessness, and genuine desire to do right all play a part. When this happens, the distress and anguish we feel easily erupt into hurtful behaviour patterns, increasing the cycles of wounding in ourselves and in those around us.

> And the cause is blindness, because he does not see God; for if he saw God continually, he would have no harmful feelings nor any kind of prompting, no sorrowing which is conducive to sin.[14]

This is neither magic nor unrealistic piety. It is the psychological realism which recognizes that a great many of our hurtful attitudes and actions are attempts to compensate for feelings of worthlessness and insecurity and anxiety. If we saw God – if we allowed ourselves to be fully receptive of his deep abiding love and protection – these harmful feelings and the inward unhappiness which easily leads to sin would be resolved.

Julian is confident that in heaven this will be fully realized. At present, however, the 'marvellous mixture' is still our lot, as we are sometimes enabled to perceive the love and enlightenment of God, and sometimes not.

> And therefore often we fail to perceive him, and presently we fall back upon ourselves, and then we find that we feel nothing at all but the opposition that is in ourselves, and that comes from the old root of our first sin, with all that follows from our own persistence; and in this we are belaboured and tempted with the feeling of sin and of pain in many different ways, spiritually and bodily, as is known to us in this life.[15]

Although we are never fully cured of our threefold blindness in this life, it is nevertheless true that through deepening awareness of the love and mercy of Christ this affliction and its consequences can be at least partially healed, even if the full honours for these wounds have to wait until the next life. He is the light that illuminates our blindness, just as there was light around the cross at the beginning of Julian's visions, though the rest of the room was dark to her. Instead of our ignorance, therefore, Julian says that because of who he is,

> we ought to have three kinds of knowledge. The first is that we know our Lord God. The second is that we know ourselves, what we are through him in nature and in grace. The third is that we know humbly that our self is opposed to our sin and to our weakness.[16]

As these three kinds of knowledge develop in us, they displace the three kinds of blindness, and the process of wounds being turned into honours is well begun.

Practical Measures

Fundamental to our spiritual growth and healing is the increasing absorption of this threefold knowledge, bringing with it a deepening security in the love of God. But there are various practical measures which we can take to facilitate the healing of the spirit, co-operating with God in his desire for our fulfilment and joy.

The first of these arises out of the recognition that our fractured personality will not be fully healed in this life, and therefore we will, in spite of our good intentions, continue to lapse into sins. Julian is instructed that this will be so, and told not to worry about it unduly, not to be too hard on herself. The Lord says to her,

> I know well that you wish to live for my love, joyfully and gladly suffering all the penance which may come to you; but since you do not live without sin, you are depressed and sorrowful ... But do not be too much aggrieved by the sin which comes to you against your will.[17]

By this is meant not only sin about which one has no choice, for that would hardly be sin at all. It is rather that, in the course of our Christian lives, in spite of the fact that we do genuinely want to live for the glory of God, we do often sin, 'through negligence, through weakness, through our own deliberate fault', as the Prayer Book puts it; and we must regularly turn to the Lord in contrition and compassion.

Julian sees that what delights the Lord is when we rejoice in his love and in the life he gives us. He does not desire us to be depressed and sorrowful, even when we have sinned, and even though we know we will sin again. This means that to the extent that it is in our power, we should avoid things that generate depression. Now, one of the things that positively invites depression is having unrealistic expectations of ourselves, requiring of ourselves a perfection beyond what is possible for us. Inevitably we cannot live up to such high standards; and then we become sorrowful and depressed at our continuous failure, with the result that the depression becomes a much greater evil than the lapse from the unrealistically high standard.

Julian is therefore cautioned not to demand of herself a sinlessness that not even God demands of her,

> For this passing life does not require us to live wholly without sin. He loves us endlessly, and we sin customarily, and he reveals it to us most gently. And then we sorrow and moan discreetly, turning to contemplate his mercy, cleaving to his love and to his goodness, seeing that he is our medicine, knowing that we only sin.[18]

We are not to expect of ourselves an impossible standard of behaviour; and when we do sin, as we will, we are to 'sorrow and moan *discreetly*' – that is, repent of our sin and be sorry for it, but not indulge in immoderate sadness because of it. Instead of concentrating on our failure, going over and over it, we are to 'turn to contemplate his mercy'. It will do us far more good to 'cleave to his love', which does not waver no matter what we do, than to wallow in despair at our sinfulness. There is a sense in which, because of the assured love of God, we can sit lightly to our sins; not in the sense that they do not matter, but in the sense that God's love and goodness matter far more, and it is on this that we need to concentrate.

Julian is speaking here out of her own experience as well as out of the tradition of the Church. She tells us that in the middle of her visions of the love of God, as she looked at Christ on the cross, God brought it to her mind that she would sin. She was so preoccupied with the delight that she found in contemplating him, however, that she failed to pay attention.[19] After a time, the delightful revelations ceased; and with their cessation came a return of the illness and pain which had been abruptly cut off with the beginning of the revelations. With the return of the pain came a total lack of spiritual consolation, so that Julian says,

> I was as barren and dry as if the consolation which I had received before were trifling, and, as the wretched creature that I am, I mourned grievously for the bodily pains which I felt, and for lack of spiritual and bodily consolation.[20]

While she was in this condition a cleric came to see her. She told him that during the day she had been raving, and it had seemed to her that the crucifix before her had bled: she trivialized the whole revelation of God's love. When the cleric became very serious at her words, she grew ashamed of them; yet she felt that she could hardly confess her wrong-doing, having just demonstrated her disbelief.

> See how wretched I was! This was a great sin and a great ingratitude, that I was so foolish, because of a little bodily pain that I had felt, as to abandon so imprudently the strength of all this blessed revelation from our Lord God.[21]

212

However, she had done it, and there was no taking it back. All she could do was lie still and trust in the mercy of God.

As soon as she fell asleep, however, she had a terrifying nightmare of the devil trying to strangle her.

> He grinned at me with a vicious look, showing me white teeth so big that it all seemed the uglier to me. His body and his hands were misshapen, but he held me by the throat with his paws, and wanted to stop my breath and kill me, but he could not.[22]

Her own unfaithfulness to what she had been taught, and her failure to confess it at once, provided the occasion for further temptation to fear and despair,[23] expressing itself in nightmare.

At last she woke up, 'more dead than alive', scarcely able to believe that the nightmare was an apparition, not an objective reality perceivable by others in the room: it was only when they denied being aware of any of the stench which she experienced that she recognized the temptation for what it was.

> And at once I had recourse to what our Lord had revealed to me on that same day, and to all the faith of Holy Church, for I regarded them both as one, and I fled to them as to my source of strength. And immediately everything vanished, and I was brought to great rest and peace, without sickness of body or fear of conscience.[24]

From this point she was able to go back and ponder the meaning of the Lord saying to her that she would sin, but that in spite of her sin, his love and mercy would continue. Therefore she should not despair at her sin; such despair merely provided occasion for further temptation. The Lord then gave her a sixteenth showing, in which he assured her that the previous ones were no hallucination; and he ended with a firm assurance, for Julian and for all her fellow-Christians: 'You will not be overcome.'

> And these words: You will not be overcome, were said very insistently and strongly, for certainty and strength against every tribulation which may come. He did not say: You will not be troubled, you will not be belaboured, you will not be disquieted; but he said: You will not be overcome. God wants us to pay attention to these words, and always to be strong in faithful trust, in well-being and in woe, for he loves us and delights in us, and so he wishes us to love him and delight in him and trust greatly in him, and all will be well.[25]

Julian, therefore, knows what she is talking about when she warns us against unreal expectations not to sin. Even after the wonderful experiences she had, she quickly betrayed them, and then made bad worse by despairing at what she had done and refusing to confess it, thereby laying herself open to the guilt and demonic temptation to despair which ensued in the nightmare. What we should do instead is, when we sin, repent promptly, and then hold on to the love and delight God has for us, rather than give our continued attention to the sin.

> And if we through our blindness and our wretchedness at any time fall, then let us quickly rise, knowing the sweet touching of grace, and willingly amend ourselves according to the teaching of Holy Church, as may fit the grievousness of the sin, and go on our way with God in love, and neither on the one side fall too low, inclining to despair, nor on the other side be too reckless, as though we did not care; but let us meekly recognize our weakness, knowing that we cannot stand for the twinkling of an eye except with the protection of grace, and let us reverently cling to God, trusting only in him.[26]

There is no use pretending that the wound is not there; but neither is there any use concentrating on the wound rather than on the healing love of Christ.

A second practical measure which will help us in the healing of our wounds is related to the first. If we are not to have a false picture of ourselves, with expectations which lead to frustration and depression, neither are we to have a false picture of God, projecting on to him the turbulence and anger which we often feel. The term 'projection' as a notion in psychoanalytic theory is relatively modern, but the concept lying behind it is one with which Julian, along with many other medieval spiritual teachers, was familiar. In projection, an individual ascribes to another person feelings which are actually his or her own, but which for some reason he or she cannot or will not recognize. Often the feeling in question is anger. Julian suggests that a frequent and harmful reaction to our sins and failings is to become very frustrated and angry with ourselves; but instead of recognizing this as our true feeling we project it on to God, saying that God is angry.

We have already seen that according to Julian this is simply not true. If God were angry even for a moment, we would 'neither have life nor place nor being'.[27] Furthermore, it is not helpful. A problem cannot be resolved if it is incorrectly identified: if we suppose that it is God who is angry, and spend our efforts trying to pacify his wrath, we fail to see that the real problem is with ourselves, and that it is our own anger, not God's, which must be dealt with.

> For I saw no wrath except on man's side, and he forgives that in us, for wrath is nothing else but a perversity and an opposition to peace and love ... For we through sin and wretchedness have in us a wrath and a constant opposition to peace and love ...[28]

Perversely, there is that in us which would cling to our anger and depression, and even project them on to God, rather than release them and find healing. They are part of the contrariness of our nature divided against iself; but the way for that fractured nature to be made whole again is neither to treasure up these negative feelings nor to project them on to God. It is rather to allow his love to find resolution for them.

How are we to do this? First, as we have seen, we are to acknowledge our negative feelings, own up to them and to the behaviour which has caused them and expressed them unwisely or hurtfully to ourselves and others. Having owned up to them, however, we are to 'quickly pass over', turning from mulling over our feelings to the steadiness of his love and longing for us. Julian says,

> When we have fallen through wickedness or blindness ... then he wants us to see our wretchedness and meekly to acknowledge it; but he does not want us to remain there, or to be much occupied in self-accusation, nor does he want us to be too full of our own misery. But he wants us quickly to attend to him, for we are his joy and his delight, and he is the remedy of our life.[29]

In this life our feelings will fluctuate, and although it is dangerous to ignore them, neither must they become the ultimate criterion of reality. Our emotions both of pain and of joy are unreliable indicators of truth, as Julian found on the occasion when she was permitted to pass violently from one to another without apparent cause. From that situation she learned that we are kept safe in God's protection whatever our feelings; and we can look forward to the time when our emotions will be fully integrated in the love and delight of God. Until then,

> It is God's will that we do all in our power to preserve our consolation, for bliss lasts forevermore, and pain is passing, and will be reduced to nothing for those who will be saved. Therefore it is not God's will that when we feel pain we should pursue it in sorrow and mourning for it, but that suddenly we should pass it over, and preserve ourselves in the endless delight which is God.[30]

This has nothing to do with repression; it is rather fixing our minds and training our emotions to focus on what is true and real, namely the love of God and our own worth in his sight, rather than hold to fixed ideas or false notions of his wrath or our worthlessness.

To enable us to do this, Julian encourages us to focus on the promises of God, and feed our minds and emotions with his love and the secure protection which he offers. This will be far more helpful than prolonged focus on our misery. If it is true that Christ gladly suffers all he can for us, then the best thing we can do for ourselves and the most pleasing to him is to draw safety and assurance from that love, feeding our sense of security in him, not nursing negative feelings. When Julian considers God's words of reassurance to her after her nightmare and her doubts about whether she could trust the experience of the love of God, she comes to believe that his instruction to accept it and to hold fast to the love and the protection he promises are more generally applicable than only to her and to that particular situation.

When he says: Accept it, he means us to fix it faithfully in our hearts; for he wants it to abide with us in faith to the end of our lives and afterwards, in fulness of joy, wishing us always to have faithful trust in his blessed promise, knowing his goodness . . .[31]

This faith is no bare recitation of creed, but is a matter of taking into ourselves his promises and his presence. It is this which ultimately effects our healing.

For above the faith no goodness is kept in this life, as I see it; and beneath the faith there is no health of soul. But in the faith is where our Lord wants us to keep ourselves, for which we are obliged by his goodness and his own action to keep ourselves in the faith, and he suffers us to have our faith tried by our spiritual enemies and to be made strong.[32]

Delight

Most important of all the ways that we can assist the process of spiritual growth and healing, where our wounds are turned into honours, is fostering in ourselves a spirit of delight in the Lord. As he loves us and takes delight in us, so we are invited to respond with gladness and delight in his unfailing love and safekeeping. We can be certain of his protection and sure of our hope for the future,

And always, the more delight and joy that we accept from this certainty, with reverence and humility, the more pleasing it is to God.[33]

God invites our rejoicing; he wants us to be happy, not just in the sense of putting a good face on carefully hidden pain, but in the far deeper sense of letting him resolve the pain, so that our joy is deep and real.

For all Julian's realism about human sin and suffering, she lends no support at all to the idea that it is somehow more spiritual to be in pain and distress, physical or mental, than to live in joy and enthusiasm. Of course it is better to own up to inner pain than to pretend it is not there and live in a superficial or dishonest cheerfulness. But as the wounds are opened to the healing love of God, we are gradually enabled to let go of the pain and depression which they caused, and enter into a life of gladness and delight which mirrors the joy of God and is a foretaste of the joy of heaven.

Julian's book is a book of joy and pleasure, in spite of its unblinking engagement with sin and suffering. She takes delight in the creation of God, the beauty of the sea valley and the hazel-nut and the intricacy of herring scales. She rejoices in the uniqueness of our bodies and their functions. Her frequent references to her 'even Christians' and her unity with them, together with her warm account of motherhood, shows her pleasure in human love. We have already seen that her life of asceticism and eventual enclosure as an anchoress in no way minimized the worth or delight of any of these things.

It is important to note that for Julian this was not a mere passive acceptance of delight as spiritually innocuous: her teaching goes much further than that. It is not that it is barely acceptable to be happy: happiness and the conditions that make for it are to be positively cultivated as a response to the delight of God in us. It is of course true that we cannot just make up our minds to be happy when we are not. Yet as our wounds are being healed, there do come occasions when we *can* 'suddenly pass over', deliberately leaving pain behind and moving forward into the joy of the Lord.

At least as important as the willingness not to nurse pains when we no longer need to, but to put them down and go forward into joy, is the deliberate development of a context in which healing and happiness are nurtured rather than undermined. This is not a matter of escaping from pain which needs to be faced, but of developing a setting in which pain can be resolved and life can be celebrated. Though Julian became an anchoress, she recognized that normally this involves a context of love for other people, so that the love and delight in God developing in ourselves can be nurtured and shared.

> Glad and merry and sweet is the blessed and lovely demeanour of our Lord towards our souls, for he saw us always living in love-longing, and he wants our souls to be gladly disposed towards him, to repay him his reward. And so I hope that by his grace he lifts up and will draw our outer disposition to our inward, and will make us all at unity with him, and each of us with others in the true, lasting joy which is Jesus.[34]

Laughter is never far from the surface in Julian's book. In the fifth revelation she saw all the powers of evil personified in the devil, and saw how by the passion of Christ the devil is rendered impotent as even his most fiendish activities are turned to good by the creativity of God.

> Because of this sight I laughed greatly, and that made those around me to laugh as well; and their laughter was pleasing to me. I thought that I wished that all my fellow Christians had seen what I saw. Then they would all have laughed with me; but I did not see Christ laughing, but I know well that it was the vision he showed me which made me laugh, for I understood that we may laugh, to comfort ourselves and rejoice in God, because the devil is overcome.[35]

Whatever the pain and difficulty that we still face, we can be confident that all will be well because of the passion of Christ and his endless love.

Though there is still 'matter for mourning' because we continue in part to suffer from blindness and wounding, there is also 'matter for

mirth' because our Lord protects us and leads us to increasing light and
wholeness.[36] In his own house and in his own Kingdom the Lord
invites us even now to the heavenly feast over which he presides:

> I saw him reign in his house as a king and fill it all full of joy and mirth,
> gladdening and consoling his dear friends with himself, very familiarly and
> courteously, with wonderful melody in endless love in his own fair blissful
> countenance, which glorious countenance fills all heaven full of the joy and
> bliss of the divinity.[37]

Heaven is not a solemn affair, but a party, full of gladness and glory; and
even now we can begin to enter into its happiness.

Notes to Chapter Ten

1. LT 39.
2. ibid.
3. LT 51, pp. 274–5.
4. LT 39.
5. LT 51, p. 267.
6. op. cit., p. 271.
7. op. cit., p. 270.
8. LT 72.
9. LT 52.
10. ibid.
11. LT. 56
12. ibid.
13. ibid.
14. LT 47.
15. ibid.
16. LT 72.
17. LT 82.
18. ibid.
19. LT 37.
20. LT 66.
21. ibid.
22. LT 67; Julian makes it quite clear that this was a nightmare, not on a par with the visions of Christ which she had had.
23. cf. LT 39, 'by our falling we give them [our enemies] occasion'.
24. LT 67.
25. LT 68.
26. LT 52.
27. LT 49.
28. LT 48.
29. LT 79.
30. LT 15.
31. LT 71.
32. ibid.
33. LT 65.

34. LT 74.
35. LT 13.
36. LT 77.
37. LT 14.

Appendix: Note on texts

Neither the Short Text nor the Long Text are extant in manuscripts dating before the mid-fifteenth century. The earliest manuscript of the Short Text is British Museum Additional 37790, probably copied in a monastic scriptorium about 1450. The earliest Long Text is in Paris, MS Bibliothèque Nationale Fonds Anglais 40, copied about 1650. Later manuscripts and printed editions, and their relations to one another, are listed and discussed in Edmund Colledge o s a and James Walsh s j, ed., *A Book of Showings to the Anchoress Julian of Norwich*, 2 vols. (Toronto, Pontifical Institute of Medieval Studies, 1978).

This edition is the nearest thing available to a modern critical edition. Though scholars find it wanting in many respects, it does give both the Short Text and the Long Text in Middle English, and lists manuscript variations.

The most readily available modern translations are as follows:

Julian of Norwich: Showings, tr. E. Colledge o s a, and James Walsh s j, Classics of Western Spirituality (London, SPCK, and New York, Paulist Press, 1978).

Julian of Norwich: Revelations of Divine Love, tr. Clifton Wolters, (Harmondsworth, Middlesex, Penguin, 1966) – Long Text only.

Revelations of Divine Love, tr. Grace Warrack (London, Methuen, 1907 edn).

Bibliography

Ackerman, Robert W., and Dahood, Roger, ed. and tr., *Ancrene Riwle: Introduction and Part I*, Medieval and Renaissance Texts and Studies vol. 31 (New York, Binghampton, 1984).

Aelred of Rievaulx, *De vita eremitica ad sororem liber* PL 32, cols. 1451–74 (incorrectly placed among St Augustine's works); also called *Regula ad sororem*, *De institutione inclusarum*. English tr., 'A Rule of Life for a Recluse', in *Treatises and the Pastoral Prayer*, Cistercian Fathers Series No. 2 (Kalamazoo, Michigan, Cistercian Publications, 1971).

Anonymous, *The Cloud of Unknowing*, Classics of Western Spirituality (London, SPCK, and New York, Paulist Press, 1981).

Anselm, *Basic Writings*, tr. S. N. Deane (La Salle, Illinois, Open Court, 1962).

——, *The Prayers and Meditations of Saint Anselm*, tr. Benedicta Ward (Harmondsworth, Middlesex, Penguin, 1973).

Anson, Peter F., *The Call of the Desert* (London, SPCK, 1961).

Athanasius, *The Life of St Antony and the Letter to Marcellinus*, Classics of Western Spirituality, tr. Robert C. Gregg (London, SPCK, and New York, Paulist Press, 1980).

Augustine of Hippo, *The Confessions of St Augustine*, tr. John K. Ryan (New York, Image, Doubleday, 1960).

——, *Selected Writings*, tr. Mary Clark, Classics of Western Spirituality (London, SPCK, and New York, Paulist Press, 1984).

——, *On the Holy Trinity, Doctrinal and Moral Treatises*, Nicene and Post Nicene Fathers (Grand Rapids, Michigan, Wm. B. Eerdmans, 1956).

Baker, Derek, ed., *Medieval Women*, Ecclesiastical History Society (Oxford, Blackwell, 1978).

Bell, Dom Maurice, ed., *Wulfric of Haselbury* by John, Abbot of Ford, Somerset Record Society vol. 47 (1932).

Bendelow-Collier, Margaret, *'Verily God is our Mother': A Study of the Doctrine of Julian of Norwich*, Pontifical Institute 'Regina Mundi' (Unpublished dissertation, Rome, 1963).

Bennett, J. A. W., *Poetry of the Passion* (London 1982).

Bernard of Clairvaux, *Apologia to Abbot William of Saint Thierry; On Precept and Dispensation*, Cistercian Fathers Series No. 1 (Kalamazoo, Michigan, 1970).

——, *On Consideration*, Cistercian Fathers Series No. 37 (Kalamazoo, Michigan, 1976).

——, *On Loving God; and On the Steps of Humility*, Cistercian Fathers Series No. 13 (Kalamazoo, Michigan, 1974).

——, *Sermons on the Song of Songs*, 4 vols. Cistercian Fathers Series Nos. 4, 7, 31, and 40 (Kalamazoo, Michigan, 1971–80).

Bibliography

Blomfield, Francis, continued by Parkin, Charles, *An Essay Towards a Topographical History of the County of Norfolk*, 5 vols. (Fersfield & Lynn 1739–75).

Bolton, J. L., *The Medieval English Economy 1150–1500* (London, J. M. Dent; and Totawa, New Jersey, Rowman & Littlefield, 1980).

Bouyer, Louis; Leclercq, Jean; and Vandenbroucke, François, *A History of Christian Spirituality: Vol. I The Spirituality of the New Testament and the Fathers; Vol. II The Spirituality of the Middle Ages; Vol. III Orthodox Spirituality and Protestant and Anglican Spirituality* (London, Burns Oates, and New York, Seabury, 1968).

Boyd, William, *The History of English Education*, 11th edn rev. Edmund J. King (London, Adam & Charles Black, 1975).

Brenan, Gerald, *St John of the Cross: His Life and Poetry* (London and New York, Cambridge University Press, 1973).

Brewer, Derek, 'The Social Context of Medieval English Literature', in Boris Ford, ed., *Medieval Literature: Chaucer and the Alliterative Tradition*, vol. I Part One of the New Pelican Guide to English Literature (Harmondsworth, Middlesex, Penguin, 1982).

Burnaby, John, *Amor Dei: A Study in the Religion of St Augustine* (London, Hodder & Stoughton, 1938).

Butler-Bowden, W., ed., *The Book of Margery Kempe*, Life and Letters Series No. 103 (London, Jonathan Cape, 1936).

Bynum, Caroline Walker, *Jesus as Mother: Studies in the Spirituality of the High Middle Ages* (Los Angeles and London, University of California Press, 1982).

Cabassut, André osb, 'Une Dévotion Médiévale peu connue, la Dévotion à Jésus notre Mère', in *Revue d'Ascétique et de Mystique* 99–100 (April-December 1949).

Chitty, Derwas, *The Desert a City* (Oxford, Blackwell, 1966).

Clay, Rotha Mary, *The Hermits and Anchorites of England* (London, Methuen, 1914; reprint Detroit, Singing Tree Press, 1968).

Colledge, E., osa and Walsh, J., sj 'Editing Julian of Norwich's *Revelations*' in *Medieval Studies* 38 (1976).

Comper, Francis M., *The Life and Lyrics of Richard Rolle* (London and Toronto, J. M. Dent; New York, E. M. Dutton, 1928).

Creighton, Charles, *A History of Epidemics in England* Vol. I (New York, Barnes & Noble, 2nd edn 1965).

Daniélou, Jean, and Marrou, Henri, *The Christian Centuries Vol. I.: The First Six Hundred Years* (London, Darton, Longman & Todd, and New York, Paulist Press, 1964).

Darwin, Francis D. S., *The English Medieval Recluse* (London, SPCK, 1944).

de Vogüe, Adalbert, *The Rule of Saint Benedict: A Doctrinal and Spiritual Commentary*, Cistercian Studies Series No. 54 (Kalamazoo, Michigan, Cistercian Publications, 1983).

Dictionary of National Biography (Oxford, Oxford University Press, 1917ff.).

Dobson, E. J., *The Origins of the Ancrene Wisse* (Oxford, Clarendon Press, 1976).

Dunn, F. I., 'Hermits, Anchorites and Recluses: A Study with Reference to Medieval Norwich', in Sayer, F. D., ed., *Julian and her Norwich*, Commemorative Essays and Handbook to the Exhibition 'Revelations of Divine Love' (Norwich 1973).

222

Bibliography

Eckhart, Meister, *The Essential Sermons, Commentaries, Treatises and Defense* Classics of Western Spirituality (London, SPCK, and New York, Paulist Press, 1981).

——, *German Sermons and Treatises Vol. I and II*, tr. M. O'C. Walshe (London and Dulverton, Watkins, 1979).

Eileen Mary SLG, 'The Place of Lady Julian of Norwich in English Literature', in *Julian of Norwich: Four Studies to Commemorate the Sixth Century of the Revelations of Divine Love* Fairacres Publication No. 28 (Oxford, SLG Press, 1973).

Elder, E. Rozanne, *The Spirituality of Western Christendom Vol. II*, Cistercian Studies Series No. 55 (Kalamazoo, Michigan, 1984).

Eriugena, John Scotus, *De Divisione Naturae*, PL 122. 125–1244.

Evans, G. R., *Augustine on Evil* (Cambridge, Cambridge University Press, 1982).

Flindall, R. A., 'The Lady Julian and her City', in Sayer, F. D., ed., *Julian and her Norwich*, Commemorative Essays and Handbook to the Exhibition 'Revelations of Divine Love' (Norwich, 1973).

Ford, Boris, ed., *Medieval Literature: Chaucer and the Alliterative Tradition.* Vol. I Part One of the New Pelican Guide to English Literature (Harmondsworth, Middlesex, Penguin, 1982).

Francis of Assisi, *Francis and Clare: The Complete Works*, Classics of Western Spirituality (London, SPCK, and New York, Paulist Press, 1982).

Fries, Maureen, 'Margery Kempe', in Szarmach, Paul, ed., *The Medieval Mystics of Europe* (Albany, New York, State University of New York Press, 1984).

Gannon, Thomas M., and Traub, George, *The Desert and the City: An Interpretation of the History of Christian Spirituality* (London, Collier-MacMillan, 1969).

Georgianna, Linda, *The Solitary Self: Individuality in the Ancrene Wisse* (London and Cambridge, Massachusetts, Harvard University Press, 1981).

Gilson, Étienne, *History of Christian Philosophy in the Middle Ages* (New York, Random House, 1955).

——, *The Mystical Theology of Saint Bernard* (London, Sheed & Ward, 1940).

Glasscoe, Marion, ed., *The Medieval Mystical Tradition in England*, Papers read at the Exeter Symposium, July 1980; Exeter Medieval English Texts and Studies, General Editor M. J. Swanton (University of Exeter Press 1980).

Gottfried, Robert S., *Epidemic Disease in Fifteenth Century England* (New Brunswick, New Jersey, Rutgers University Press, 1978).

Gray, Douglas, *Themes and Images in the Medieval English Religious Lyric* (London and Boston, Routledge & Kegan Paul, 1972).

Grayson, Janet, *Structure and Imagery in Ancrene Wisse* (Hanover, New Hampshire, University Press of New England, 1974).

Grimlaic, *Regulae Solitariorum*, in PL 103 cols. 575–664.

Hadewijch, *The Complete Works*, Classics of Western Spirituality (London, SPCK, and New York, Paulist Press, 1980).

Hatcher, Jon, *Plague, Population and the English Economy 1348–1530* (London and New York, Macmillan, 1977).

Heufelder, Emmanuel, OSB, *The Way to God According to the Rule of St Benedict*, Cistercian Studies Series No. 49 (Kalamazoo, Michigan, Cistercian Publications, 1983).

Hilton, Walter, *The Goad of Love* (tr. with additions of *The Stimulus Amoris* of James of Milan) ed. Clare Kirchberger (London, Faber & Faber, 1952).

223

Bibliography

——, *The Scale of Perfection*, ed. Evelyn Underhill (London, John M. Watkins, 1957).

——, *The Scale of Perfection*, tr. Gerard Sitwell OSB (London, Burns Oates, 1953).

Holdsworth, Christopher J., 'Christina of Markyate', in Baker, Derek, ed., *Medieval Women*, Ecclesiastical History Society (Oxford, Blackwell, 1978).

Hugh of St Victor, *De Sacramentum* PL 176.

Hussey, S. S., 'Walter Hilton: Traditionalist?', in Glasscoe, Marion, ed., *The Medieval Mystical Tradition in England*, Papers read at the Exeter Symposium, July 1980; Exeter Medieval English Texts and Studies, General Editor M. J. Swanton (University of Exeter Press 1980).

Hyman, Arthur, and Walsh, James J., ed., *Philosophy in the Middle Ages: The Christian, Islamic, and Jewish Traditions* (Indianapolis, Hackett, 1973).

Ignatius of Antioch, *Epistle to the Romans*, in The Ante-Nicene Fathers Vol. I: *The Apostolic Fathers – Justin Martyr – Irenaeus* (Grand Rapids, Michigan, Wm. B. Eerdmans, 1957, reprint of the Edinburgh 1867 edn).

Isabel Mary SLG, 'The Knights of God: Citeaux and the Quest of the Holy Grail', in Benedicta Ward SLG, ed., *The Influence of St Bernard* (Oxford, SLG Press, 1976).

Jacobs, Louis, *Jewish Mystical Testimonies* (New York, Schocken, 1976).

James, William, *The Varieties of Religious Experience* (Glasgow, Collins, Fontana, 1977; first publ. 1902).

Janson, H. W., *History of Art* (Englewood Cliffs, New Jersey, Prentice-Hall, and New York, Henry N. Abrams, 1969).

Jantzen, Grace M., 'Ethics and Mysticism: Friends or Foes?', in *Nederlands Theologisch Tijdschrift*, vol. 3 No. 4 (1985).

——, *God's World God's Body* (London, Darton, Longman & Todd, and Philadelphia, Westminster, 1984).

——, 'Luther and the Mystics', in *King's Theological Review* vol. VIII No. 2 (1985).

John of the Cross, *The Complete Works: 3 Vols.*, tr. E. Allison Peers (London, Burns Oates & Washbourne, 1953 rev. edn).

Katz, Stephen, ed., *Mysticism and Philosophical Analysis* (London, Sheldon, 1978).

Knowles, David, and Obolensky, Dimitri, *The Christian Centuries: Vol. II The Middle Ages* (London, Darton, Longman & Todd, and New York, Paulist Press, 1969).

——, *The English Mystical Tradition* (New York, Harper & Brothers, 1961).

——, *The English Mystics* (London, Burns & Oates, 1927).

——, *The Religious Orders in England: Vols. I–III* (Cambridge, Cambridge University Press, 1948–59).

Lagorio, Valerie M., 'The Medieval Continental Women Mystics', in Szarmach, Paul, ed., *An Introduction to the Medieval Mystics of Europe* (Albany, New York, State University of New York Press, 1984).

Langland, William, *Piers the Ploughman*, tr. J. F. Goodridge (Harmondsworth, Middlesex, Penguin, 1959).

Leclercq, Jean, *Bernard of Clairvaux and the Cistercian Spirit* Cistercian Studies Series No. 16 (Kalamazoo, Michigan, Cistercian Publications, 1976).

——, *The Love of Learning and the Desire for God* (London, SPCK, and New York, Fordham University Press, 1961).

Little, A. G., 'The First Hundred Years of the Franciscan School at Oxford', in

Bibliography

Seton, Walter, ed., *St Francis of Assisi 1226–1926: Essays in Commemoration* (London, University of London Press, 1926).

Llewelyn, Robert, ed., *Julian, Woman of our Day* (London, Darton, Longman & Todd, 1985).

——, *Love Bade Me Welcome* (London, Darton, Longman & Todd, 1984).

——, *With Pity Not With Blame* (London, Darton, Longman & Todd, 1982).

Louth, Andrew, *The Origins of the Christian Mystical Tradition from Plato to Denys* (Oxford, Clarendon, 1981).

Macquarrie, John, *Principles of Christian Theology* (London, SCM, rev. edn 1977).

Madigan, Mary Felicitas IBVM, *The Passio Domini Theme in the Works of Richard Rolle: His Personal Contribution in its Religious, Cultural, and Literary Context*, Elizabethan and Renaissance Studies, ed., James Hogg, Salzburg Studies in English Literature (Institut für Englische Sprache und Literatur, Universität Salzburg, 1978).

Maisonneuve, Roland, *L'Univers Visionnaire de Julian of Norwich*, Thèse Presentée Devant L'Université de Paris IV, 1979 (Atelier National de Reproduction des Thèses, Université de Lille III, 1982).

Mallard, W., 'John Wyclif and the Tradition of Biblical Authority', in *Church History* 30 (1961).

Martin, C. B., *Religious Belief* (Ithaca, New York, Cornell University Press, 1959).

Mary Paul SLG, 'Julian of Norwich and the Bible', in *Julian of Norwich: Four Studies to Commemorate the Sixth Centenary of the Revelations of Divine Love* Fairacres Publication No. 28 (Oxford, SLG Press, 1973).

McCann, Dom Justin, ed., *The Golden Epistle of Abbot William of St Thierry to the Carthusians of Mont Dieu*, tr. Walter Shewring (London, Sheed & Ward, 1930).

McGinn, Bernard, 'St Bernard and Meister Eckhart', in *Cîteaux Com. Cist.* vol. I (1980).

McIlwain, James T., 'The "Bodelye Syeknes" of Julian of Norwich', in *Journal of Medieval History*, vol. X No. 3 (September 1984).

McKisack, May, *The Fourteenth Century 1307–1399*. The Oxford History of England vol. 5 (Oxford, Clarendon, 1959).

McLean, Michael, *Guidebook to St Julian's Church and Lady Julian's Cell* (Norwich 1979, rev. 1981).

McNeill, John T., *A History of the Cure of Souls* (New York, Harper & Row, 1951).

Mechthild of Magdeburg, *The Flowing Light of the Godhead*, tr. Lucy Menzies, *The Revelations of Mechthild of Magdeburg* (London and New York, Longmans Green, 1953).

Meisel, Anthony C., and del Mastro, M. L., tr., *The Rule of St Benedict* (New York, Image Books, Doubleday, 1975).

Merton, Thomas, *Conjectures of a Guilty Bystander* (New York, Doubleday, 1966).

——, *Mystics and Zen Masters* (New York, Farrar, Straus & Giroux, 1967).

Miles, Margaret, *Augustine on the Body*, AAR Dissertation Series No. 31 (Missoula, Montana, Scholar's Press, 1979).

Molinari, Paul, *Julian of Norwich, The Teaching of a 14th Century English Mystic* (London and New York, Longmans Green, 1958).

Moltmann, Jürgen, *The Crucified God* (London, SCM, 1974).

Bibliography

Moorman, John, *A History of the Franciscan Order From Its Origins to the Year 1517* (Oxford, Clarendon Press, 1968).

Morton, James, ed., *The Ancrene Riwle* (London, Chatto & Windus, and Boston, John W. Luce, 1907).

Origen, *An Exhortation to Martyrdom, Prayer and Selected Works*, Classics of Western Spirituality (London, SPCK, and New York, Paulist Press, 1979).

Owst, G. R., *Preaching in Medieval England: An Introduction to the Sermon Manuscripts of the Period c. 1350–1450* (New York, Russell & Russell, 1965).

Pagels, Elaine, *The Gnostic Gospels* (Harmondsworth, Middlesex, Pelican, 1982).

Passmore, John, *The Perfectibility of Man* (London, Duckworth, 1970).

Pelikan, Jaroslav, *The Christian Tradition: A History of the Development of Doctrine: Vol. I The Emergence of the Catholic Tradition (100–600); Vol. II The Spirit of Eastern Christendom (600–1700); Vol. III The Growth of Medieval Theology (600–1300)* (London and Chicago, The University of Chicago Press, 1971–8).

Pelphrey, Brant, *Love was His Meaning: The Theology and Mysticism of Julian of Norwich*, Salzburg Studies in English Literature (Institut für Anglistik und Amerikanistik, Universität Salzburg, Austria, 1982).

Pepler, Conrad OP, *The English Religious Heritage* (London, Blackfriars, 1958).

Powers, Eileen, *Medieval English Nunneries c.1275 to 1535* (London, Hafner, and New York, Biblo & Tannen, 1922 rep. 1964).

Reynolds, Anna Maria CP, *A Showing of God's Love, The Shorter Version of Sixteen Revelations of Divine Love by Julian of Norwich* (London, Longmans Green, 1958).

——, 'Some Literary Influences in the "Revelations" of Julian of Norwich', in *Leeds Studies in English and Kindred Languages*, Nos. 7 and 8 (1952).

Rickert, M., *Painting in Britain: The Middle Ages* (London 1954).

Riehle, Wolfgang, *The Middle English Mystics* (London, Routledge & Kegan Paul, 1981).

Rolle, Richard, *The Fire of Love and the Mending of Life*, tr. Francis Comper (London, Methuen, 2nd edn 1920).

——, *The Fire of Love*, tr. Clifton Wolters (Harmondsworth, Middlesex, Penguin, 1973).

Sayer, F. D., ed., *Julian and her Norwich*, Commemorative Essays and Handbook to the Exhibition 'Revelations of Divine Love' (Norwich 1973).

Scholem, Gershom G., *Major Trends in Jewish Mysticism* (New York, Schocken, 3rd edn 1961).

Scott James, Bruno, ed., *The Letters of Saint Bernard of Clairvaux* (London, Burns Oates, 1953).

Seton, Walter, ed., *St Francis of Assisi 1226–1926: Essays in Commemoration* (London, University of London Press, 1926).

Sherry, Patrick, *Spirit, Saints, and Immortality* (London, Macmillan, 1984).

Southern, R. W., *The Making of the Middle Ages* (London and New Haven, Yale University Press, 1953).

——, *Western Society and the Church in the Middle Ages*, The Pelican History of the Church Vol. II (Harmondsworth, Middlesex, Penguin, 1970).

Squire, Aelred, *Aelred of Rievaulx: A Study* (London, SPCK, 1969).

Stace, Walter Terence, *Mysticism and Philosophy* (London, MacMillan, 1961).

Bibliography

Sutherland, Stewart, *God, Jesus and Belief* (London, SCM, 1985).

Szarmach, Paul, ed., *An Introduction to the Medieval Mystics of Europe* (Albany, New York, State University of New York Press, 1984).

Tanner, Norman P., *Popular Religion in Norwich with Special Reference to the Evidence of Wills, 1370–1532* (Oxford, D. Phil. Dissertation, 1973).

Teresa of Jesus, *The Complete Works*, 3 volumes, tr. E. Allison Peers (London, Sheed & Ward, 1949).

Thomas Aquinas, *Basic Writings of St Thomas Aquinas*, 2 vols, ed. Anton C. Pegis (New York, Random House, 1945).

Thompson, E. Margaret, *The Carthusian Order in England* (London, SPCK, 1930).

Thouless, R. H., *The Lady Julian: A Psychological Study* (London 1924).

Trevelyan, G. M., *England in the Age of Wycliffe* (London, Longman, 1972; first publ. 1899).

Tugwell, Simon, *Ways of Imperfection* (London, Darton, Longman & Todd, 1984).

Underhill, Evelyn, *Cambridge Medieval History*, vol. VII, ed. Tanner, et al. (Cambridge, Cambridge University Press, 1949).

——, *Mysticism* (London and Dutton, New York, 12th edn 1930; first publ. 1911).

Vann, Gerald, *The Divine Pity* (London, Fontana, 1956).

Vinje, Patricia Mary, *An Understanding of Love According to the Anchoress Julian of Norwich*, Elizabethan and Renaissance Studies (Salzburg, Austria, Institut Für Anglistik und Amerikanistik, Universität Salzburg, 1983).

Ward, Benedicta SLG., ed., *The Influence of St Bernard* (Oxford, SLG Press, 1976).

——, '"Faith Seeking Understanding": Anselm of Canterbury and Julian of Norwich', in *Julian of Norwich*, Fairacres Publication No. 28 (Oxford SLG Press, 1973).

William of St Thierry, *The Golden Epistle to the Carthusians of Mont Dieu*, ed. Dom Justin McCann; tr. Walter Shewring (London, Sheed & Ward, 1930).

——, *The Golden Epistle to the Carthusians of Mont Dieu* Cistercian Fathers Series No. 12 (Kalamazoo, Michigan, 1974).

——, *On Contemplating God, Prayer, and Meditations* Cistercian Fathers Series No. 3 (Kalamazoo, Michigan, 1977).

Williams, Rowan, *The Wound of Knowledge* (London, Darton, Longman & Todd, 1979).

Wolters, Clifton, *Julian of Norwich: Revelations of Divine Love* (Harmondsworth, Middlesex, Penguin, 1966).

Woolf, Rosemary, *The English Religious Lyric in the Middle Ages* (Oxford, Clarendon, 1968).

Index

Aelred, of Rievaulx   ch 3 *passim*, 49n, 57, 66, 99, 118
alienation   150, 153, 170
anchoritic life: bishop assesses candidate   9, 39, 46; daily timetable   42; evolution of   28–9
Ancrene Riwle   30, ch. 3 *passim*, 49n, 118
Anselm, St, Archbishop of Canterbury   55–6, 66, 68, 71n, 113–14, 117
apophatic tradition   94, 110, 154–6, 160
Aquinas, Thomas   17, 20, 112–14, 130, 172, 197
Augustine, St, Bishop of Hippo, augustinian theology   16–17, 26n, 68, 99, 111–14, 124n, 128, 148, 161, 164n, 172, 182, 196, 201n
Augustinian Friars   19

Beghards   7
Béguines   7, 20, 22
Benedict, St   36
Benedict XIII, Pope   5
Benedictines   17–19, 22, 57, 118
Bernard of Clairvaux   20, 42, 48n, 55, 62–3, 71n, 99, 117, 158–9, 163n, 201–2nn
Black Death   7–8, 14n, 24–5, 59, 146
Black Prince   6
Blomfield, Francis   21
body, attitudes to   31, 37, 40–2; *see also* sensuality; substance
Brunton, Thomas   17

Carmelites   19
Carrow Abbey   18–19, 22–3, 38
Cecilia, St   62
Chaucer   15
Cistercians   17, 48n, 63, 117, 119
Cloud of Unknowing   40, 59, 94, 106n, 110, 154–6, 160
Colledge, E., and Walsh, J.   13n, 16, 26n, 98–9, 124n
Conisford   7
corruption, church   9–10, 97, 100
counsel, counselling   29, 31, 33, 35–6, 38–9, 45, 47–8, 68, 205
crusade, Norwich   9–10, 100, 189

Despenser, Henry, Bishop of Norwich   9–12, 39, 81, 189
Dominicans   19
Dream of the Rood   54

Easton, Adam   17
Eckhart, Meister   19, 63, 140–1, 158–9, 163n
Edward III, King   5–6
enclosure, rite of   33
Erigena, John Scotus   94, 161n
erotic imagery   72n; *see also* wounds, spirituality of

fasting   36–7, 41
forgetting, spirituality of   *see* apophatic tradition
Francis of Assisi, St   64, 131
Franciscans   7, 19, 72n

Georgianna, Linda   30, 50n

Index

Gerald of Wales 45
Golden Epistle see William of St Thierry
Gregory the Great, St 16
Grimlaic 30

Henry IV, King 11
heresy 7, 10–11
Hilton, Walter 56, 58–9, 69, 118, 157
Hugh of St Victor 112

indulgences 9–10, 100
intercession 29, 45–6
Isabella, Queen 5

John of Beverley 188–9, 203
John of the Cross, St 64, 140–1
John of Gaunt 6
John XXII, Pope 5
Julian groups 12n
Julian of Norwich: and Bible 16–17, 98–100, 107n; on 'courtesy of God' 132–4; creation, theology of 76, 127–37, 153–4, 161; date of birth 4, 13n; date of visions 20; death of 21; on 'godly will' 150–2, 187, 206; on 'great deed', 'great mystery' 102, 125n, 173–80; identifies with human suffering 61, 64–5, 68, 169; illness of 3–4, 21, 23–5, 53, 61, 64, 74–8, 85n, 184–5; knowledge of God, criteria for 93, 106; lord and servant, parable 76–7, 98–9, 121, 132–3, 175, 190–201, 206–10; loyalty to 'Holy Church' 10–11, 96–7, 100–6, 174, 178–9, 191–2, 198–200, 213; her name 4, 20–1; on natural reason ('kyndly reson') 93–6, 100, 105, 114, 142; on passion of Christ 53, 58–61, 64–9, ch. 5 passim, 90–2, 134–6, 138, 154, 167–70, 186–7; on personhood 92–3, 134, 137–61;

'three wounds' 17, 53, 61–2, 68–9, 187–8, 204; 'a woman, ignorant, weak and frail' 15, 80–1; writes in English 11, 17, 26n; see also motherhood of God; sensuality; substance; visions, assessment of
Julian, St, church of 4, 7, 18

Kempe, Margery 3, 29, 40, 63, 72n, 81, 157–8

Langland 54
Litster, Geoffrey 8–9, 34
Lollards 10–11, 80, 101

Macquarrie, John 162n
martyrdom 55, 71n
Mechthild of Magdeburg 63
Merton, Thomas 90
Molinari, Paul 74
motherhood of God 90, 104, 111, 115–24, 130, 143, 158
mysticism, interpretation of 78–85; see also visions, assessment of

Norwich: religious communities 17, 19; social and economic condition of town 5–6, 8

Origen 62, 71n

pantheism 132–4
passion of Christ, in spirituality 54–8, 65–7, 68
Passmore, John 45
Paul, St 42, 55, 64, 83, 116–17, 130, 140, 171, 184, 202n
Peasants' Revolt 8–10, 97, 133
Philip IV, King of France 5
philosophy, and mysticism x, 82–3
plague see Black Death
projection 214–15
Pseudo-Dionysius 94, 110
Regula Solitariorum 30

229

Index

Rhineland, influence of   19, 63, 159
Richard II, King   6, 48n
Rolle, Richard   56, 112

sensuality, sensual nature   111, 121,
   142–51, 170–3, 180, 187, 205–6
sexuality   35–6, 63, 157–8, 164n
substance, substantial nature   111,
   121, 140–51, 170–3, 180–1, 205–6
Suso, Henry, 63

Tauler, Johannes   19, 63
Teresa of Avila, St   22, 139
Tugwell, Simon   15
Tyler, Wat   8, 48n

Underhill, Evelyn   72n
universalism   178–9
Urban VI, Pope   9–10, 17

Vann, Gerald   131
visions, assessment of   53, 60–1,
   77–85, 105
Vulgate Bible   16–17

Wensum, River   4
William of St Thierry   16, 20, 55,
   71n, 94
wills   20–1, 38
wool trade   6–7
wounds, spirituality of   62–7, 122,
   172, 199–200, 203–5, 208–10, 214,
   216–17
Wulfric of Haselbury, St   24, 29, 36,
   38, 40
Wyclif, John   10–11, 26n

Zohar   117